IMAGES
of Modern America

Rio Rancho

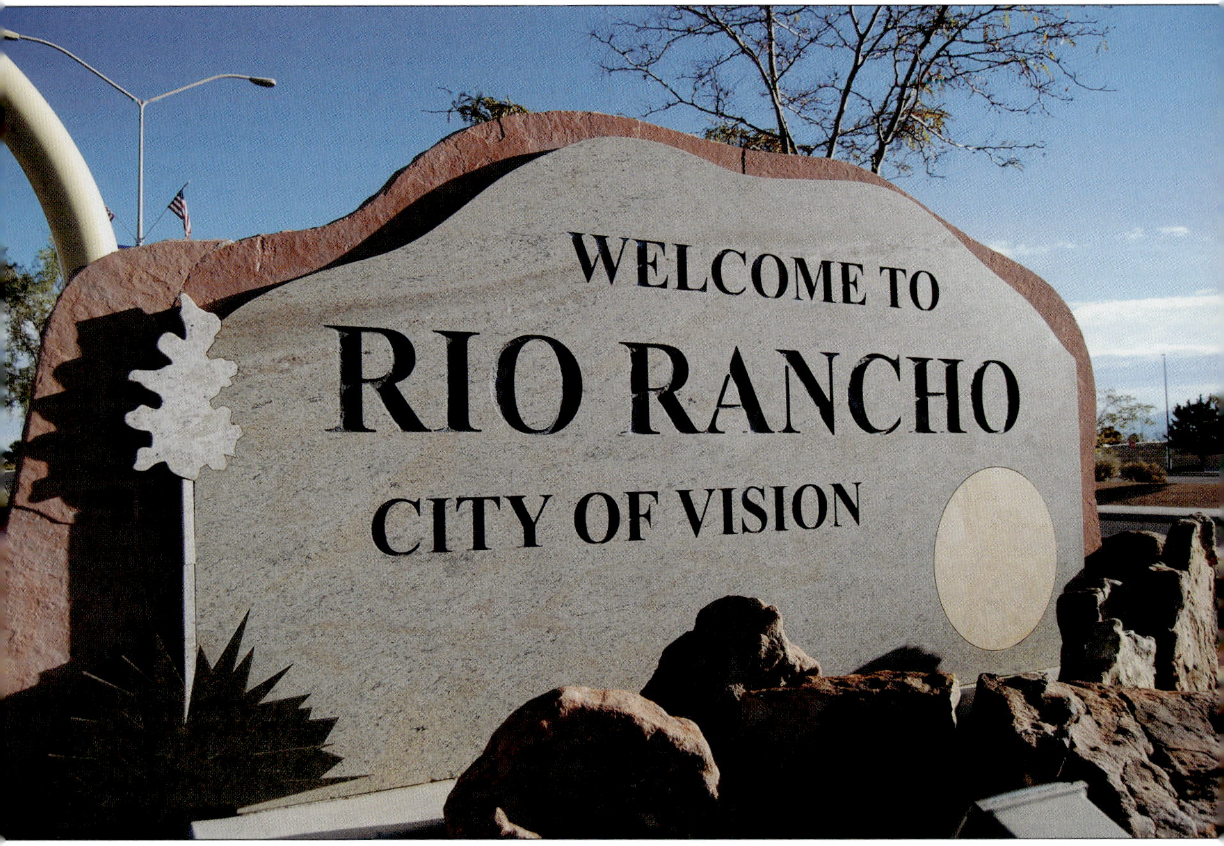

Greeting drivers headed north on three major arterials entering Rio Rancho—New Mexico State Road (NM) 528, Golf Course Road, and Unser Boulevard—the "City of Vision" welcomes them and states, "See you soon," on the opposite side. (Author's collection.)

On the Front Cover: Clockwise, from the top left, Rio Grande Estates visitors deplane from a flight into Albuquerque; a welcome sign at a highway entrance into Rio Rancho; an early groundbreaking; the silhouette of an infantryman at the city's Veterans Monument Park; and the metro area's showplace, Santa Ana Star Center. (All courtesy of AMREP Southwest.)

On the Back Cover: From left to right, successful attempt to enter the Guinness Book of World Records for jack-o'-lantern carving in Rio Rancho in October 2013; a Fourth of July parade down Southern Boulevard; and an earlier Fourth of July celebration at the Rio Rancho Sports Complex. (All courtesy of AMREP Southwest.)

IMAGES
of Modern America

RIO RANCHO

Gary Herron

ARCADIA
PUBLISHING

ISBN 978-1-4671-3368-5

Published by Arcadia Publishing
Charleston, South Carolina

Printed in the United States of America

Library of Congress Control Number: 2015941078

For all general information, please contact Arcadia Publishing:
Telephone 843-853-2070
Fax 843-853-0044
E-mail sales@arcadiapublishing.com
For customer service and orders:
Toll-Free 1-888-313-2665

Visit us on the Internet at www.arcadiapublishing.com

Contents

Acknowledgments

Working for the *Rio Rancho Observer* on two occasions in my journalistic life, I have had the pleasure of being close to the action of this dynamic city.

My first stint, which lasted just seven months (1985–1986), gave me a taste of the growing city before it had many of its current amenities. It was the worst job I ever had—with one issue coming out a week, I literally went into the office at 8:00 a.m. on Mondays and did not leave until about 8:00 a.m. on Tuesdays, working around the clock with a small staff and, needless to say, not getting much sleep.

My second stint began in May 2000 and was just the opposite. Although my business card notes I am the sports editor, I have written about and photographed much more than sports in the "City of Vision": elections, crime, ground-breakings and ribbon-cuttings, school board meetings, high school graduations, hundreds of events at Santa Ana Star Center, and—my favorite—writing feature stories about people with interesting stories.

Although I have never lived in Rio Rancho, I have a "buy-in" there, being employed there and as a charter member of the Rio Rancho Sports Advisory Council and a former board member, for a year each, for Cibola Little League and Friends of the Library of Rio Rancho.

Thanks to all the people who made this effort possible: Rockford Hayes, the publisher of the *Observer*, who gave me the go-ahead to use photographs and stories; Dawn Hite at Loma Colorado Main Library, who gave me access to the Rio Rancho History Room; AMREP Southwest, which permitted me to borrow and scan some images from its files; longtime resident Donna Benedetto; and early resident Glenda Mowry, who had the pleasure of meeting and writing about many of the city's new residents as they arrived here in the early 1970s.

Unless otherwise credited, images appear courtesy of Gary Herron and the *Rio Rancho Observer*.

INTRODUCTION

Although most people consider 1981 as the beginning of Rio Rancho's history, when it became incorporated, and others believe the 1960s migration of mostly New Yorkers and Midwesterners to the area as their place to enjoy retirement, generations of Native Americans had been residing in the area since the 1300s. In fact, generations of Kuauans, who had begun building their adobe structures that century, had evolved to an approximately 1,200-room settlement, known as Kuaua (and by today's residents as Coronado Historic Site), in the 1500s.

In February 1540, an event occurred that permanently changed the way of life for residents at Kuaua, as well as their neighbors along the Rio Grande and beyond. An army of Spanish explorers, led by Francisco Vázquez de Coronado, began its march northward from some 1,400 miles away, in the frontier town of Compostela, Mexico. They were hoping to find treasures similar to those discovered by Hernán Cortés among the Aztecs, seeking the legendary Seven Cities of Cibola. Coronado and close to 300 soldiers, six Franciscan friars, and an estimated 1,000 Indian allies and slaves, plus about 1,500 head of livestock, ventured north into that uncharted territory.

They followed ancient roads that had made trade among Native American tribes possible for centuries. In September 1540, with most of Coronado's army engaged in defeating the Zuni and Acoma pueblos to the west, an advanced guard of Spaniards arrived in the Tiwa-speaking region along the Rio Grande, which they called Tiguex. One village's inhabitants, forced out by soldiers, had to find refuge in neighboring communities; small pueblos were also located at Alameda, now covered by Alameda Elementary, and just north of what is now known as Rio Rancho's River's Edge III residential neighborhood.

After acts of brutality by these European intruders—and the resulting retaliation by the natives—all-out warfare ensued. The Spaniards' expedition to the plains of Kansas, still seeking that fabled wealth, was followed by continued unrest and intermittent fighting with the Pueblo Indians, all ending with Coronado being ordered out of the Tiguex area in the spring of 1542.

Jumping ahead to the 1930s, archeologists from three New Mexico state institutions retraced the footsteps of Adolph Bandelier and Charles Lummis, who had excavated sites near Bernalillo in the late 1880s. Teams from the University of New Mexico, the Museum of New Mexico, and the School of American Research, thanks to New Deal financial assistance, excavated Kuaua and a site two miles to the south, which scientists hoped would prove Coronado's army had spent time there. Despite that ambitious project, there is no evidence uncovered that indicates Kuaua indeed was the village Coronado's army commandeered.

Flash ahead again two decades; it is the 1950s, and young entrepreneurs Chester Carrity and Henry Hoffman started a mail-order business in New York. Their first product was rose bushes. Other products were added over the years, and the company finally emerged as the American Real Estate and Petroleum Corporation (AMREP). When AMREP purchased the Koontz Ranch in the early 1960s, the lands northwest of Albuquerque were home to 500 head of cattle. The company began to market and develop the 90,000 acres by selling homesites to people in the

East and Midwest. It was one of the most widely marketed land-development programs in the United States.

Between 1961—the first building in the city was AMREP's on Grande Boulevard in 1961—and 1977, AMREP sold more than 75,000 lots to thousands of people through advertising, free dinners, movies, and slide shows. It offered people a dream of leaving crowded cities and moving west, with dramatic views and endless opportunities.

One of the first couples to buy a lot in 1961, John and Marjorie Cannizzaro, made their first trip to the estates in 1965, finding only the land office and five homes in existence. The couple moved to Rio Rancho in 1972, and in 1974, Marjorie—a great-granddaughter of Pres. William Taft—made an unsuccessful run for Sandoval County clerk.

Model home construction began in 1962, and the first residents, Mr. and Mrs. Ray Palmer, moved here in 1963. AMREP built six homes in 1963; the first streets with homes on them were Twenty-third Avenue, Leonard Street, and Grande Boulevard. The Palmers were followed by the Parkers from Kansas, the McCrones from Florida, the Lundys from Oklahoma, and the Emersons from England.

In June 1964, official dedication ceremonies of Rio Rancho Estates took place at the clubhouse. New Mexico secretary of state Alberta Miller, representing Gov. Jack Campbell, spoke and predicted Rio Rancho Estates would have a major role in advancing the prosperity of the state; state senator A.T. Montoya praised the area for attracting a fine caliber of people.

The first issue of what subsequently turned out to be the *Roadrunner* consisted of one sheet of legal-sized paper, no title, and this headline: "Rio Rancho Estates Now Has a Recreation Director." It was Zelda Haynes.

In 1964, the city had a population of about 75 people; in 1969, there were 1,500 residents, and by 1974 there were 5,377 people living in the city. Until early 1970, residents had an address in Albuquerque; in February 1970, they were instructed to tell folks they lived in Rio Rancho Estates, New Mexico, with the zip code 87124.

In September 1971, the first newspaper (*Rio Rancho Roadrunner*) began monthly publication. The *Roadrunner* "Carries ALL the news of Rio Rancho Estates" and was printed by and for the residents of the "Community That Has Everything." A year's subscription cost $3. Its forte was introducing new residents of Rio Rancho Estates, telling where they came from. Later, Glenda Mowry served as a reporter; she would gather new residents at the Sabana Grande Community Center Auditorium to have photographs taken and obtain some information on the newcomers. AMREP's James Colegrove, director of public affairs for AMREP Southwest, was the first publisher; Abe J. Perilman was the editor.

In February 1972, a Foodway grocery store came to Rio Rancho Estates Shopping Center. Toward the end of 1972, residents no longer referred to their neighborhoods as Unit 16, where the first homes were built, or Unit 11; they became Clearview and Star Heights, respectively, after residents voted. Rio Rancho Estates became officially known as merely Rio Rancho.

Incorporation studies had been conducted in 1974 and again in 1976, but on November 8, 1977, the 2,700 residents who went to the polls for the first time on the matter of incorporation voted against the measure. On August 8, 1978, incorporation lost again, this time 1,628 to 1,098.

In 1980, despite three years of local controversy, city residents—by now totaling about 10,000 people—voted to become an incorporated city and begin taking charge of their own destiny. The proverbial third time worked like a charm, as 60 percent voted in favor of incorporation on September 3, 1980, with the decision approved 2,330 to 1,544.

One

Rio Rancho Estates

Perhaps the real irony about what is now known as Rio Rancho, the City of Vision, is the story about the city's origins. Properly, it should have been called Rancho del Rio, adhering to the Spanish used in the state, meaning "ranch by the river."

By then, thousands of residents in New York—an alternative nickname for the City of Vision has been Little New York—had been taking advantage of free dinners, courtesy of AMREP Corporation, and sales pitches to retire to New Mexico and enjoy 360 days of sunshine a year. That sounded great to people weary of shoveling snow and seeking inexpensive housing and a new start.

Once they had taken advantage of AMREP's sales pitch, which included a flight and accommodations in Albuquerque, to visit where their next home could be, who would not love the Sandia Mountains to the east and wide, open spaces? Many no doubt, had to be intrigued from their love of movies with a Western bent.

It became sort of the "If you build it, they will come" mantra made famous in the movie *Field of Dreams*. AMREP had more than three dozen home styles, something to appeal to everyone.

Rio Grande Estates grew steadily, initially as a bedroom community of Albuquerque. There, people shopped and got their entertainment: movie houses, college and professional sports, stage plays, concerts, and more.

What AMREP officials originally had in mind—a thriving community—became a reality when the city incorporated. Before too many years had passed in the 21st century, what had once been wide-open desert with nothing but cacti and scrub brush had become New Mexico's third-largest city.

Today, it is much more than a retirement community: most of the original inhabitants have passed away, with many of their children opting to stay here and raise their own children.

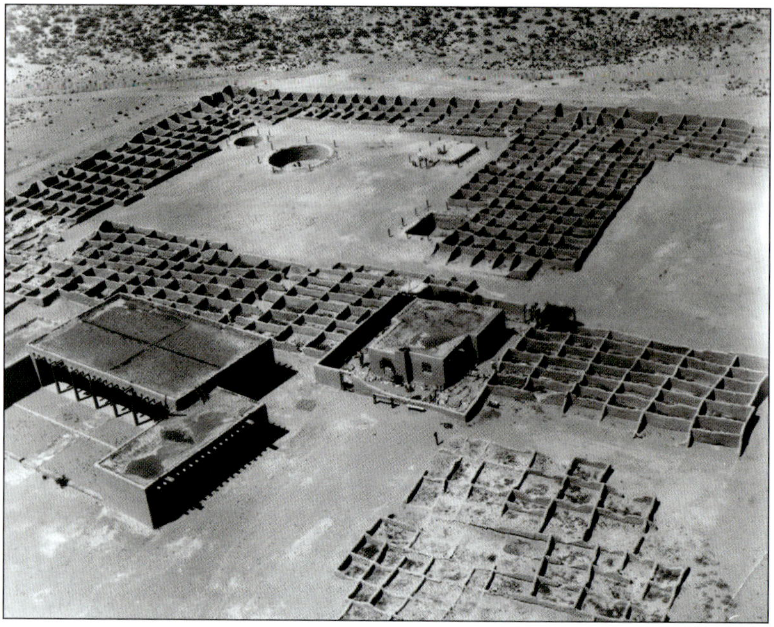

This is an aerial photograph of the Coronado Historic Site captured by the New Mexico Department of Development in August 1964. It is believed Spanish explorer Francisco Vázquez de Coronado visited here in the winter of 1541, and he and his men probably trekked along the west bank of the Rio Grande. (Courtesy of the Gary Herron Collection.)

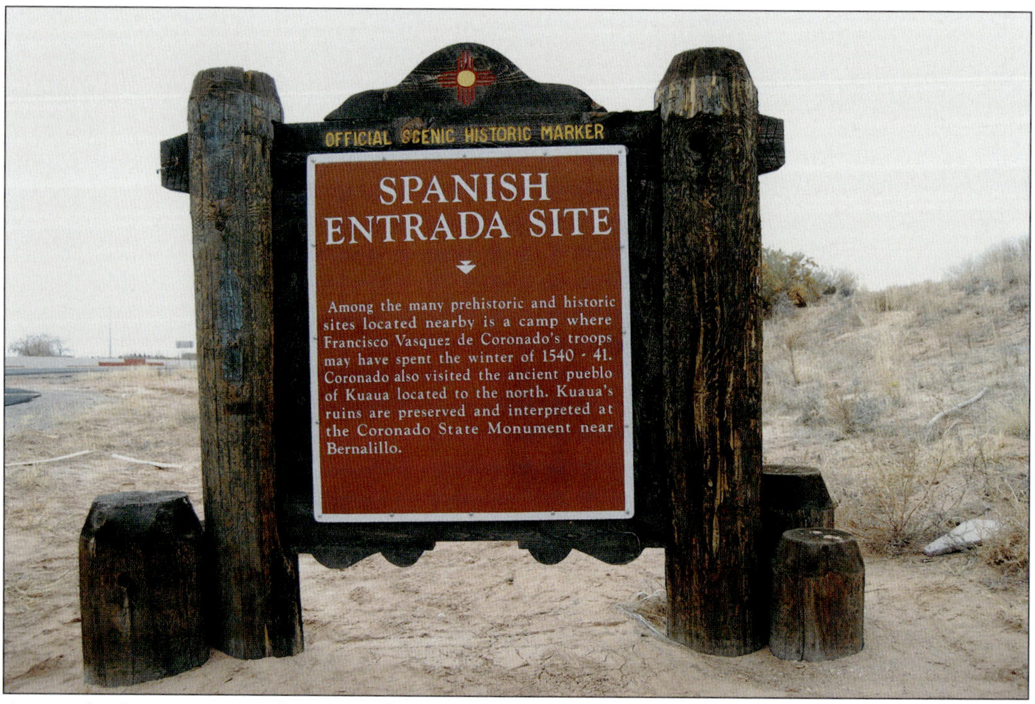

A state highway sign, on the west side of New Mexico State Road (NM) 528, just south of Idalia Road, tells that an army led by Francisco Vázquez de Coronado very likely passed through here in 1540–1541. Not far from this sign is an untouched site of a small pueblo at the north end of River's Edge III.

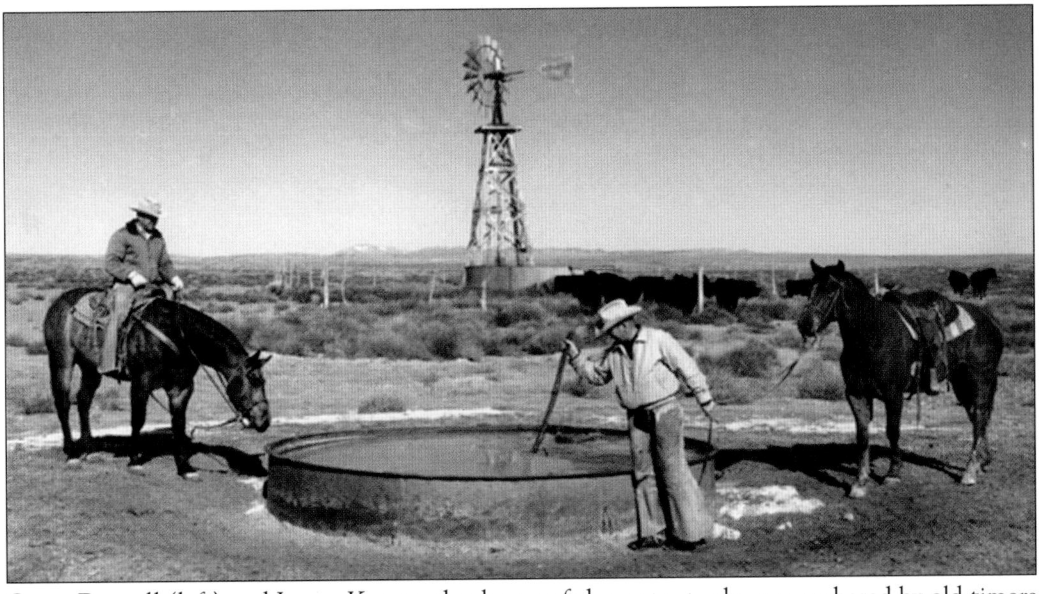

Casey Darnell (left) and Jasper Koontz check one of the water tanks, remembered by old-timers as one of the few structures on the mesa and also a great swimming hole near what would several decades later be Rio Rancho. This site may have been out near what today is Northern Meadows. (Courtesy of Koontz family and Caplin Estate.)

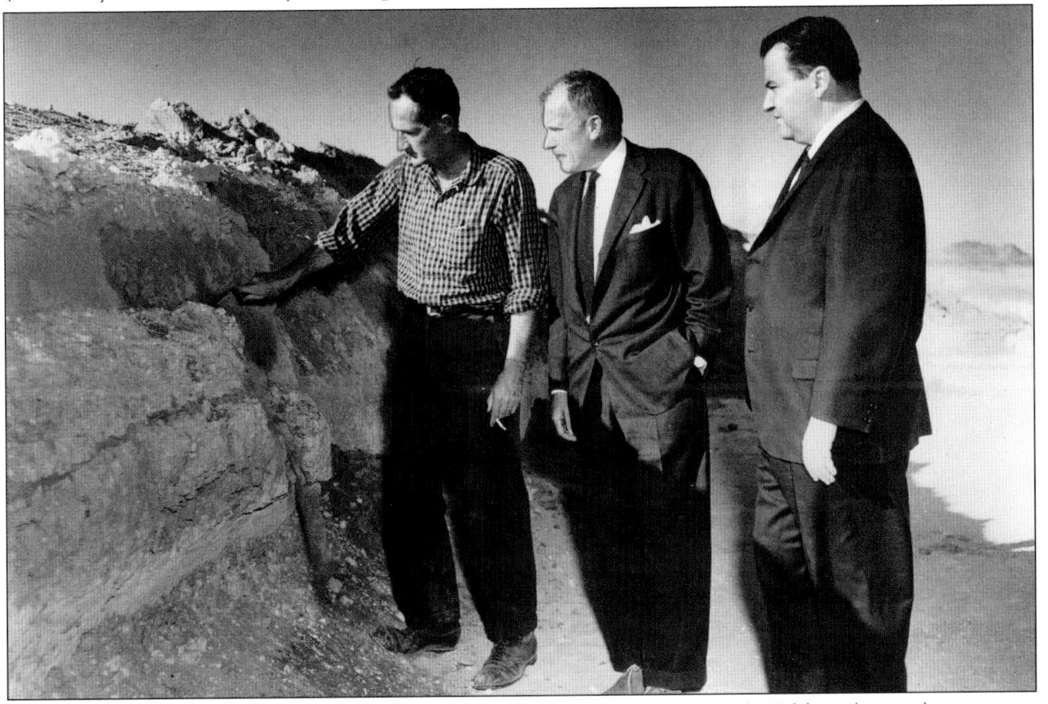

Renowned archeologist and University of New Mexico professor Frank Hibben (center) examines the side of a trench at Rio Rancho Estates in March 1965. The Lakewood, Ohio, native loved New Mexico so much that he completed his master's degree at the University of New Mexico in 1936 and followed that up with a doctorate from Harvard in archeology. (Courtesy of *Cleveland Press*/author's collection.)

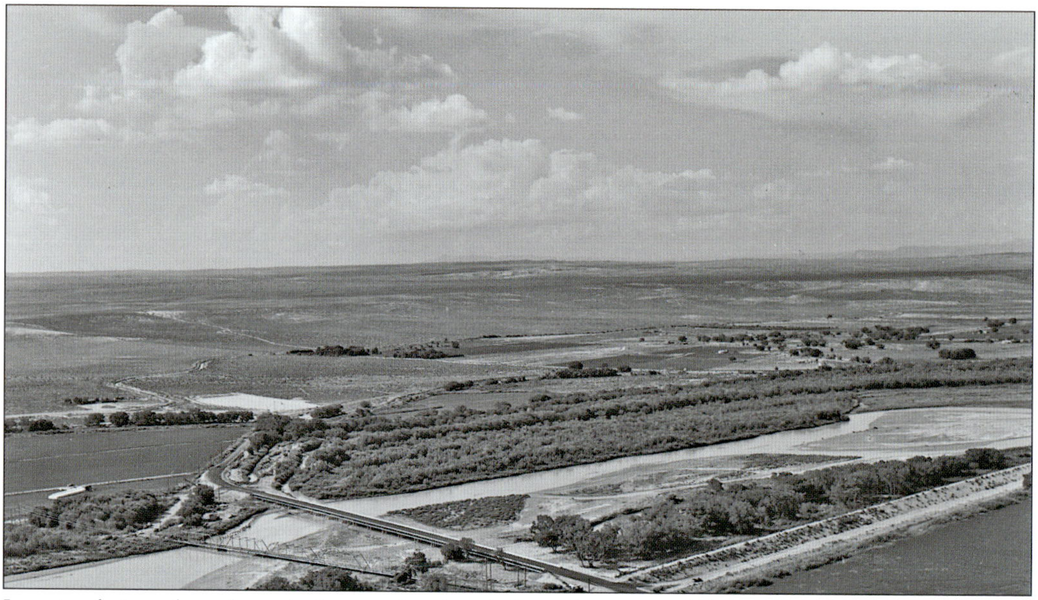

Imagine being aboard an airplane today, headed northwest, and about to cross the Rio Grande: this is what the future Rio Rancho looked like in 1956. At the time photographer Dick Kent took this image, the Corrales Bridge was under construction; the Rio Grande and bosque have not changed. (Courtesy of Mary Davis and the Corrales Historical Society.)

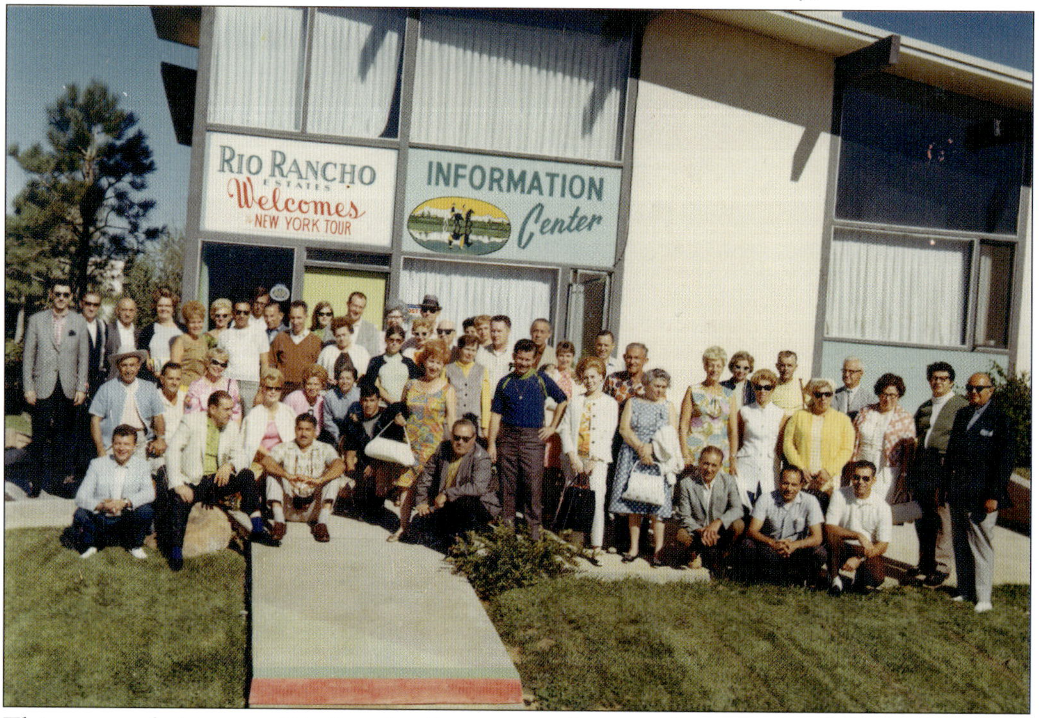

This group of visitors to Rio Rancho Estates was flown in from New York in August 1968. Included in this photograph is Diane Benedetto, wearing sunglasses and sitting on the sidewalk. She and her husband liked what they saw and bought a home on Rose Circle, where they raised six children. (Courtesy of Diane Benedetto.)

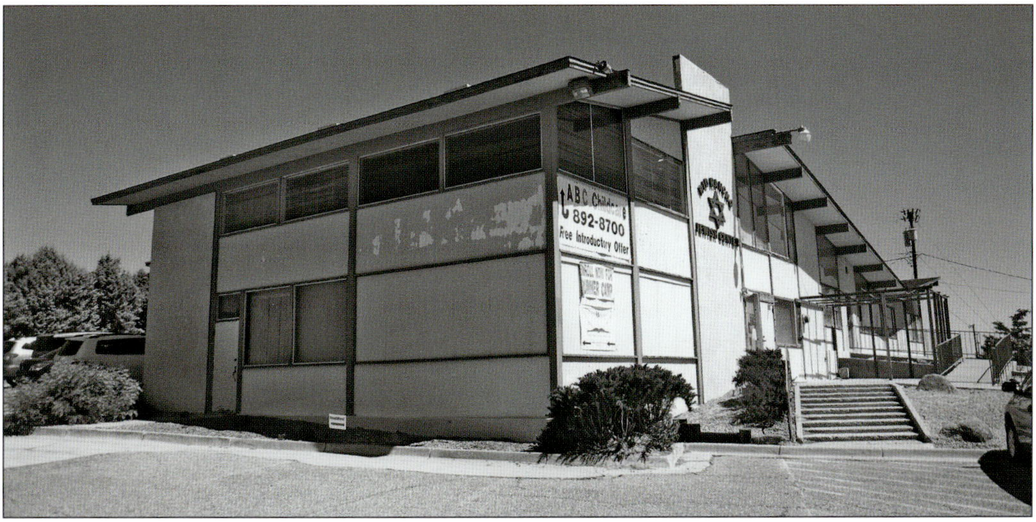

Pictured here in 2014 is the original AMREP sales office, on Grande Boulevard across from Haynes Park, in Rio Rancho Estates. It is the same building that Rio Rancho Estates visitors posed in front of in the 1960s image on the previous page. Among its tenants in 2014 were ReadWest and the Jewish Center.

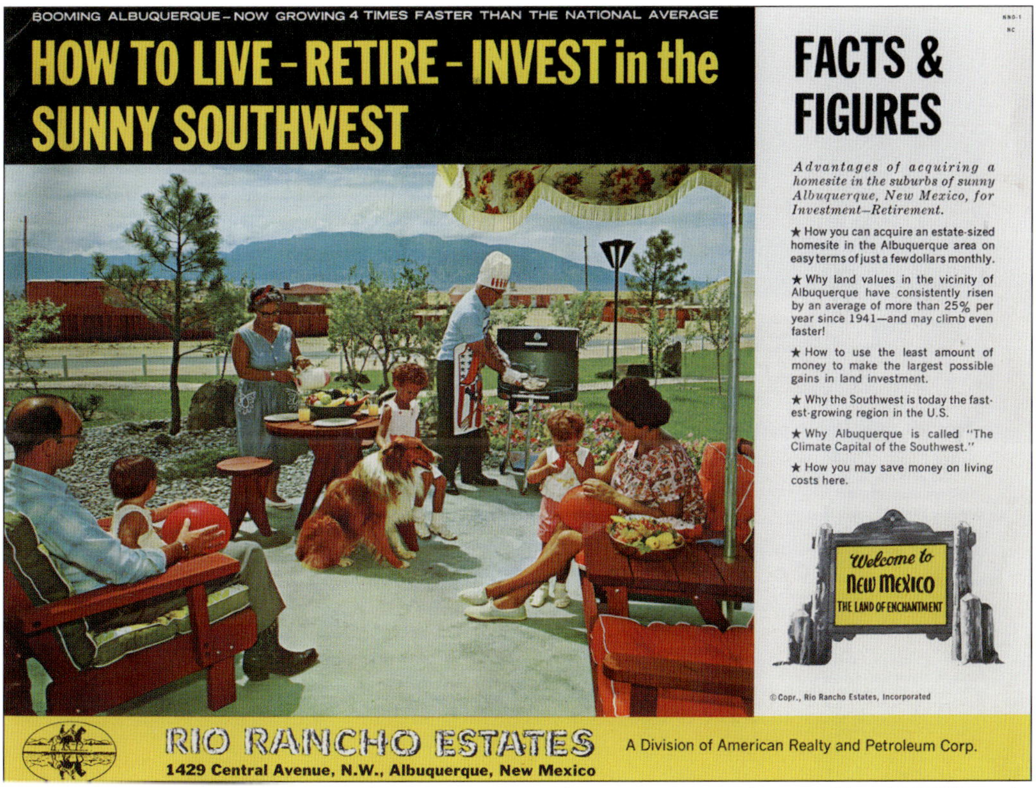

"Your golden future" was one of the ways Rio Rancho Estates was advertised by AMREP in its many brochures, most depicting myriad ways people could have fun here. Who would not trade rain in the spring and summer and snow in the winter for 360 days of sunshine a year? (Courtesy of Diane Benedetto.)

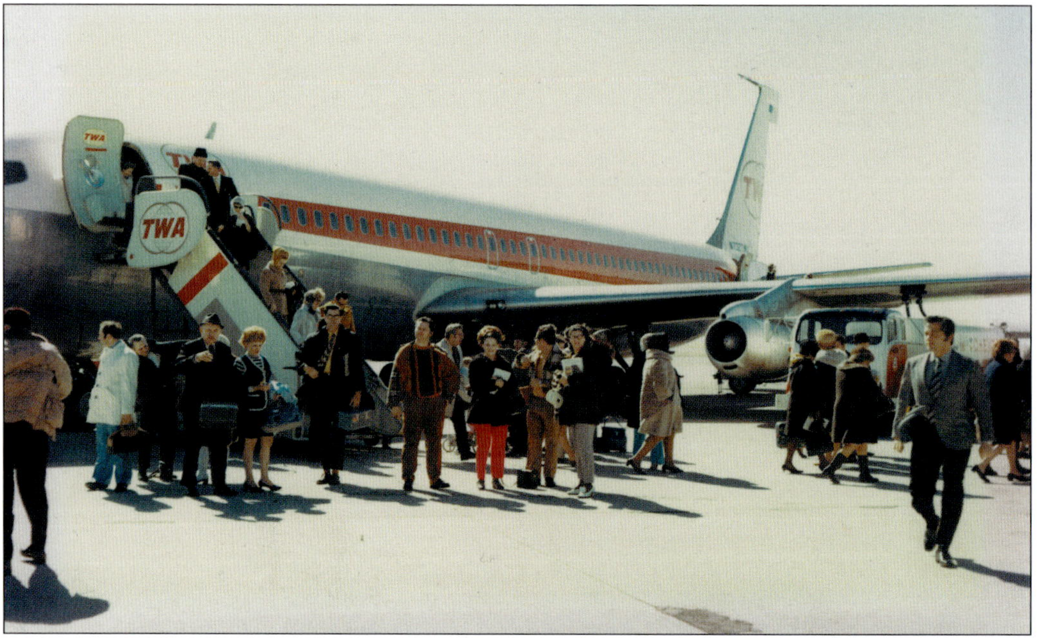

People flew into the airport in Albuquerque, got off the plane and onto the tarmac, and proceeded to board large buses that would transport them to the development (AMREP Southwest had 27 units) to get a the lay of the land. All of the visitors were wined and dined. (Courtesy of AMREP Southwest.)

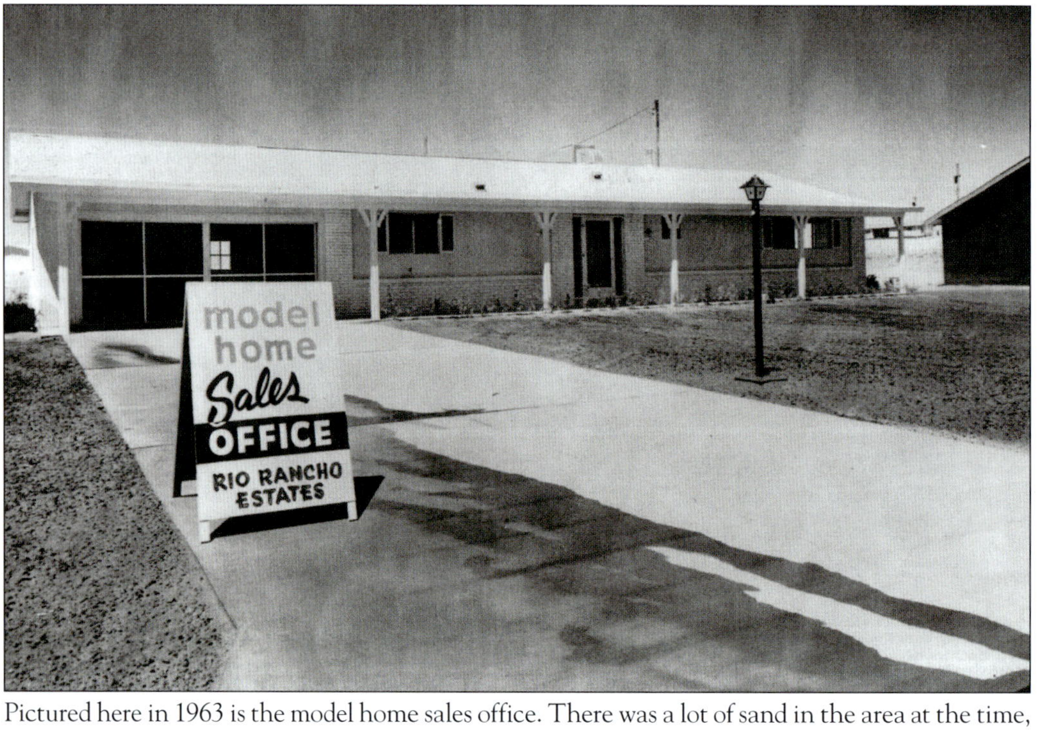

Pictured here in 1963 is the model home sales office. There was a lot of sand in the area at the time, as there is now. Today, this area is near Haynes Park, a lush park enjoyed for decades, with a pool, basketball courts, playground, and tennis courts. (Courtesy of Loma Colorado Main Library.)

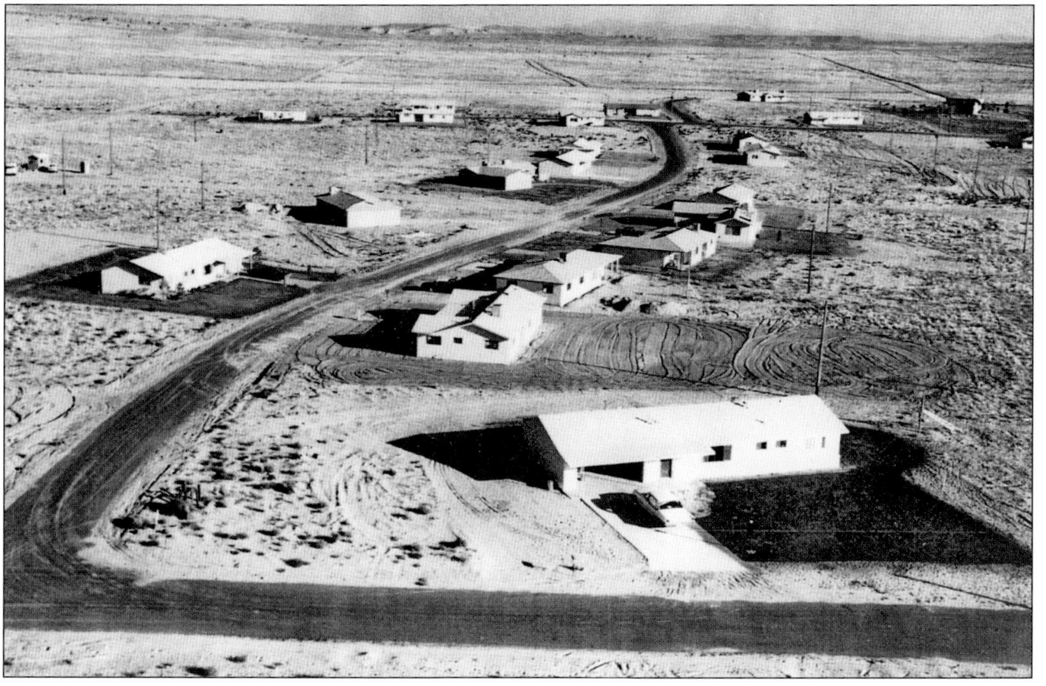

This 1964 aerial photograph shows Leonard Street heading north off Twenty-third Avenue, running east and west at the bottom, which then had only model homes for potential buyers to check out. Today, it is near the southernmost border of Rio Rancho and Sandoval County. (Courtesy of Loma Colorado Main Library.)

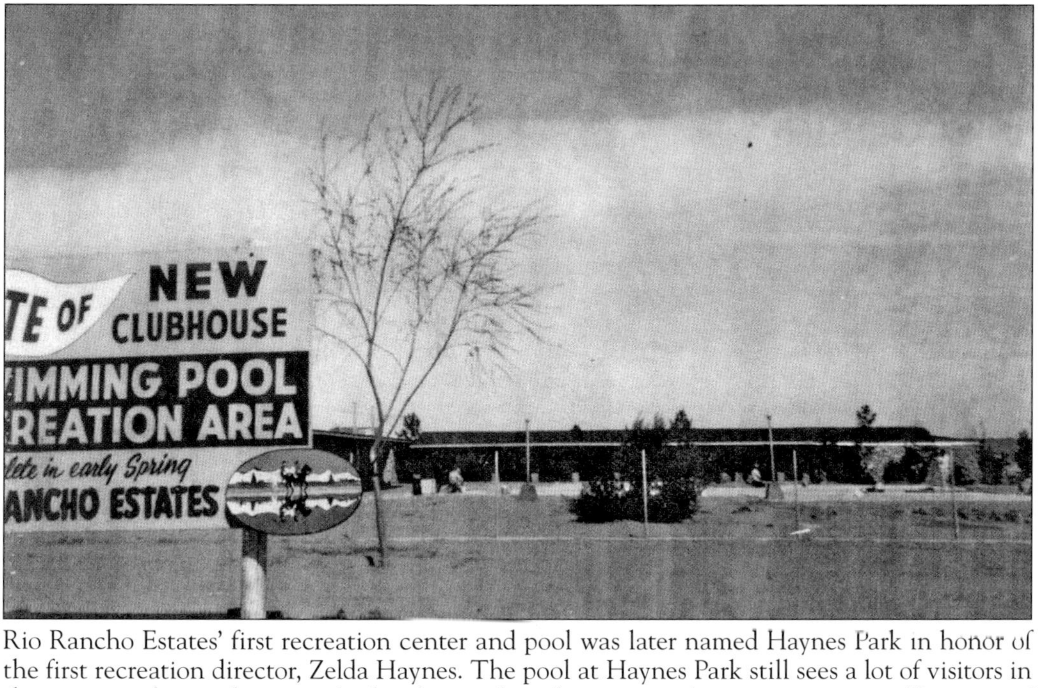

Rio Rancho Estates' first recreation center and pool was later named Haynes Park in honor of the first recreation director, Zelda Haynes. The pool at Haynes Park still sees a lot of visitors in the summer; the city has since built other pools and even an indoor aquatic center. (Courtesy of Loma Colorado Main Library.)

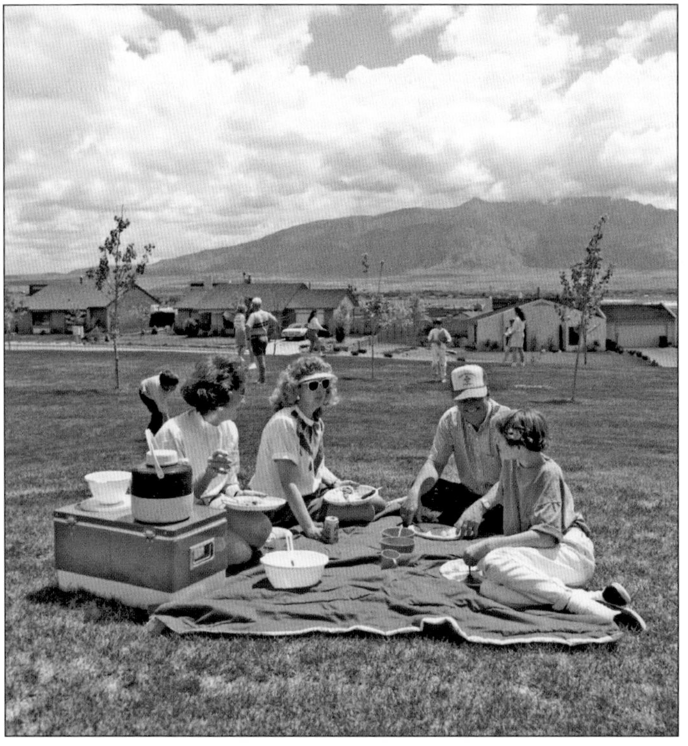

Who would not think Rio Rancho Estates looked like a great place to live, especially during a cold winter or rainy spring back East? The mountains and sunbathing must have seemed viable and appealing alternatives. An enjoyable day then or even today can be spent taking the tram or driving to Sandia Peak. (Courtesy of AMREP Southwest.)

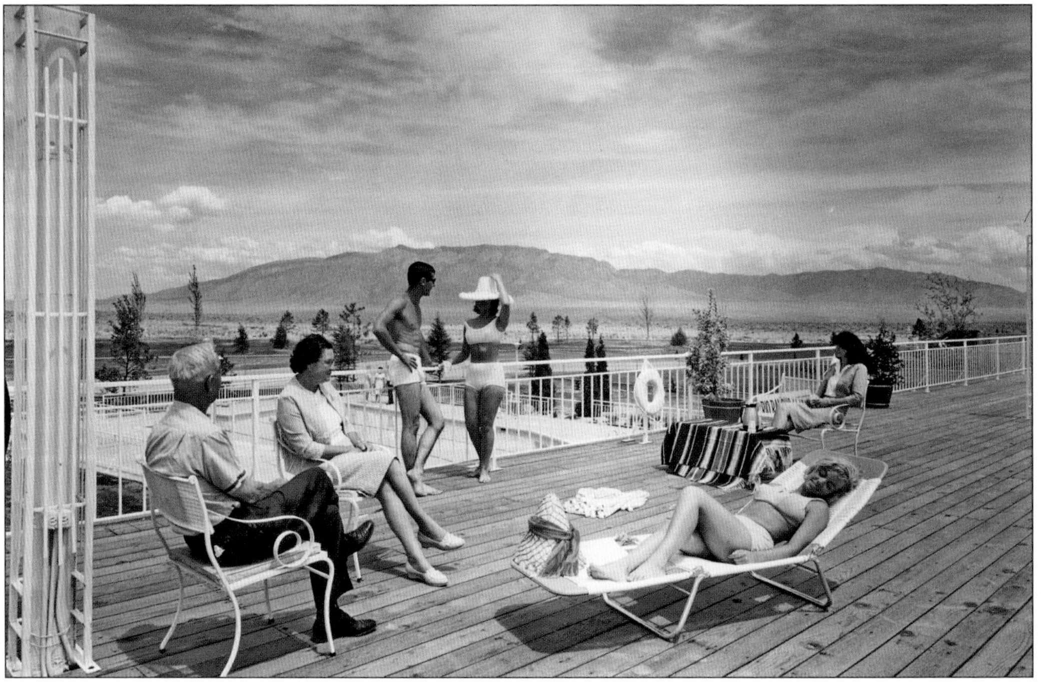

This is another of AMREP's promotional photographs, with the Sandia Mountains looming in the east. People from back East were no doubt surprised to discover they could ski up in the Sandias or near Santa Fe and play tennis in Rio Rancho on the same January day. (Courtesy of AMREP Southwest.)

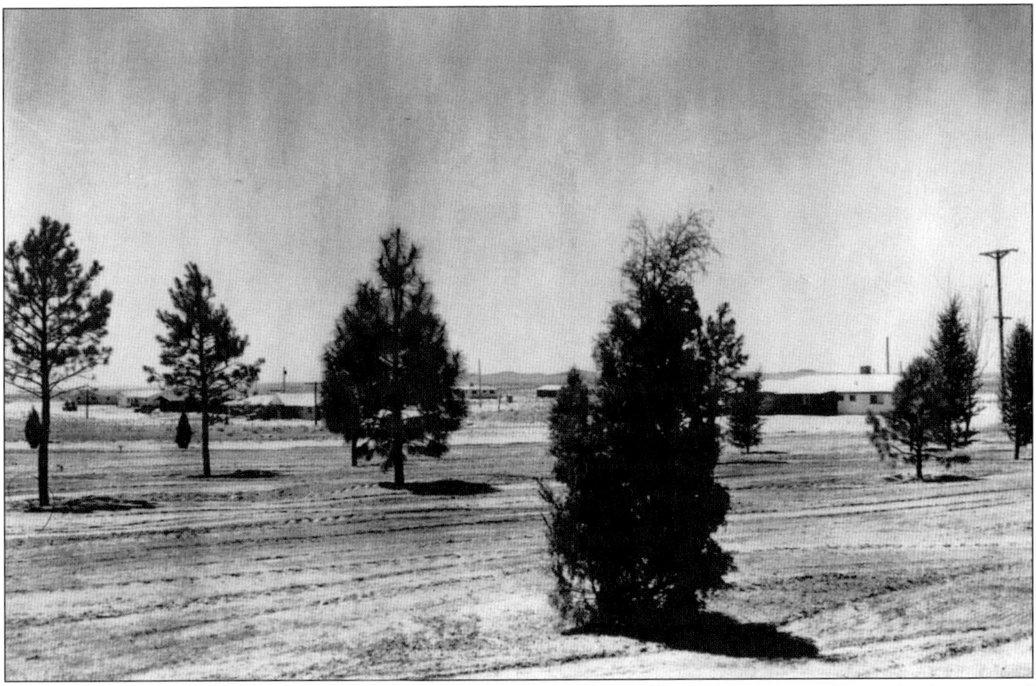

There were not a lot of trees in Rio Rancho Estates back in the mid-1960s, and people discovered when the wind blew—most of the time, it seemed—there would be a lot of dirt and dust in the air. Today, there are still breezy, dusty days but a lot more trees. (Courtesy of Loma Colorado Main Library.)

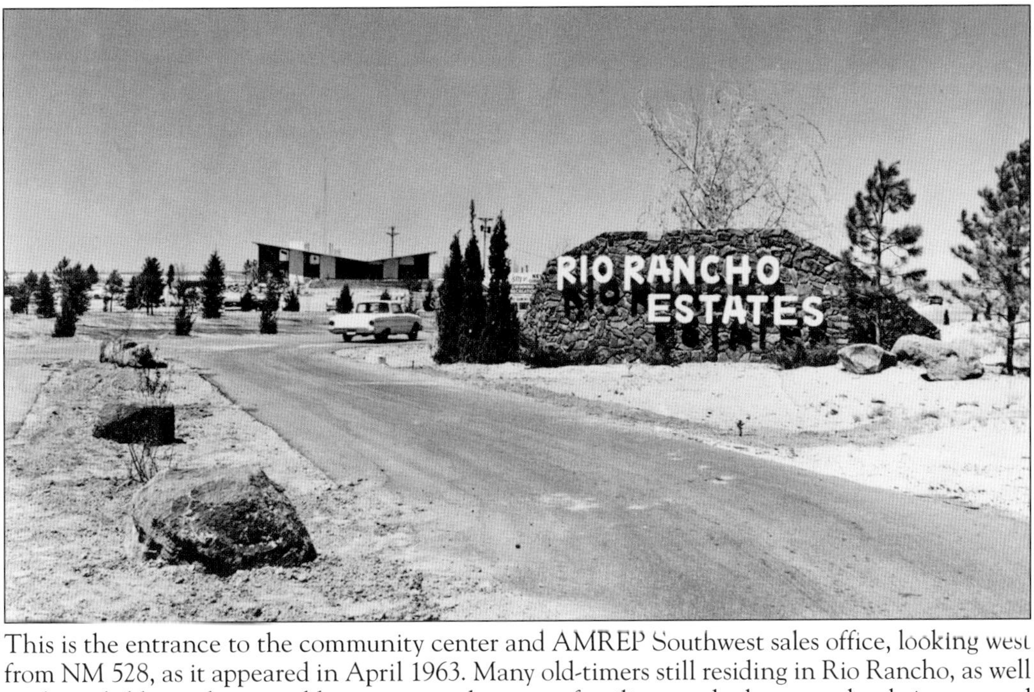

This is the entrance to the community center and AMREP Southwest sales office, looking west from NM 528, as it appeared in April 1963. Many old-timers still residing in Rio Rancho, as well as their children who stayed here to raise their own families, no doubt remember being greeted by this sign. (Courtesy of Loma Colorado Main Library.)

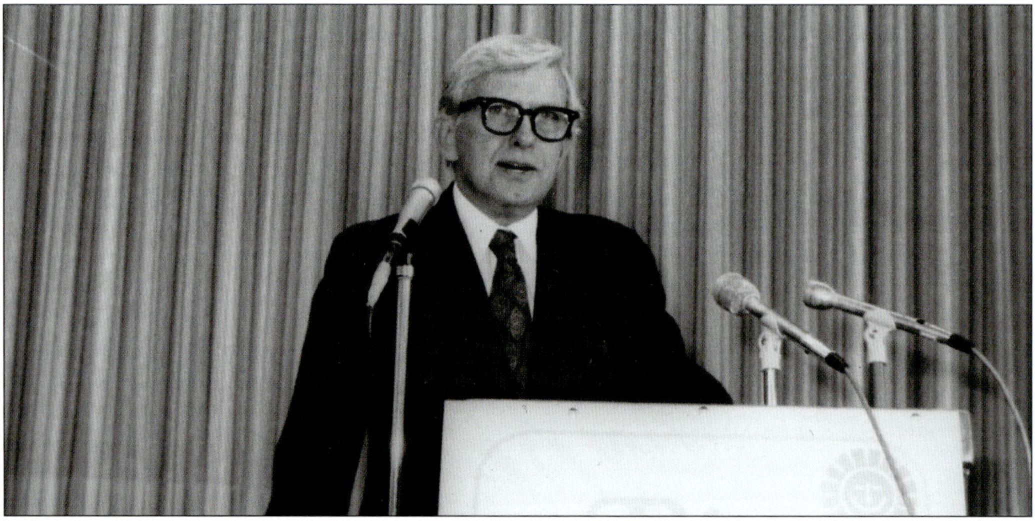

Many old-timers have fond memories of Jim Colegrove, who put a lot of work into the *Roadrunner*, the first newspaper in Rio Rancho Estates, and also served as the director of public affairs for AMREP Southwest. Often, Colegrove would be one of the first people new residents met. (Courtesy of AMREP Southwest.)

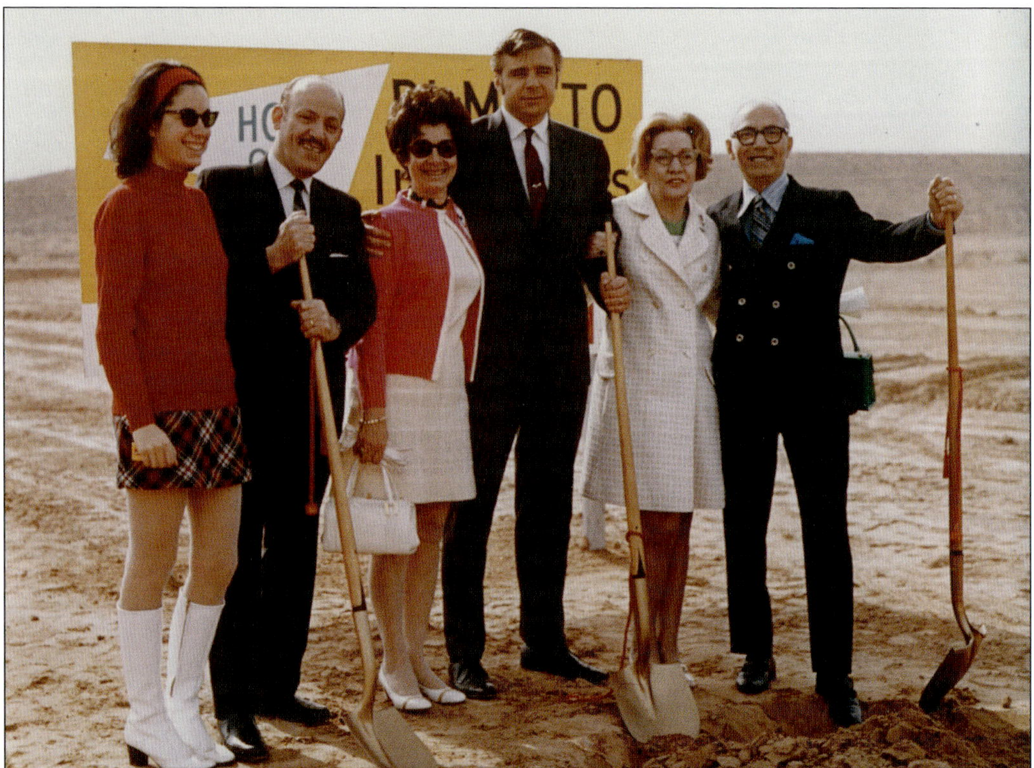

This is an AMREP publicity shot of a Rio Rancho Estate ground-breaking in the 1960s, as evidenced by the go-go boots worn by the woman on the left. Ground-breakings and ribbon-cuttings are still big in Rio Rancho, publicized well in advance by the Rio Rancho Regional Chamber of Commerce. (Courtesy of AMREP Southwest.)

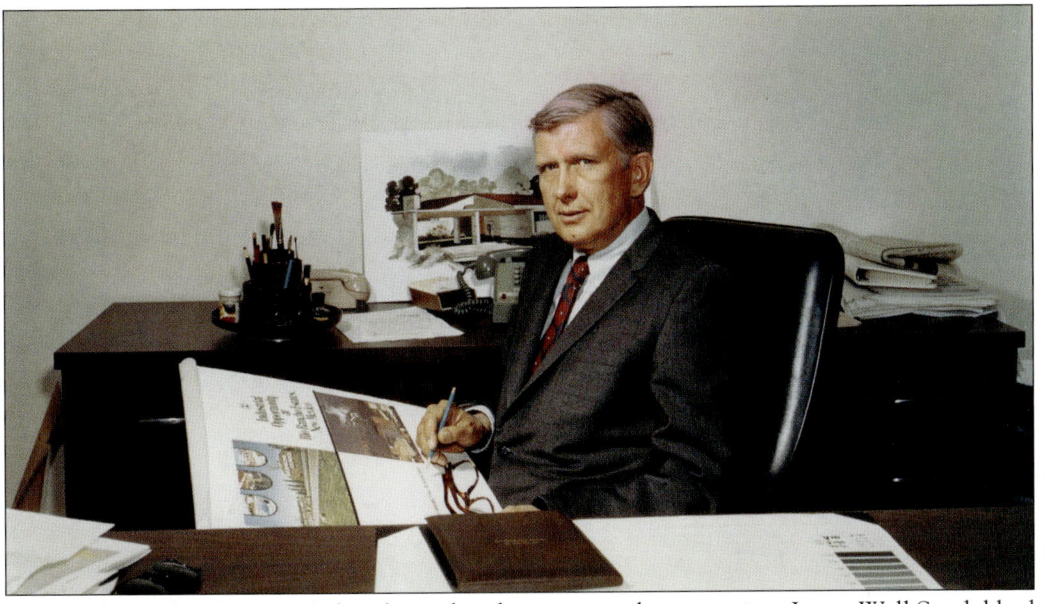

Born and raised in Denver, Colorado, with a degree in civil engineering, James Wall Sr., dubbed the "Father of Rio Rancho," began with AMREP in 1968 and was originally involved in tour packages and the marketing program. Later, in property management, he rose through the ranks and became responsible for the entire development. (Courtesy of AMREP Southwest.)

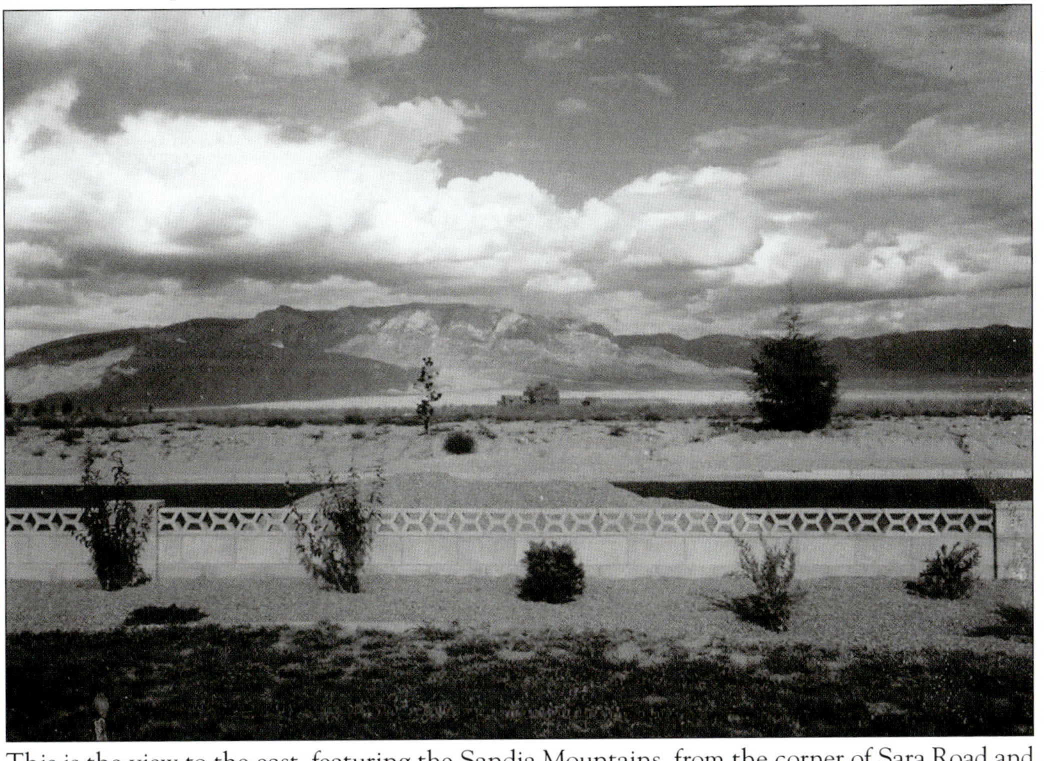

This is the view to the east, featuring the Sandia Mountains, from the corner of Sara Road and Grande Boulevard in August 1969. There is no Hilltop Plaza, Intel, or much of anything else to block the view. Drive by there today and see how much has changed. (Courtesy of Diane Benedetto.)

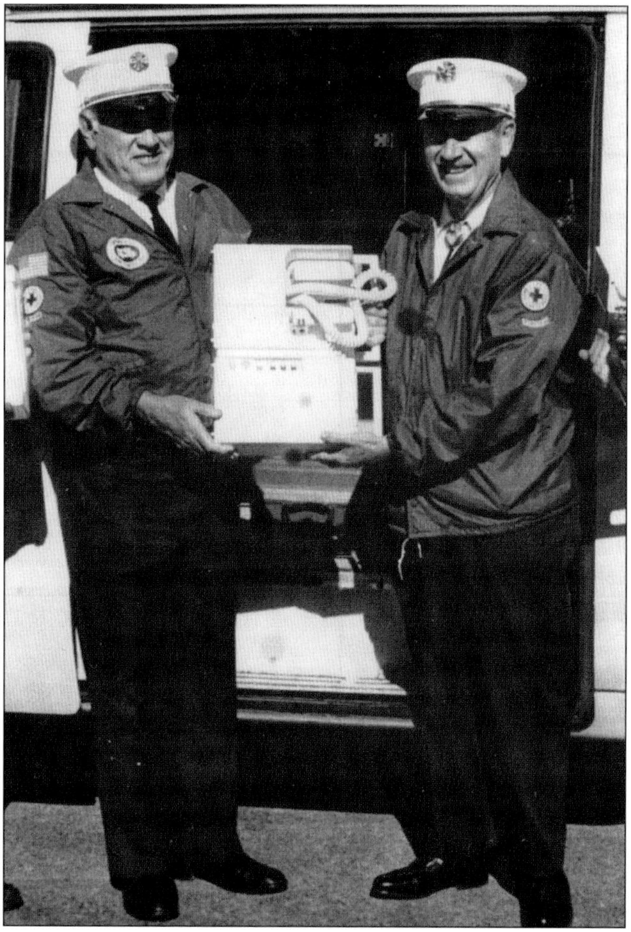

Pictured here is the first fire chief in Rio Grande Estates, John Kearney (left), with deputy chief Bob Peterson. The fire station on Southern Boulevard, just west of the intersection with Golf Course Road, was named after Kearney many years later. A man who also migrated from back East, Kearney made firefighting a priority for Rio Rancho Estates. (Courtesy of Diane Benedetto.)

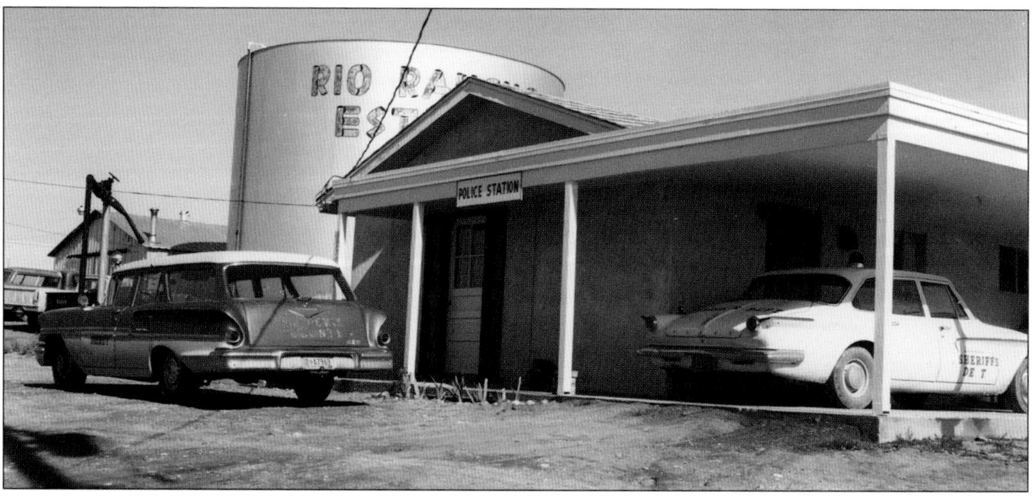

Rio Rancho Estates' first police department, built courtesy of AMREP and staffed by Sandoval County deputies, was on Twenty-first Avenue on what was then the southern edge of the populated area. In 2014, the city's main police station and municipal court were on Quantum Road in the center of the city. (Courtesy of Loma Colorado Main Library.)

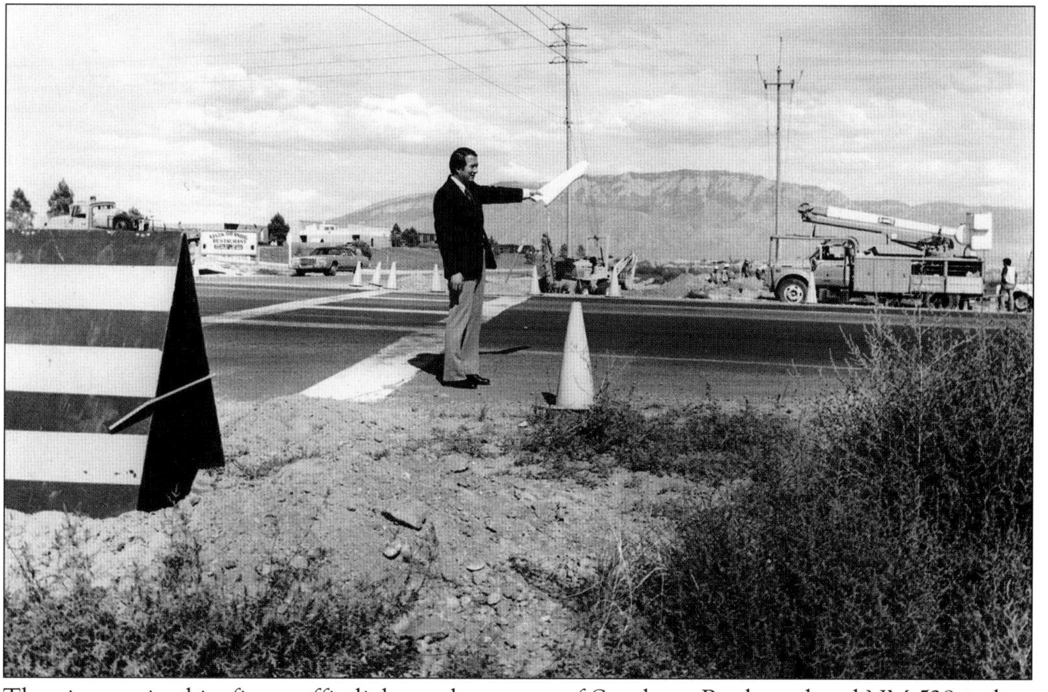

The city received its first traffic light at the corner of Southern Boulevard and NM 528 in late 1975. The state highway department footed the $34,000 bill. As of early 2015, between Westside Boulevard, the city's southern limits, and Northern Boulevard, there are a dozen traffic lights.

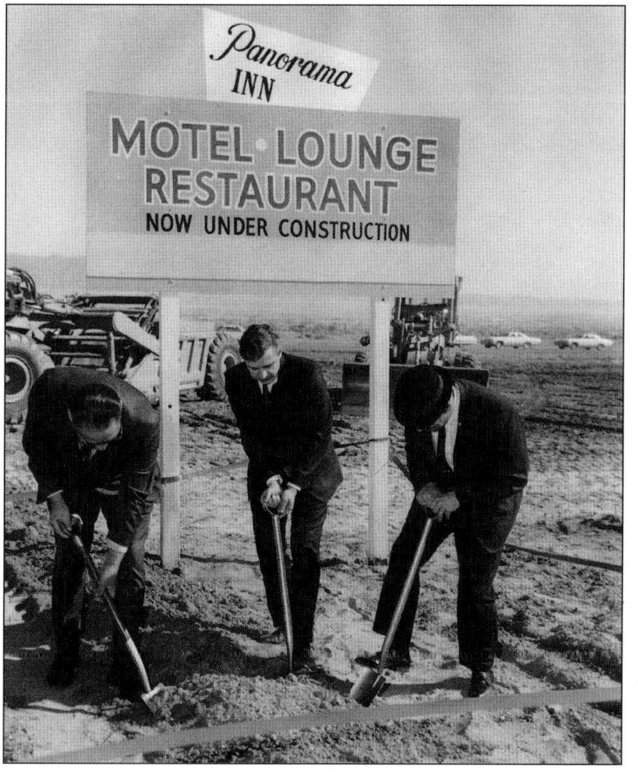

Pictured here is the groundbreaking ceremony for the Panorama Inn, "the place to be" in Rio Rancho Estates' early days. The inn was finished and opened in 1967, and many first-time visitors spent a night there. Note the images on page 22 to see how the inn has changed since it opened. (Courtesy of Loma Colorado Main Library.)

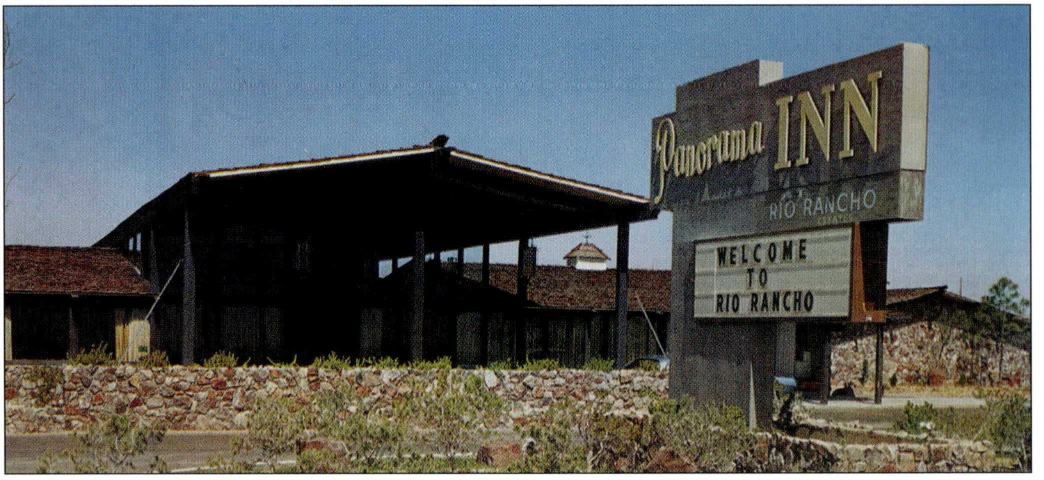

The Panorama Inn is pictured here on a postcard from about 1970. The Palmer family operated the first store in the city here in 1968, carrying sundry items. As they looked at property, first-time visitors often spent a night or two at the Panorama Inn, which opened on September 30, 1967. (Courtesy of Diane Benedetto.)

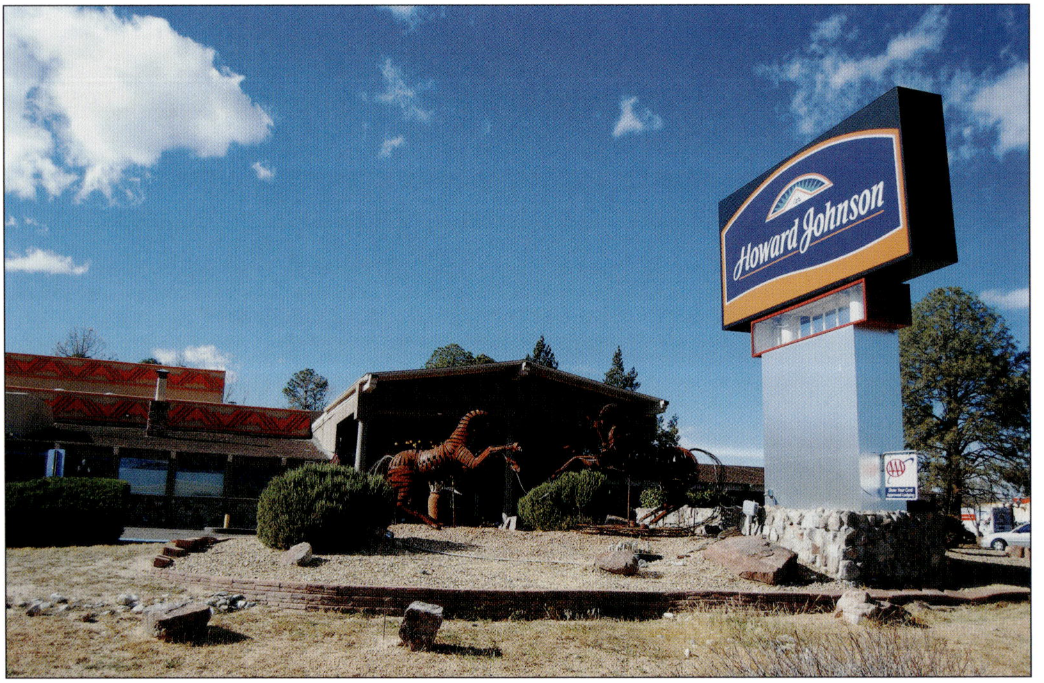

The landmark Panorama Inn became a Howard Johnson's Hotel in early 2014, when this photograph was taken. There were almost 600 motel and hotel rooms in the city in 2015, and the inn remained busy, with high school teams registering there for state tournament events at the high schools and Star Center.

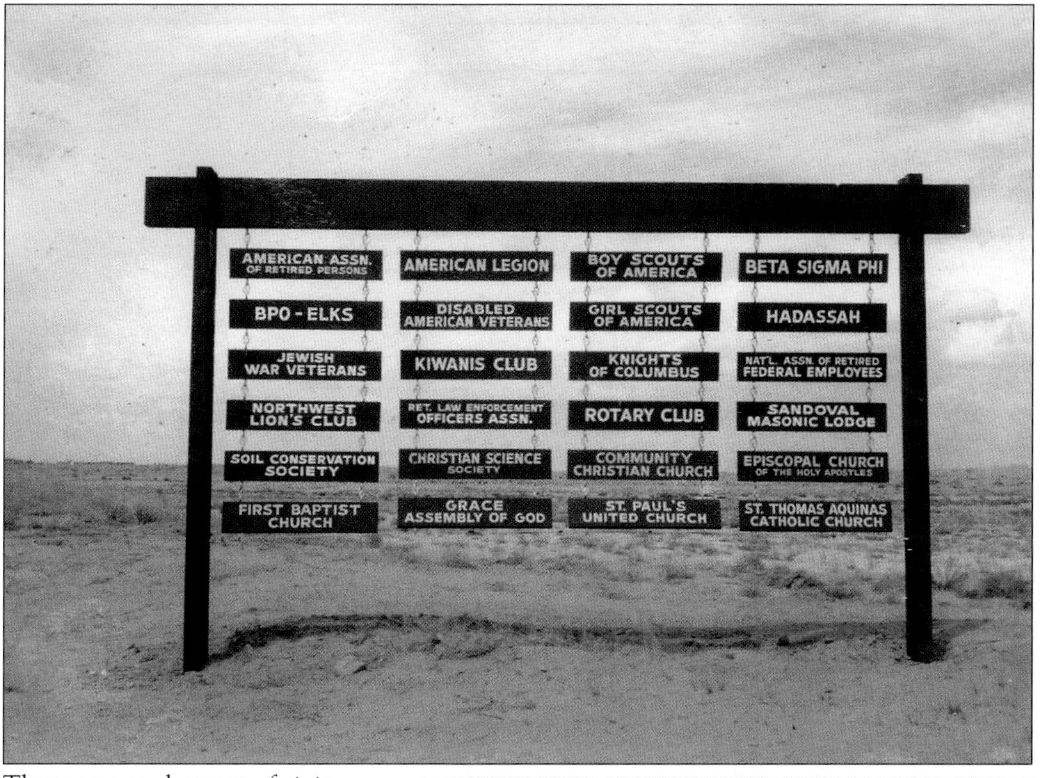

There was no shortage of civic organizations and clubs in Rio Rancho Estates' early days. In this photograph believed to have been taken in 1976, there are 24 listed. Some have come and gone, but Boy Scouts, Girl Scouts, Kiwanis, and Rotary International are going strong.

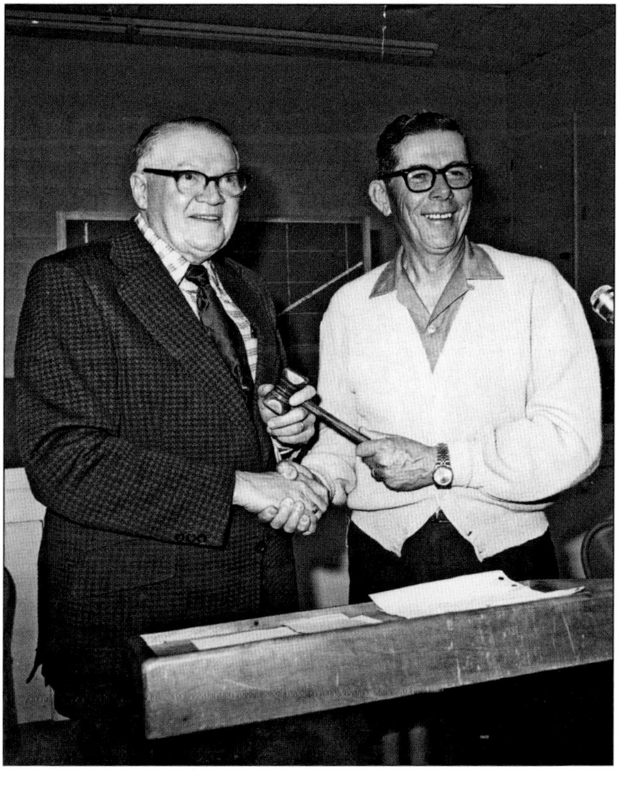

Homer Knearl (left) and Grover Nash were members of the Rio Rancho Homeowners Civic Association and early proponents for incorporation of Rio Grande Estates. Although residents did not support incorporation the first two times, it came before the voters again, and the proverbial third time was the charm.

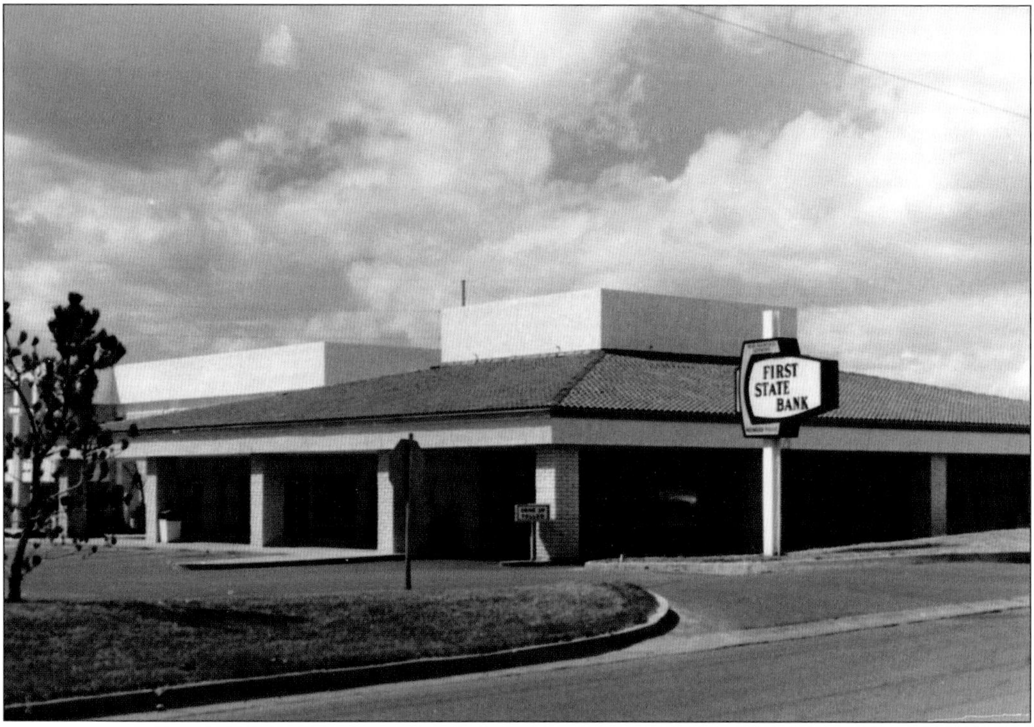

First State Bank, on Southern Boulevard west NM of 528, was at the northwest corner of the Rio Rancho Shopping Center and today is an MVD Express. Immediately south was the Blum Building, which served as city hall until a new city hall was built. The old city hall was razed in 2014.

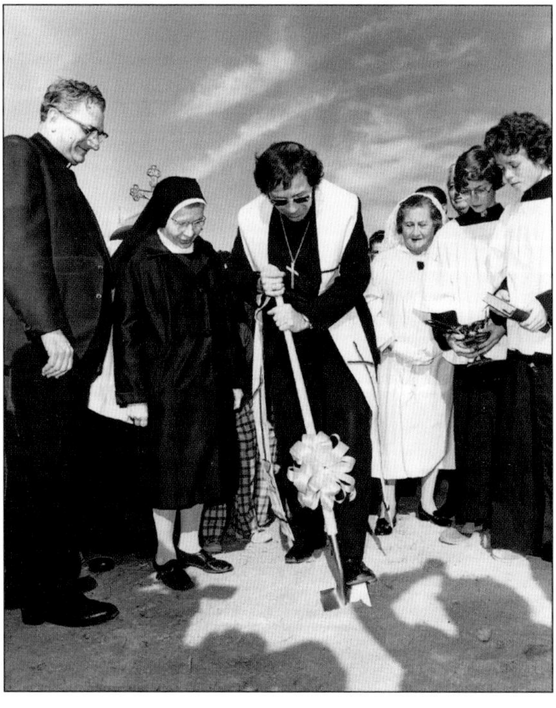

Archbishop Robert Sanchez wielded the shovel when ground-breaking for St. Thomas Aquinas Catholic Church on Sara Road took place in March 1974. The $400,000 building would seat 400 parishioners. The parish was founded by the families of Kenneth Corbett, fire chief John Kearney, Raymond Blaschke, George Canham, and Anthony Rokosz.

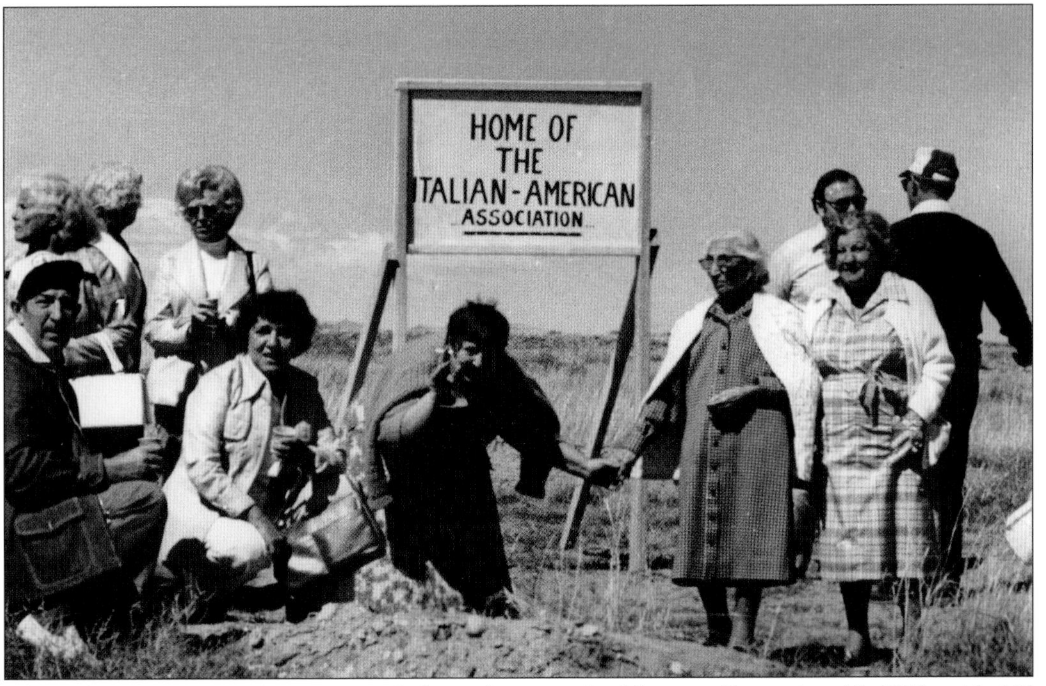

The Italian-American Association dedicated its new building on December 16, 1978, with US senator Pete Domenici and governor-elect Bruce King participating in the ceremonies. The association sold bonds to finance the $125,000 building. The structure, on Sara Road, still sees considerable use for banquets, art exhibits, and much more.

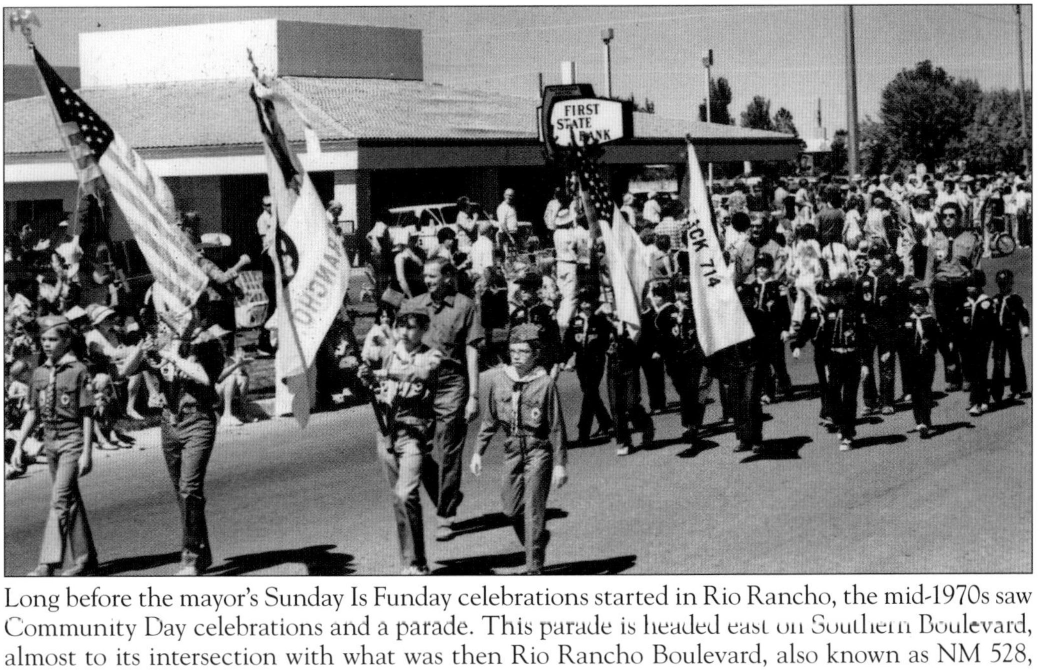

Long before the mayor's Sunday Is Funday celebrations started in Rio Rancho, the mid-1970s saw Community Day celebrations and a parade. This parade is headed east on Southern Boulevard, almost to its intersection with what was then Rio Rancho Boulevard, also known as NM 528, near what today is MVD Express.

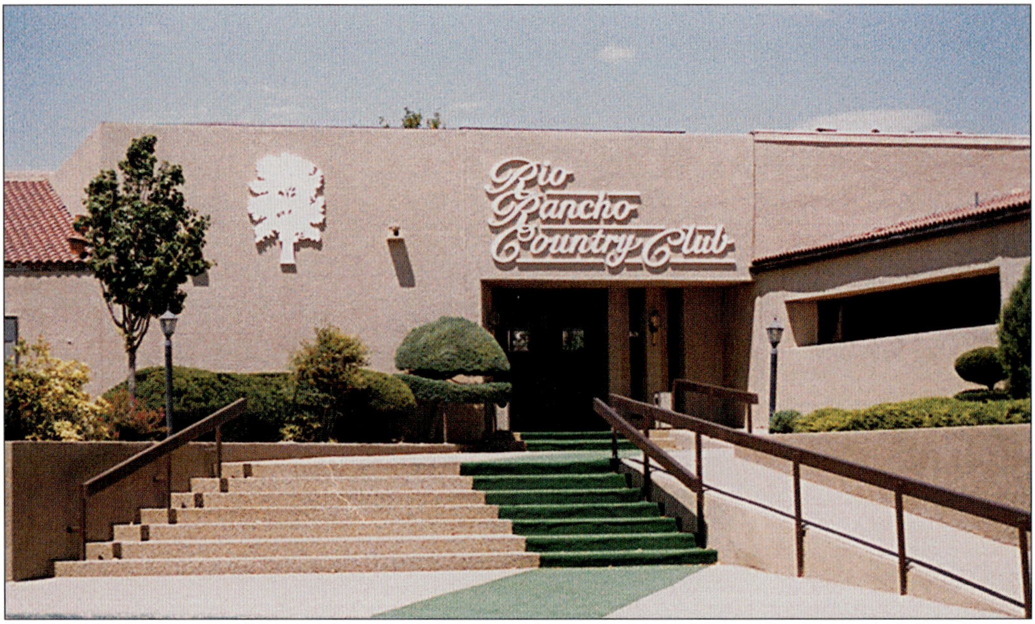

Originally known as Panorama Country Club when it opened in 1971, this was the place to be in the city for club meetings, dances, banquets, weddings, and much more. Later, the country club was known as Rio Rancho Country Club, Chamisa Hills Country Club, and finally Club Rio Rancho.

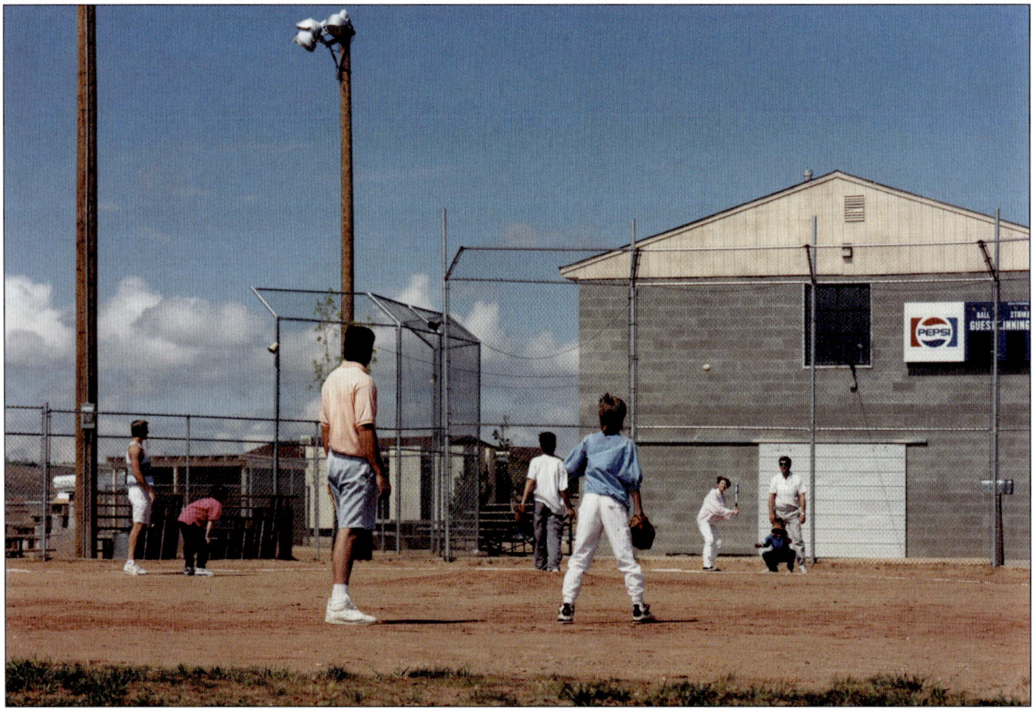

Rio Rancho Little League finally got its own home after years on Roskos Field at Haynes Park. This Little League complex was built on Sundt Road, west of NM 528. It was later involved in a property swap, with the city's two Little Leagues, Sunset and Cibola, getting different sites.

Two

Incorporation and Beyond

After residents approved incorporation on the third try, a new pride took over, and Rio Rancho started to feel like any other American city, just without Main Street.

Today, Rio Rancho is divided into six council districts, with one councilor representing each district. Rio Rancho's mayor is elected at-large by all of the city's voters to serve a four-year term, and the office is designated by city charter as a "weak mayor." That is, the mayor only casts a vote on the governing body when there is a tie vote among the six councilors. The city council and mayor are non-partisan offices. Councilors are elected to serve staggered four-year terms, with three district seats up for election every two years. There are no term limits in Rio Rancho.

Dencil Haycox became the first police chief of the Rio Rancho Police Department, which became operational on October 31, 1981, with seven officers, six civilian personnel, and a patrol sergeant serving under Haycox. In December 1985, the police and fire departments, along with animal control, fleet maintenance, emergency medical services, and emergency management, combined to form the department of public safety. By then, the population had more than doubled from 1981—so had the number of police officers, with 27 officers and 20 civilian employees.

Between 1980 and 1990, the population more than tripled, and business expanded to meet the growing demand. By the 1990 census, Rio Rancho was the sixth-largest city in New Mexico; 20 years later, it was the third largest, behind Albuquerque and Las Cruces. In the mid-1980s, AMREP established an economic development department and worked with the city to recruit business and industry to Rio Rancho.

In 1992, voters approved a home rule charter for the city, giving it more ability to govern itself and make its own rules and regulations. Rio Rancho's population, according to the 2000 census, was 51,765. According to Albuquerque Business First in December 2014, Rio Rancho has grown by 72.12 percent since 2000—more than five times the average national growth rate.

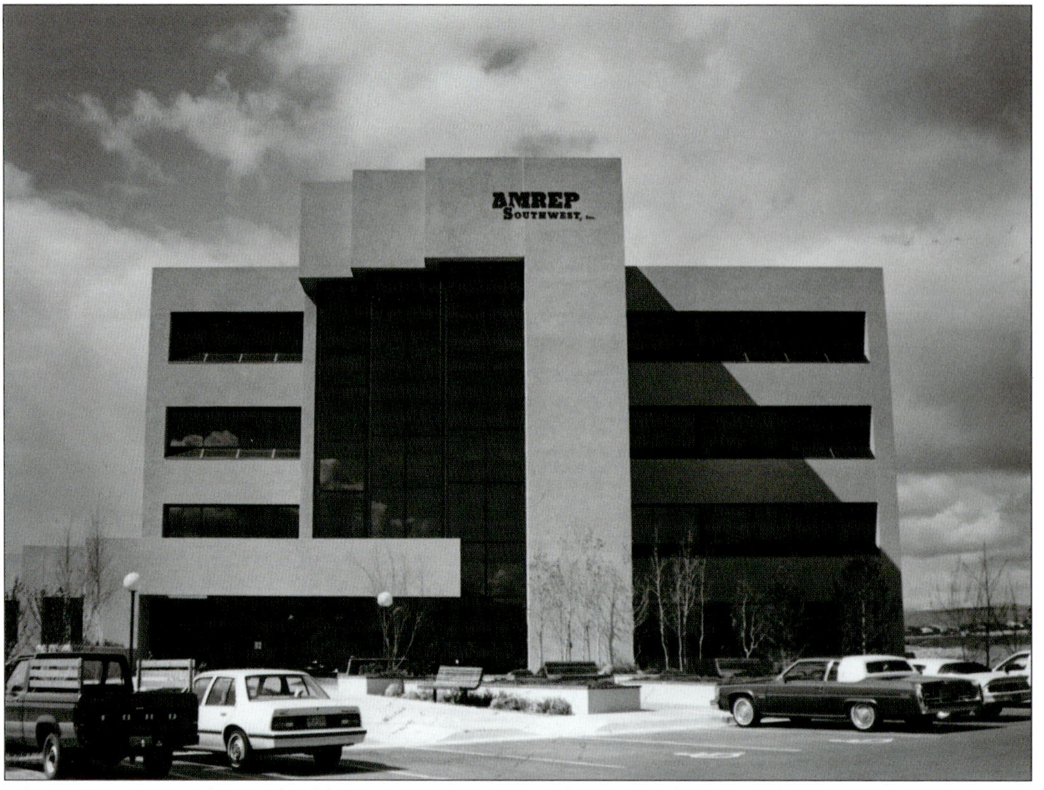

The AMREP Southwest building, on NM 528 south of Northern Boulevard, is referred to by locals as Rio Rancho's first skyscraper, though it is only four stories high. AMREP still has offices on the top floor. Sometimes, the building is used for rappelling exercises by the Rio Rancho Police Department.

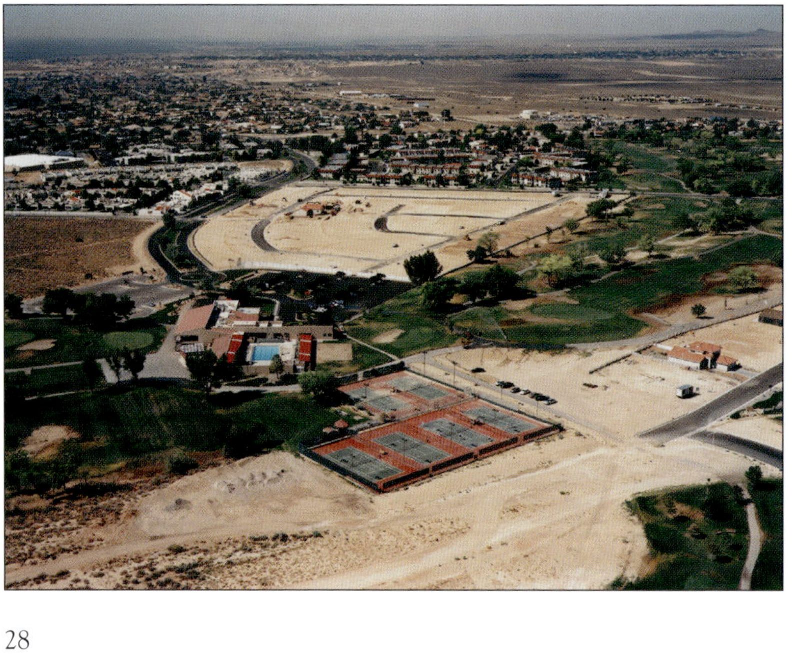

This aerial photograph, taken by Cal Mowry about 1986, depicts the country club and its six tennis courts surrounding then-undeveloped land. There has been a lot more development, and little bare land remains. (Courtesy of Glenda Mowry.)

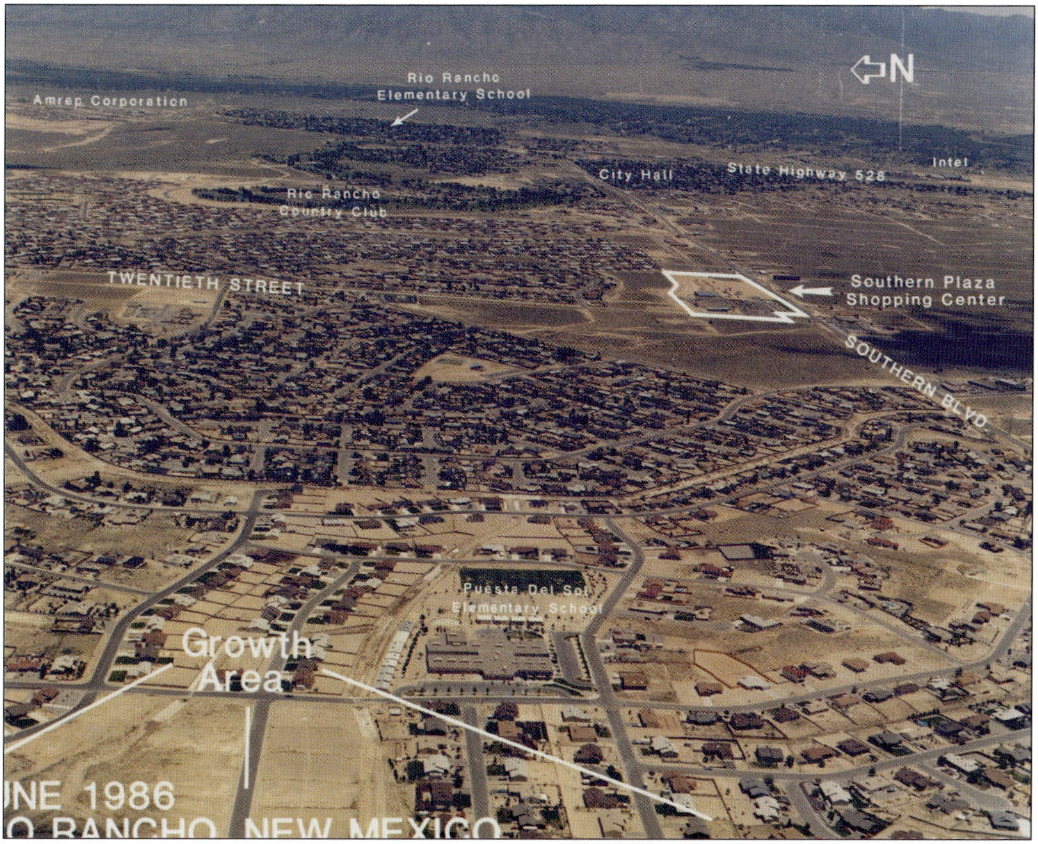

This aerial shot was taken from the west side of Rio Rancho in 1986 and shows the former site of Puesta del Sol Elementary and many other to-be-developed areas since built upon and inhabited. The original Puesta del Sol building is the current home for St. Thomas Aquinas Catholic School. (Courtesy of AMREP.)

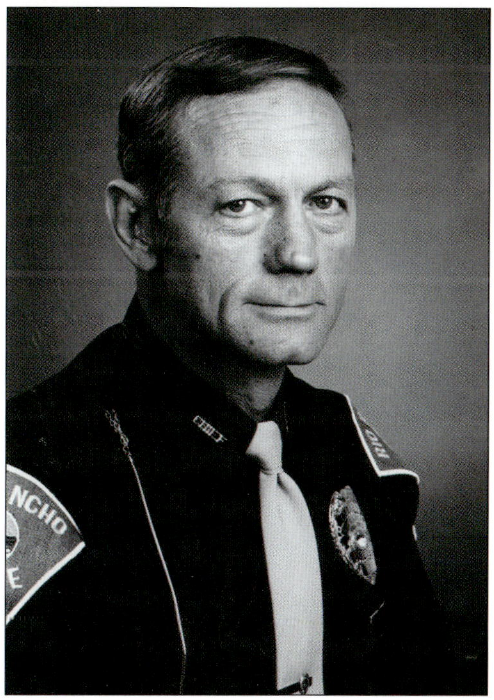

Dencil Haycox was Rio Rancho's first chief of police; he oversaw the merger of the police and fire departments into the department of public safety, and he remained chief until 2001. Haycox was popular among city fathers and residents. The department of public safety later changed into separate police and fire departments.

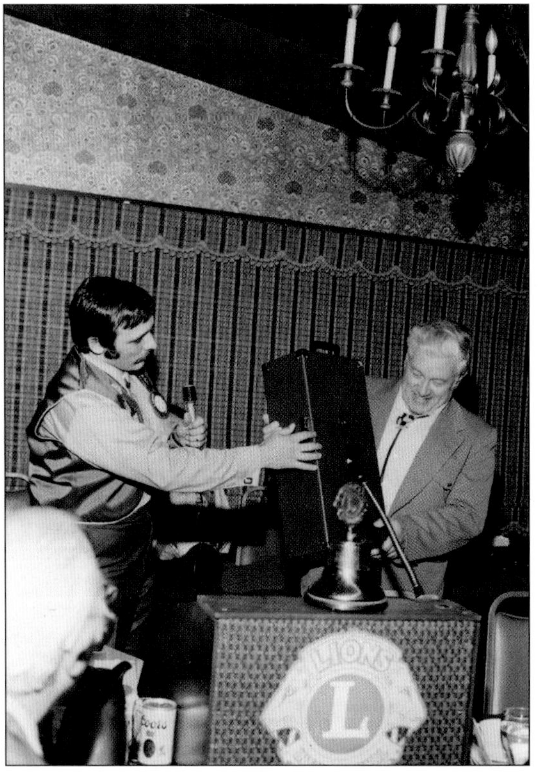

Fire chief John Kearney (right) accepts the donation of a speaker from the Lions Club in this undated photograph. Kearney moved to Rio Rancho from New York and was the catalyst for an efficient fire department. On August 25, 2004, Fire Station 1 was named John B. Kearney Memorial Station.

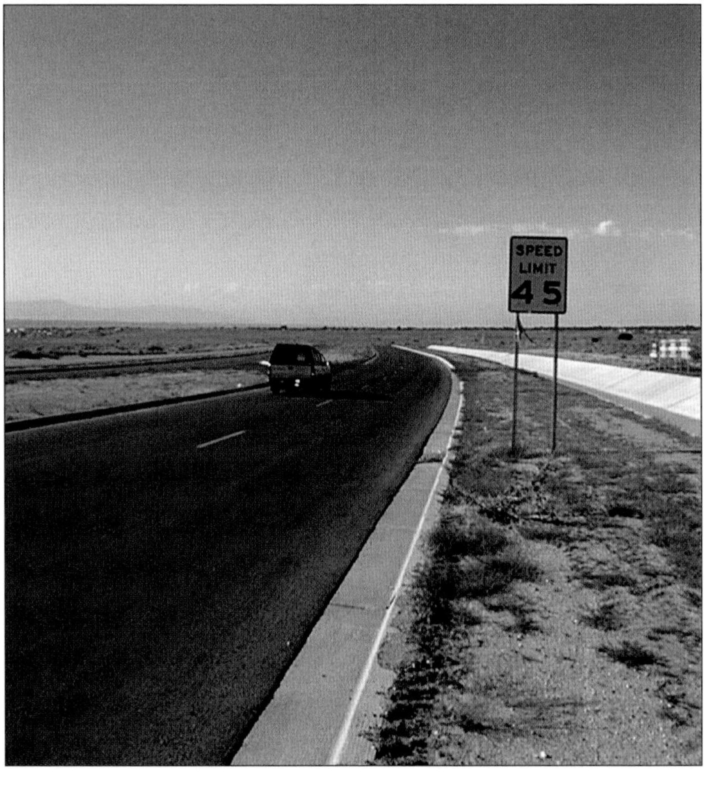

Unser Boulevard is pictured here in 1998. Development on both sides of the thoroughfare through Rio Rancho has taken place since this photograph was taken, making it almost unrecognizable. Also, in recent years, Unser Boulevard was completed and connects US 550, north of Rio Rancho, to I-40.

Here are two of the hardest-working politicians, who both served Rio Rancho for decades. Pauline Eisenstadt lives in Corrales and had Rio Rancho in her district during her time Santa Fe, where she served as state representative and state senator. Posing with Eisenstadt is US senator Tom Udall. Both are Democrats.

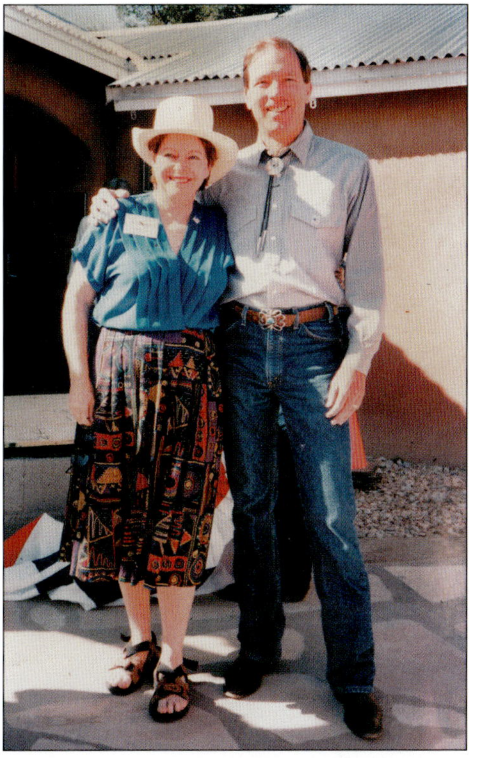

The Hilton Garden Inn, on NM 528 just north of Albuquerque, opened in 1998 and is one of the city's finest hotels, providing lodging and a pool and exercise room for high school sports teams, entertainers, movie crews, and much more. A remodeling project took place there in 2014.

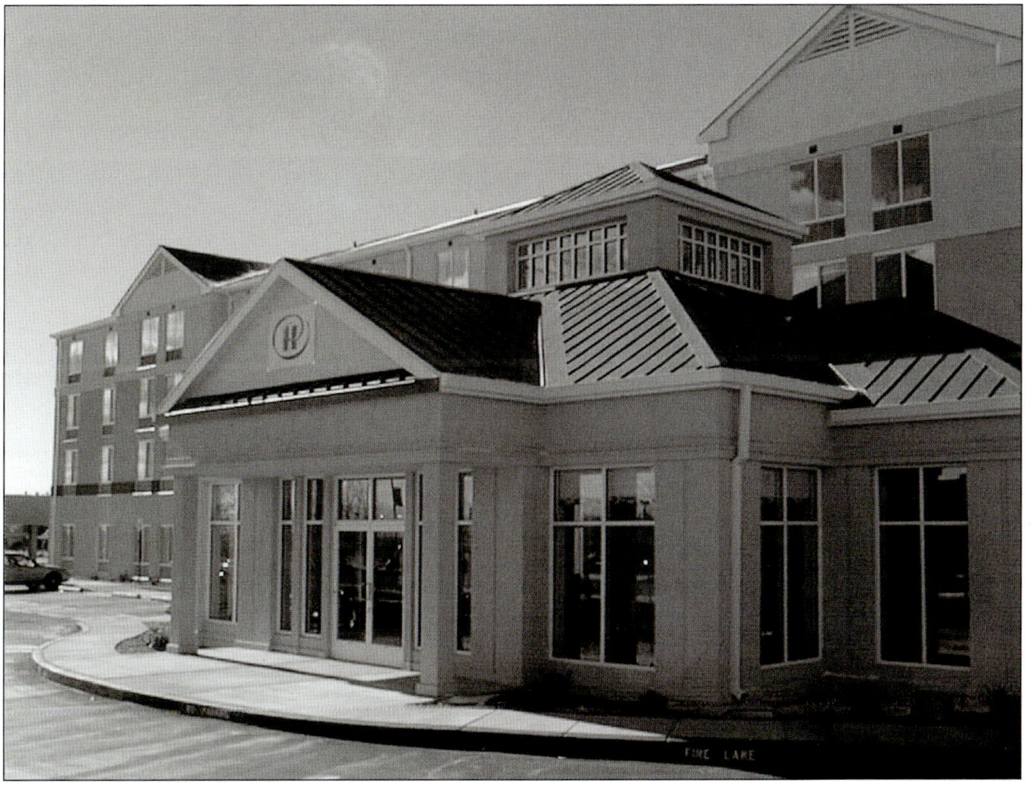

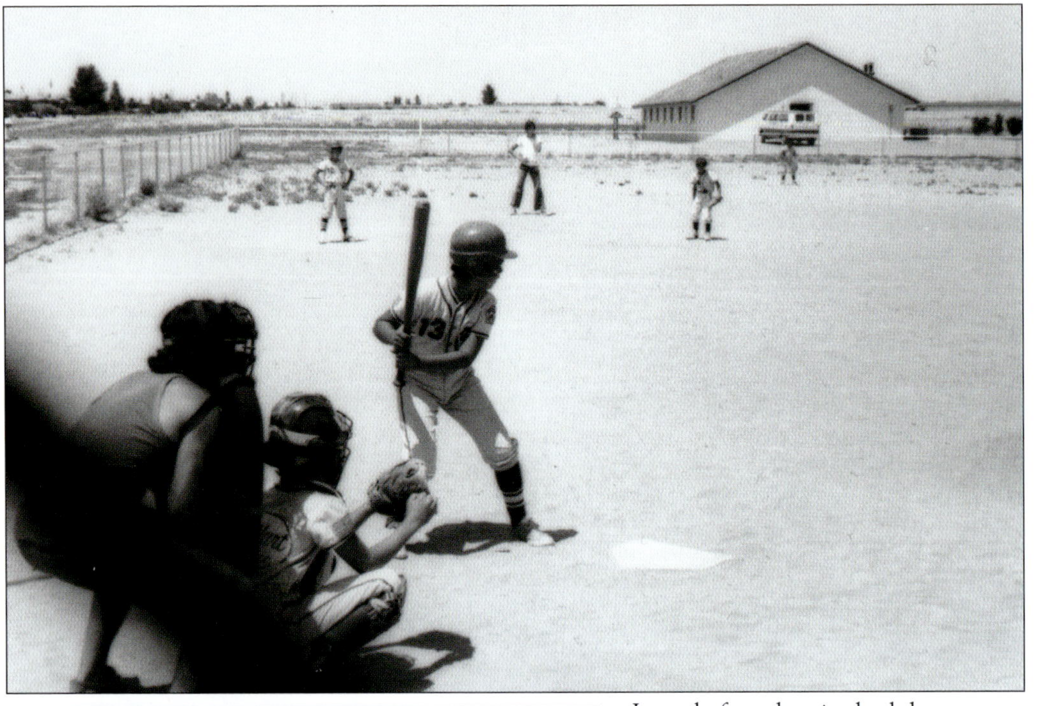

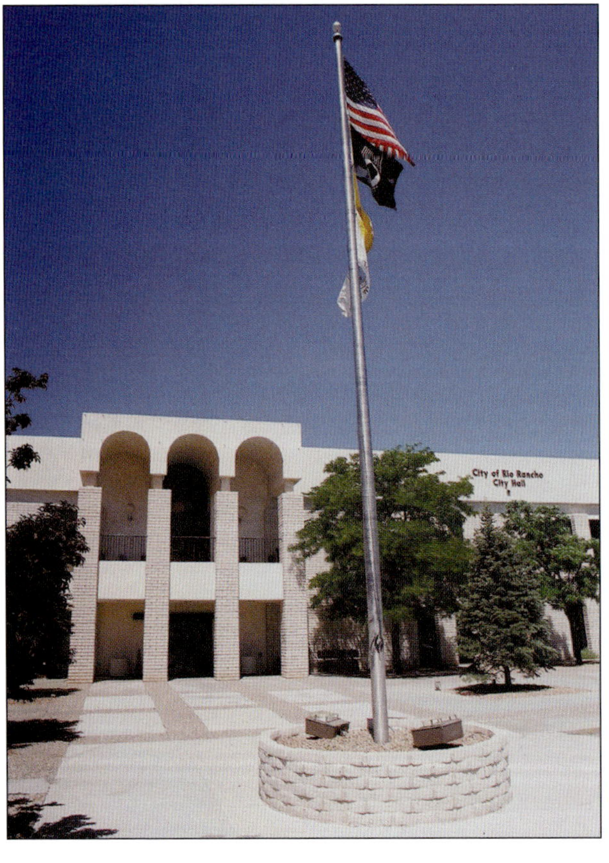

Long before the city had decent baseball fields, one lone diamond at Haynes Park, known as Roskos Field, served for the Rio Rancho Little League. In the distance is First Baptist Church on Nineteenth Avenue, a possible target here for batter Carey Moots, today a well-known videographer. (Courtesy of Dick Moots.)

The Blum Building served initially as AMREP Southwest headquarters, was sold to the city, and then was used as city hall starting in 1983. The library was once housed here, along with the parks and recreation department. In 2014, several years after the new city hall opened in City Center, this building was razed.

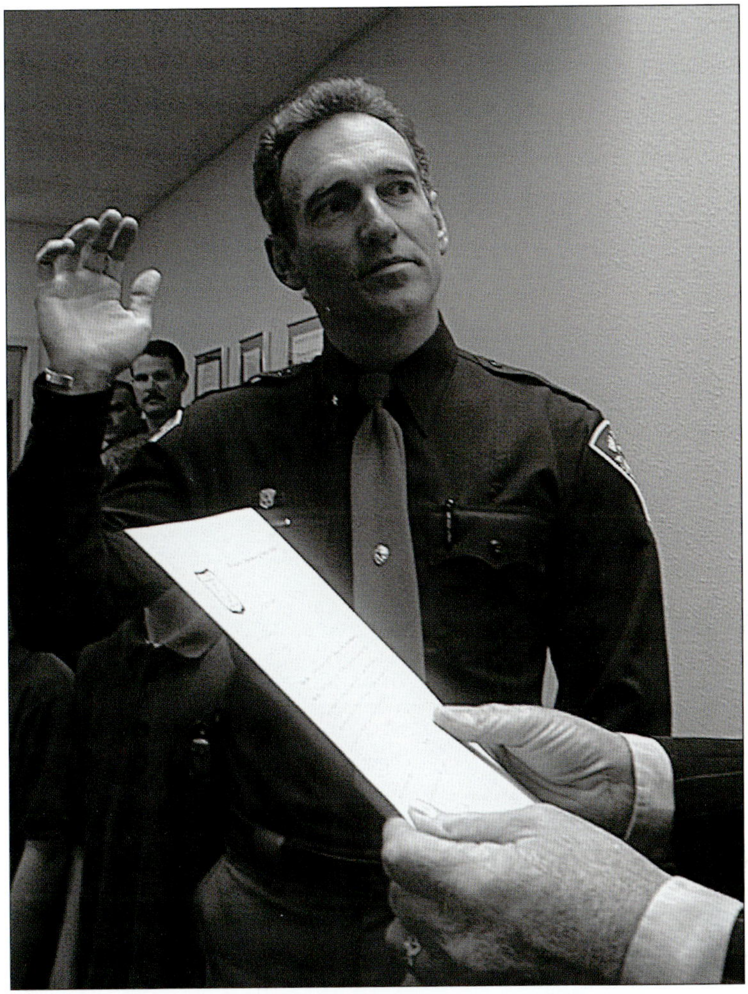

Michael Baker was sworn in as police chief in November 2001 and served in that capacity until December 2004, when Robert G. Boone succeeded him. Boone retired in November 2013, and he was followed by Michael Geier. In 2013, Baker became the Rio Rancho Public Schools director of safety and security.

Less than two months after the terrorist attacks that took place on September 11, 2001, this huge flag was painted on the playing field at the Rio Rancho Sports Complex. Rio Rancho, which originated with New Yorkers and has a large population of proud veterans, was shocked by the 9/11 events.

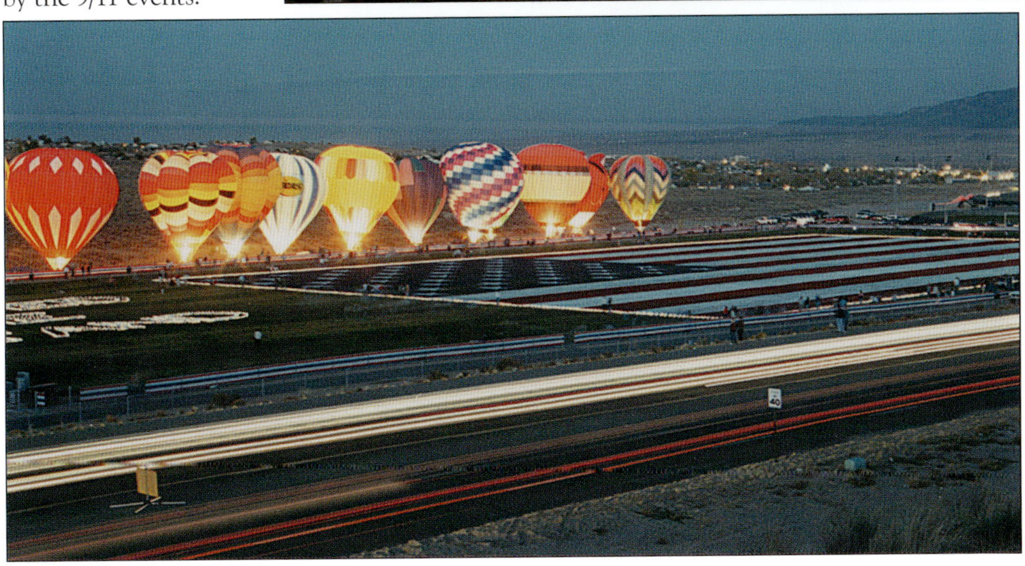

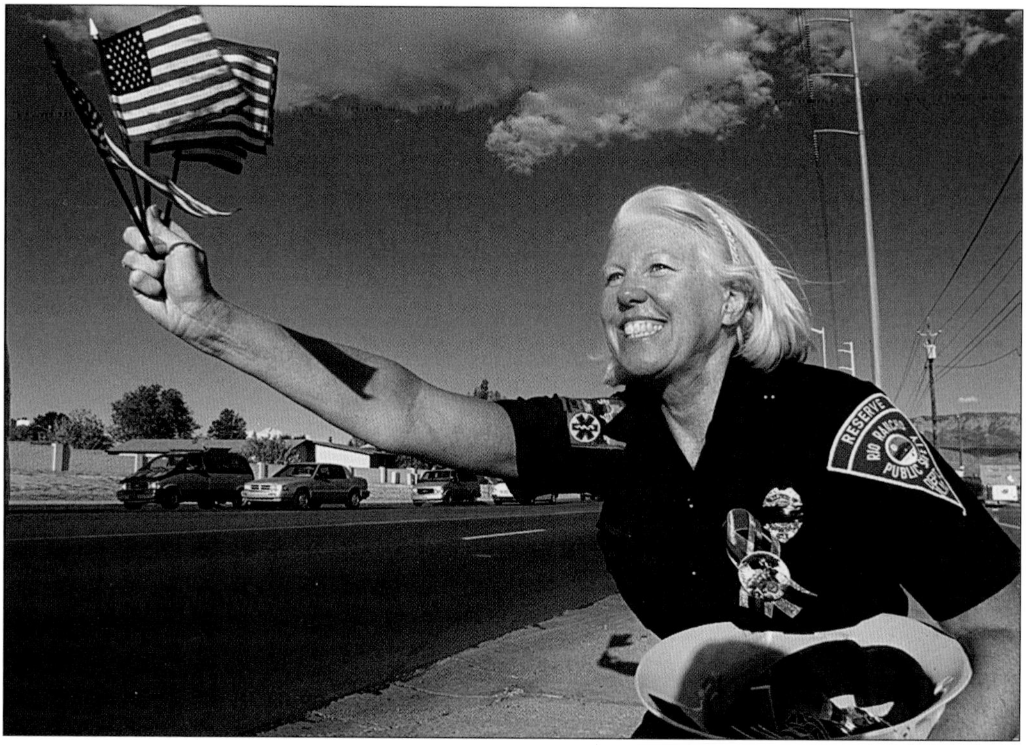

Rio Rancho Department of Public Service reserve officer Peggy Hartz handed out flags, buttons, and pins on September 21, 2001, to those who made donations to the emergency response relief fund, helping those in New York City and Washington, DC, following the 9/11 terrorist attacks.

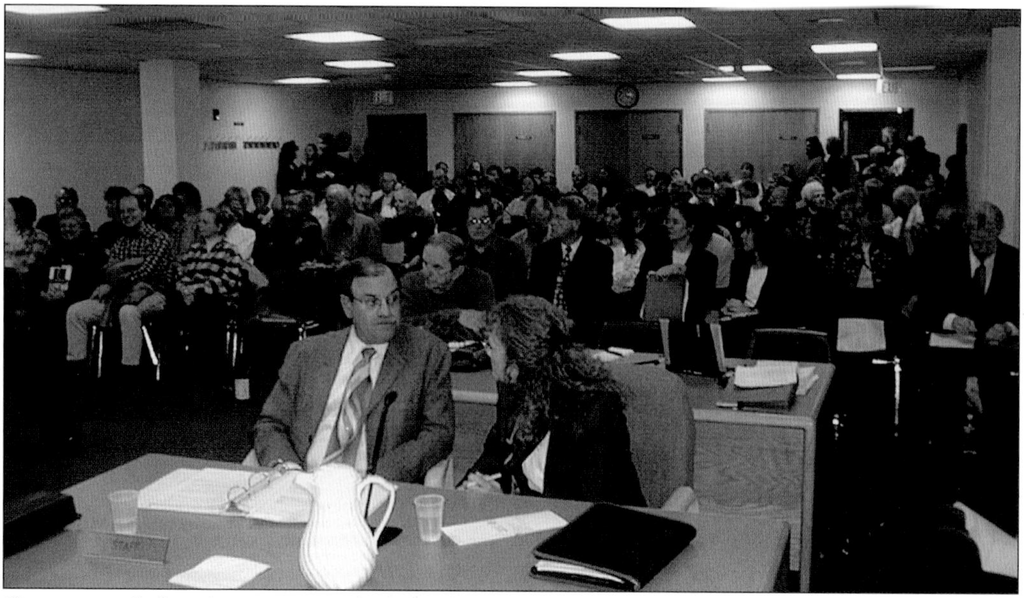

City council chambers were packed for this November 2002 meeting of the governing body. Most of the attendees lived in River's Edge I and opposed Walmart building a new store in their neighborhood. The dissenters got their way, and a new super Walmart was built within the town limits of Bernalillo.

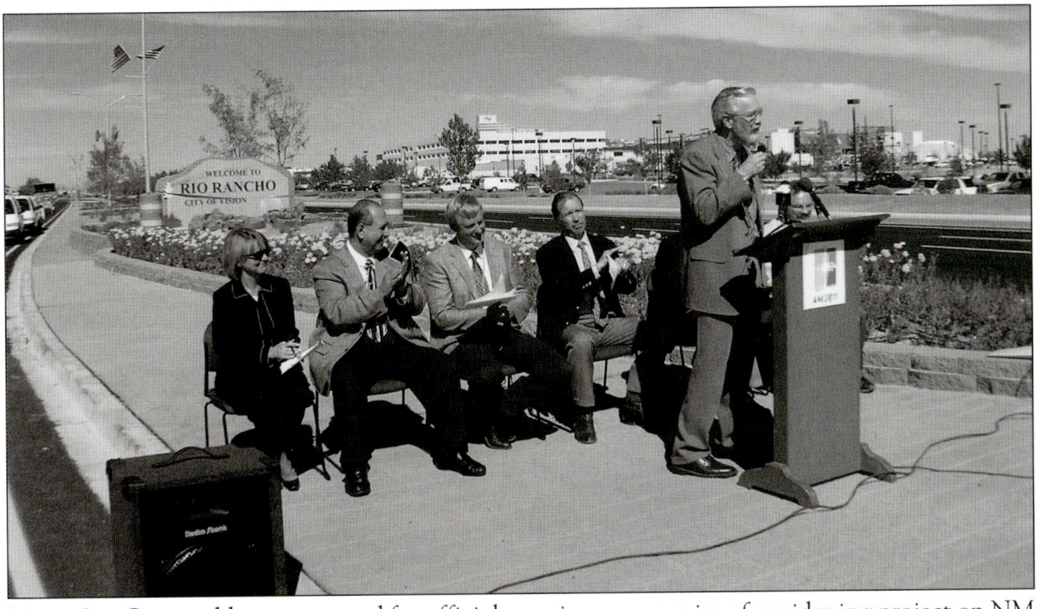

Mayor Jim Owen addresses a crowd for official opening ceremonies of a widening project on NM 528 in October 2003, north of the city limits, to Southern Boulevard. Another widening project on NM 528, between Southern Boulevard and Ridgecrest Drive, was completed in late 2014. More NM 528 widening is in the plans.

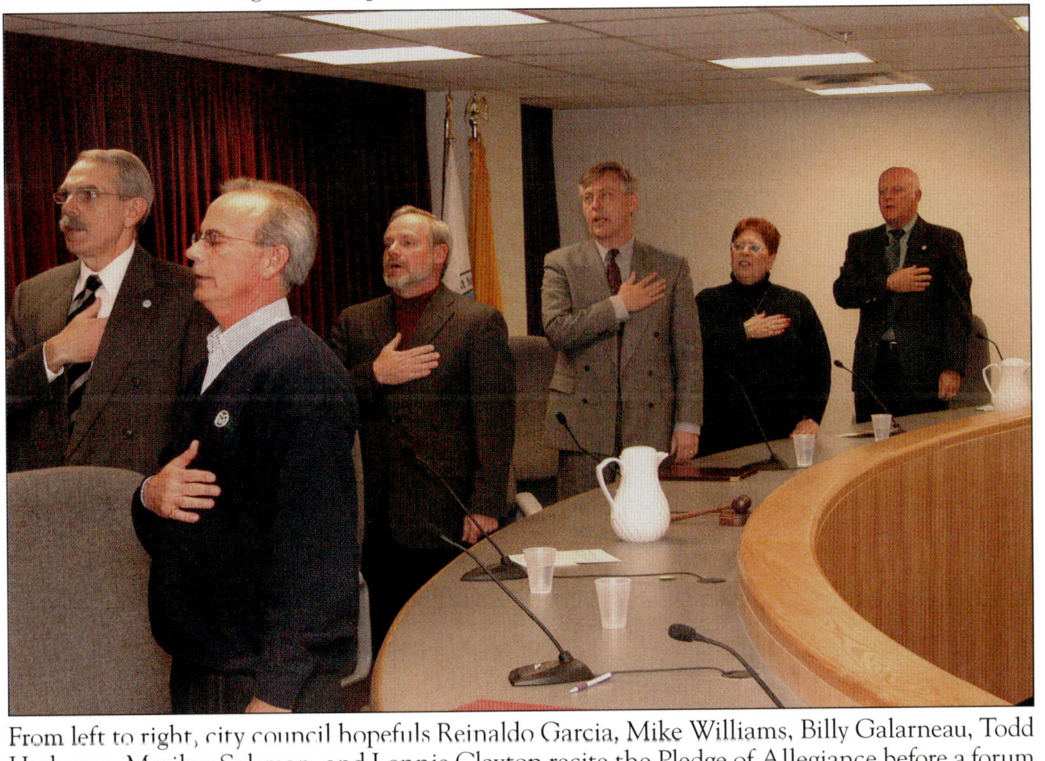

From left to right, city council hopefuls Reinaldo Garcia, Mike Williams, Billy Galarneau, Todd Hathorne, Marilyn Salzman, and Lonnie Clayton recite the Pledge of Allegiance before a forum in February 2004. Garcia spent many years on the Rio Rancho Public School Board of Education; Williams, Salzman, and Clayton spent time on the city council.

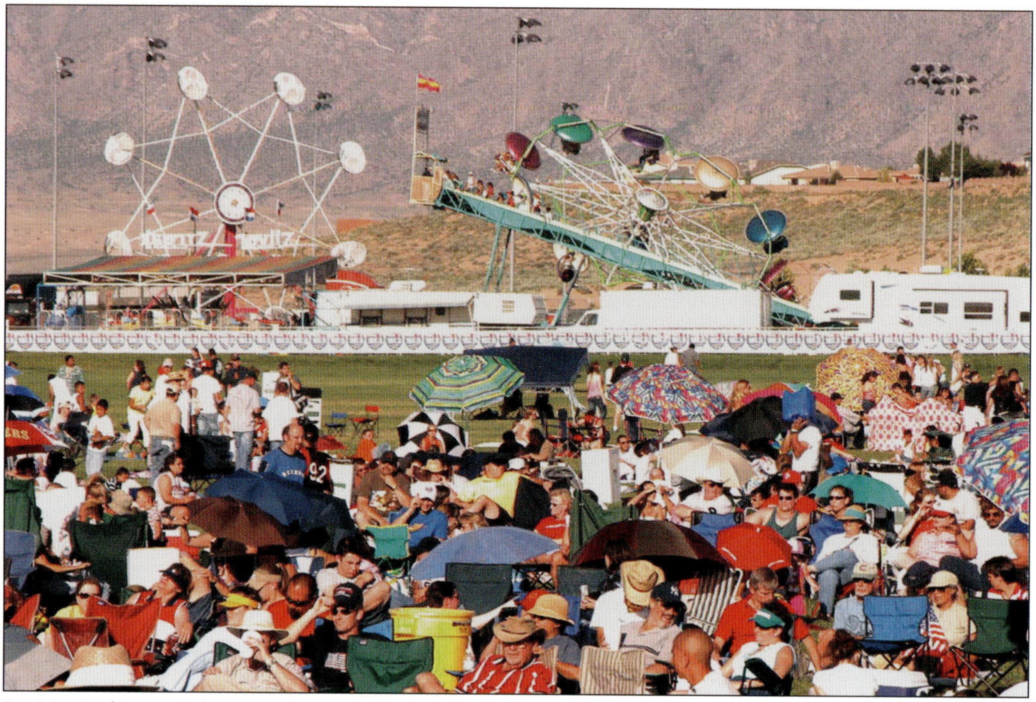

In 2005, the Fourth of July featured a huge celebration, with a carnival-like atmosphere and a country music concert, all held at the Rio Rancho Sports Complex. Fourth of July celebrations have since been pared down, but there are still a parade and fireworks. The city also holds Memorial Day parades.

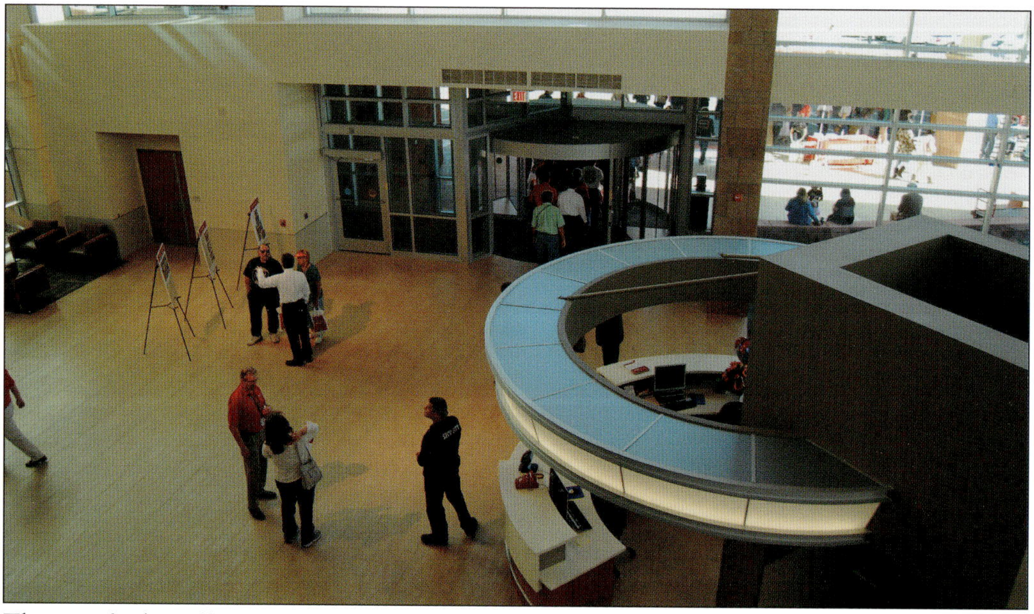

This new facility off Unser Boulevard opened in October 2011 and was named, in honor of donors Jack and Donna Rust, Presbyterian Rust Medical Center. In addition to the 2,500 jobs created over its two years of construction, the new medical center produced more than 490 permanent jobs for residents.

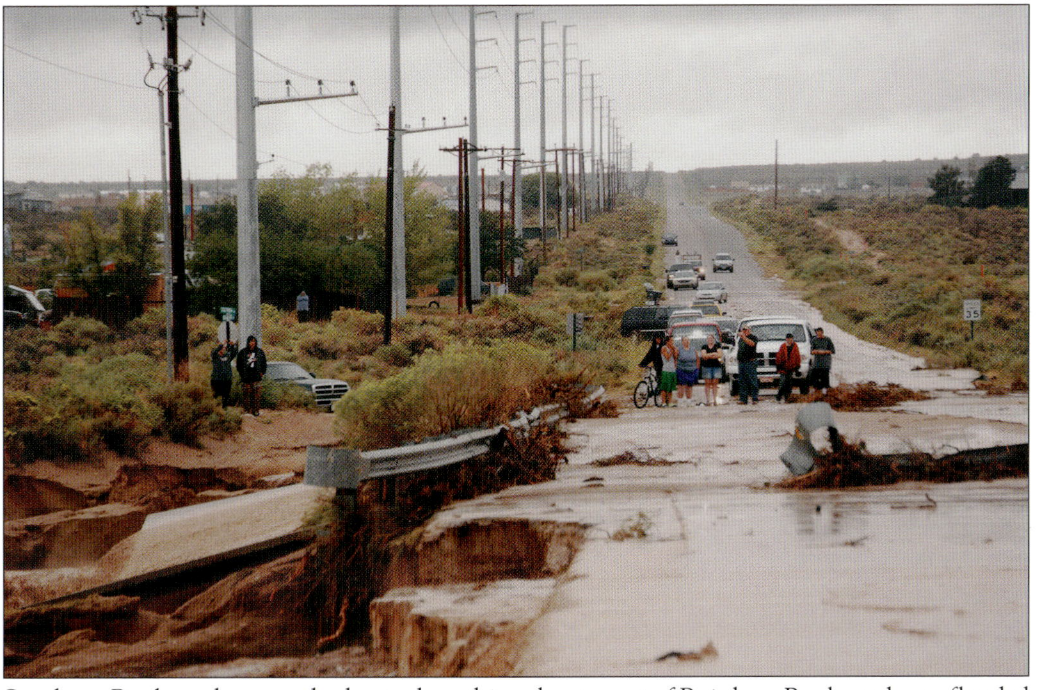

Southern Boulevard was washed out when this culvert, west of Rainbow Boulevard, was flooded after a rare heavy rainfall in September 2013. Fortunately, the roadway was opened the next day, and there had been no dire emergencies in the city's western extremities and unincorporated areas of Sandoval County.

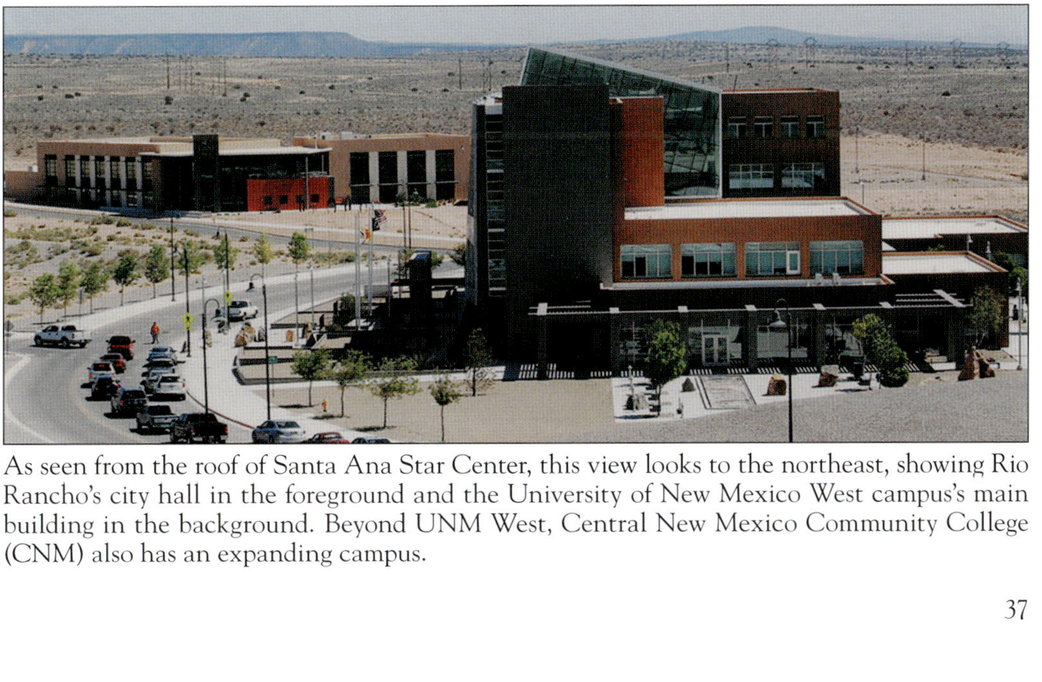

As seen from the roof of Santa Ana Star Center, this view looks to the northeast, showing Rio Rancho's city hall in the foreground and the University of New Mexico West campus's main building in the background. Beyond UNM West, Central New Mexico Community College (CNM) also has an expanding campus.

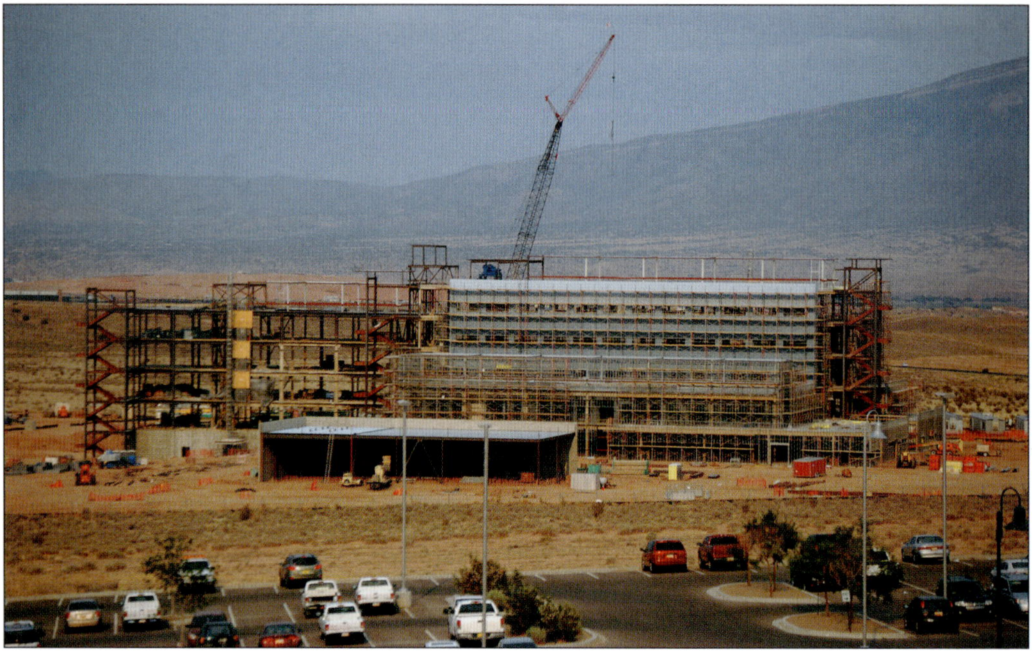

UNM Sandoval County Regional Medical Center is a teaching hospital, pictured here in 2011 under construction on Paseo del Volcan, just east of City Center. The Sandia Mountains are in the distance. Completed and opened in 2013, the facility has a helipad.

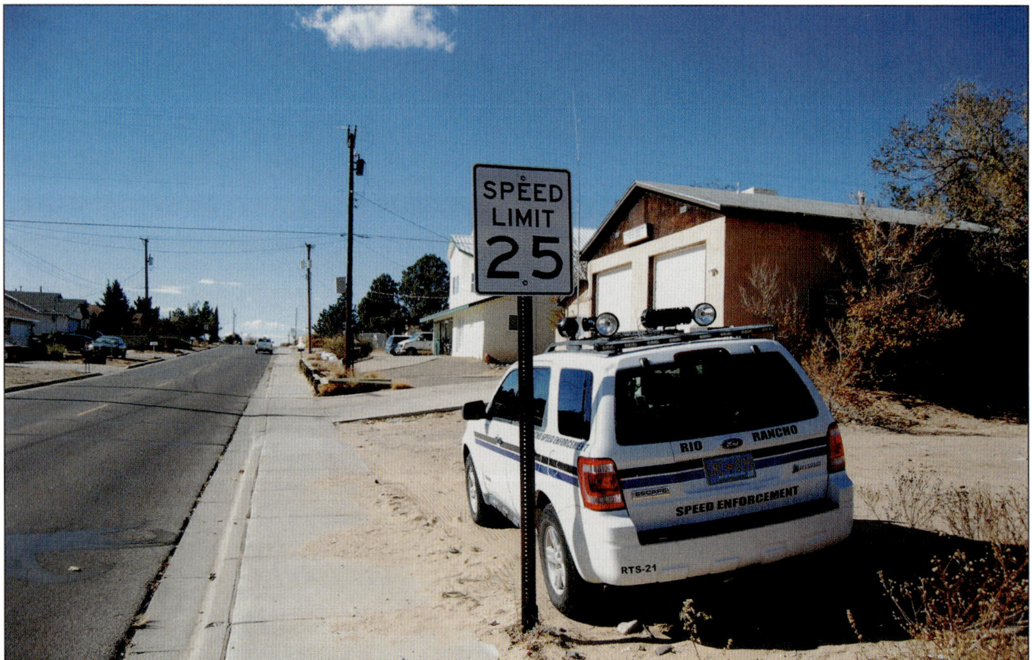

This is a Rio Rancho Police Department's unmanned speed van, which officers move around the city. They seem to be effective speed deterrents, but many residents think they are used by the city to generate funds. The city also has red-light cameras at the Unser-Southern and Unser-Northern intersections.

William Howden presided over the first meeting of the governing body on February 23, 1981. During his tenure, the city gained criminal and traffic codes, an animal ordinance, and a street-maintenance program, but he was later disgraced and arrested for child abuse in 2011.

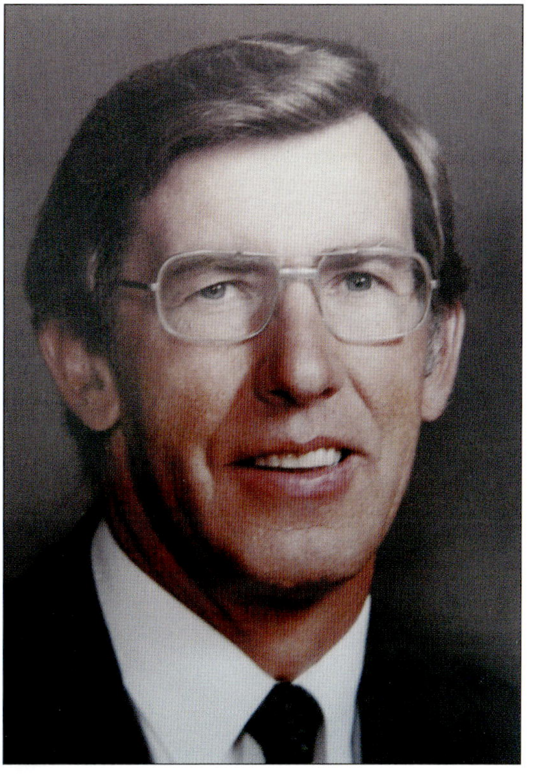

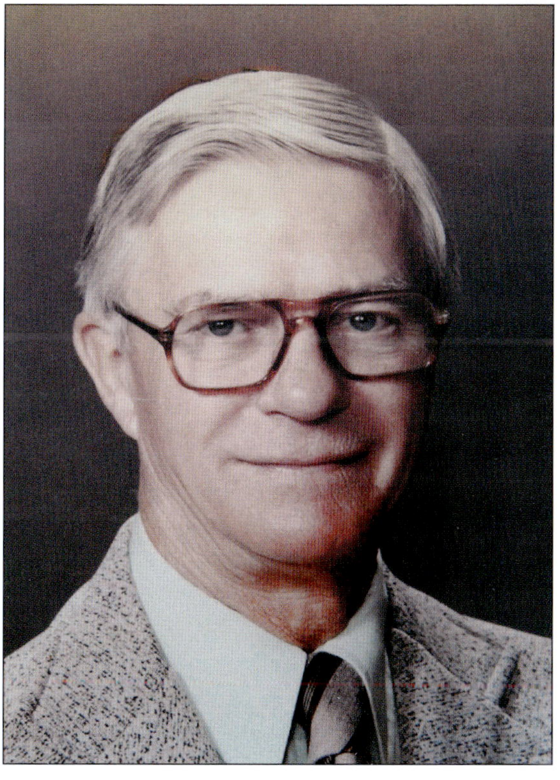

David Bruening moved here from Florida in 1980 and served as the second mayor (1982–1985), leaving office due to health reasons. His administration oversaw the city's purchase of the Blum Building in 1983. He was in office for the first bond issue, used to build a fire station on Southern Boulevard.

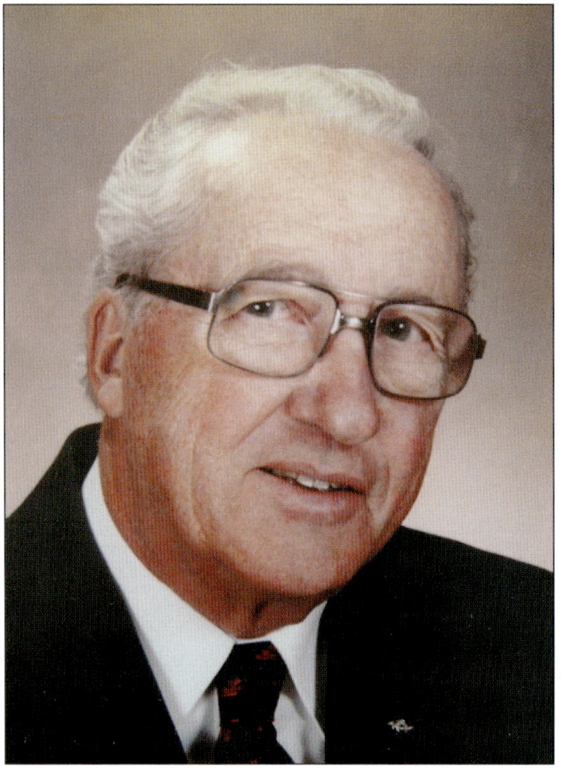

A retired judge and lawyer, Richard Wiles came to Rio Rancho Estates in the 1960s, served as a charter member of the planning and zoning commission, won election to the city council in 1982, and was named to succeed Mayor David Bruening in 1985. Wiles later served as municipal judge.

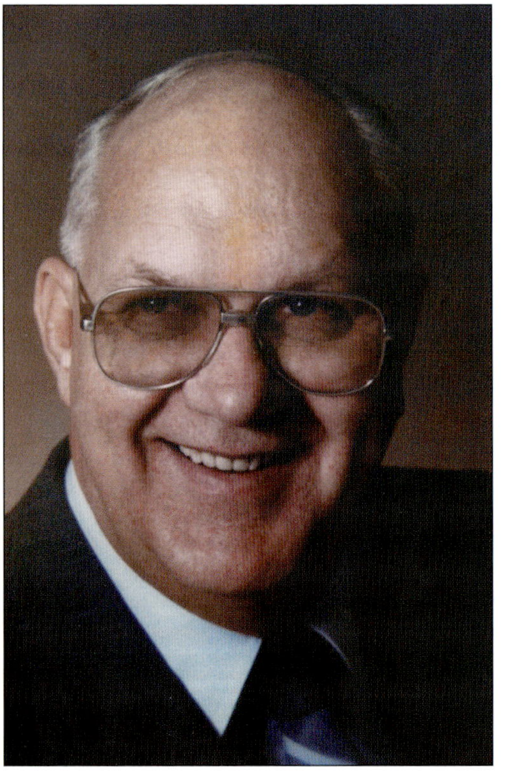

Terry Griffin was elected mayor in 1986 and served for 13 months before resigning on March 31, 1987, after clashes with the governing body. The city council filed a civil complaint seeking his removal from office for malfeasance in December 1986; he denied those allegations but stepped down before a trial.

Grover Nash worked with Homer Knearl on the incorporation issue and won a second term on the city council when named to succeed Terry Griffin as mayor in 1987. Nash served as mayor until the 1990 election. In the late 1990s, Nash was on a committee that reviewed the city charter.

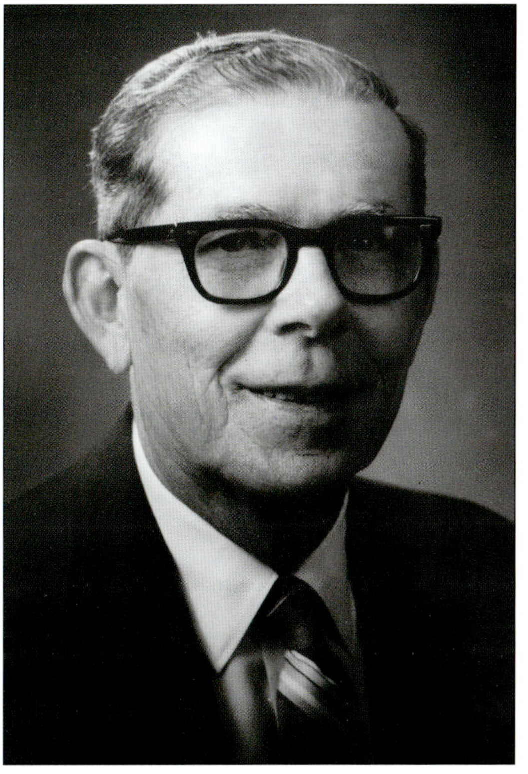

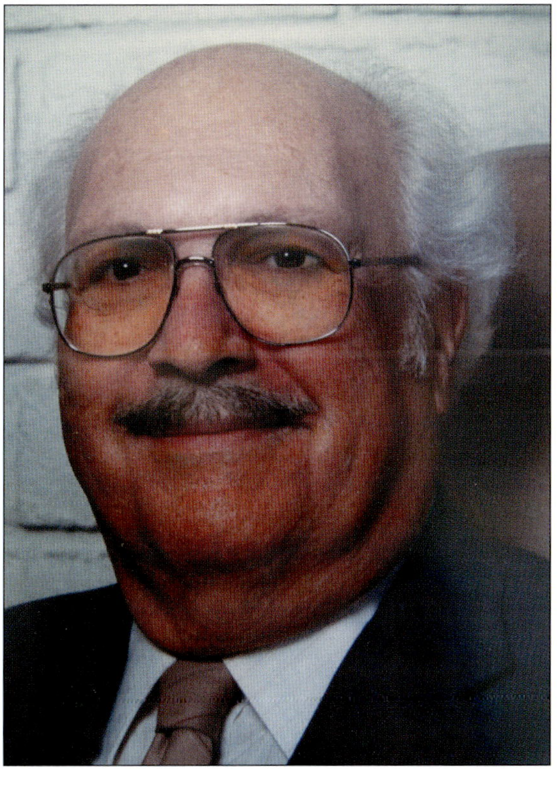

The only mayor of Rio Rancho with a highway named after him, Pat D'Arco served from 1990 to 1994 and was first known as a prolific letter-writer to local newspapers. He was appointed to his stint on the city council when he was appointed to replace Grover Nash, who assumed the reins after the Terry Griffin resignation.

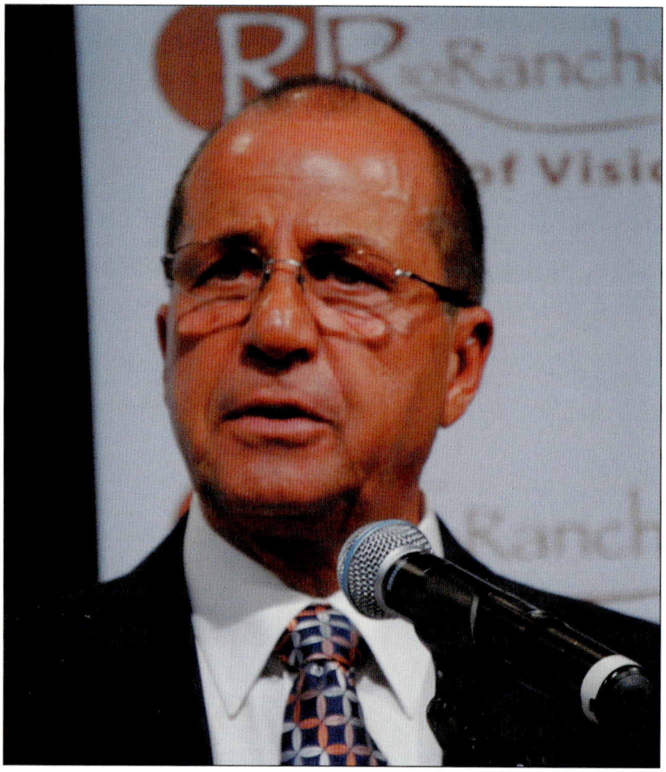

Thomas Swisstack was on the Sandoval County Commission and head of the Bernalillo County Juvenile Detention Center when he won the 1994 mayoral election. He did not run in 1998 and was elected to the state's house of representatives in 2002. After two terms, Swisstack won the mayoral race again in 2010.

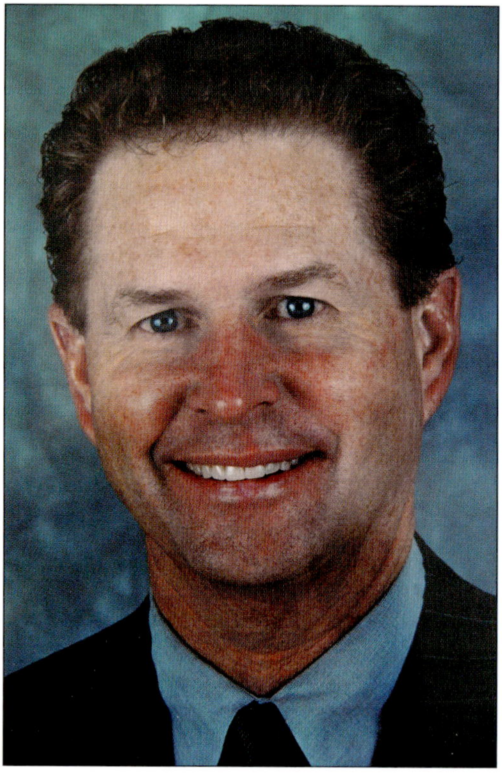

John Jennings served as mayor from 1998 to 2002. The onetime banker looked back on his administration and is proudest of a partnership with Intel and the state, along with a $5-million city bond issue that led to the widening of NM 528, restoration of the Paseo del Volcan alignment, and redevelopment of Unit 16.

Jim Owen was elected mayor in 2002, and two years later he had a hand in the plans for Santa Ana Star Center and City Center. Owen, once the site manager at Intel's Rio Rancho plant, was defeated by Kevin Jackson in 2006 and ran unsuccessfully in 2010 and 2014.

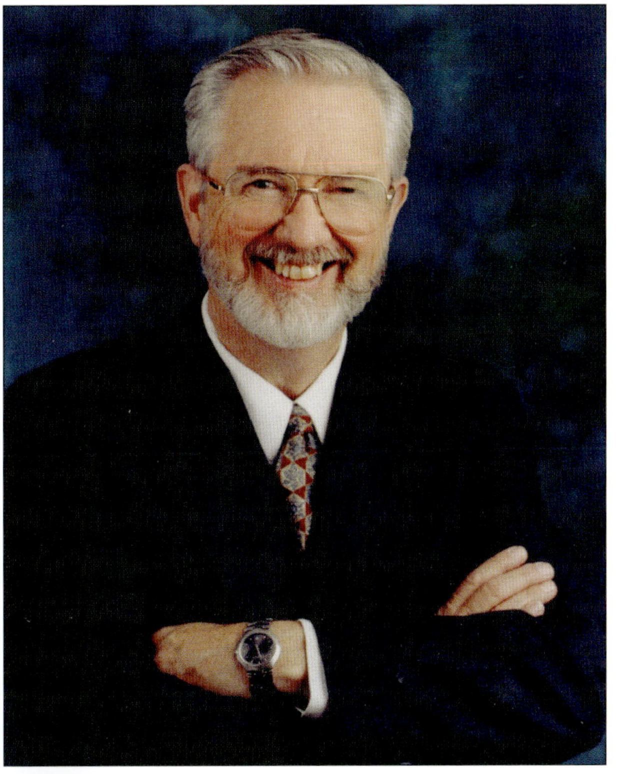

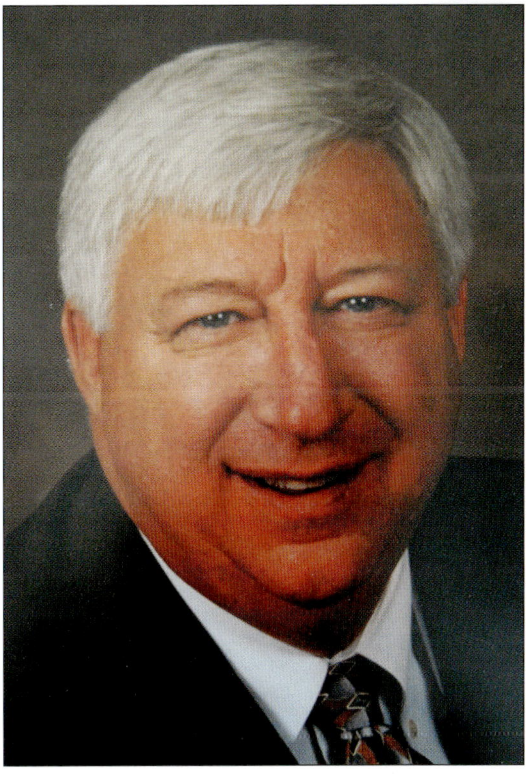

Kevin Jackson grew up in Rio Rancho, was a track and field athlete at West Mesa High School, and attended West Point. Back in Rio Rancho, he became involved with nonprofit organizations, including the New Mexico Family Council, and won election as mayor in 2006. Jackson resigned in 2007 amid allegations of fraud.

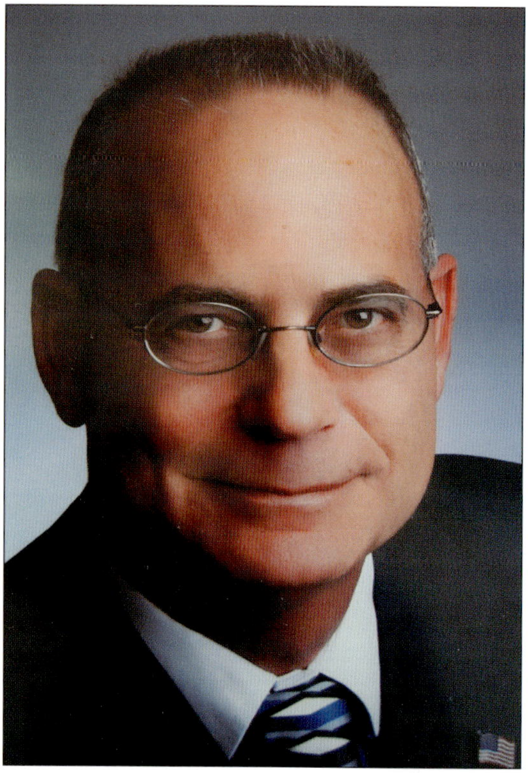

Michael Williams served as interim mayor after Kevin Jackson resigned his position. Williams, a District 1 councilor, lost mayoral elections in 2010 and 2014, the latter when he was defeated by Gregg Hull in a runoff election, which was necessary when no mayoral candidate received more than half of the total votes cast.

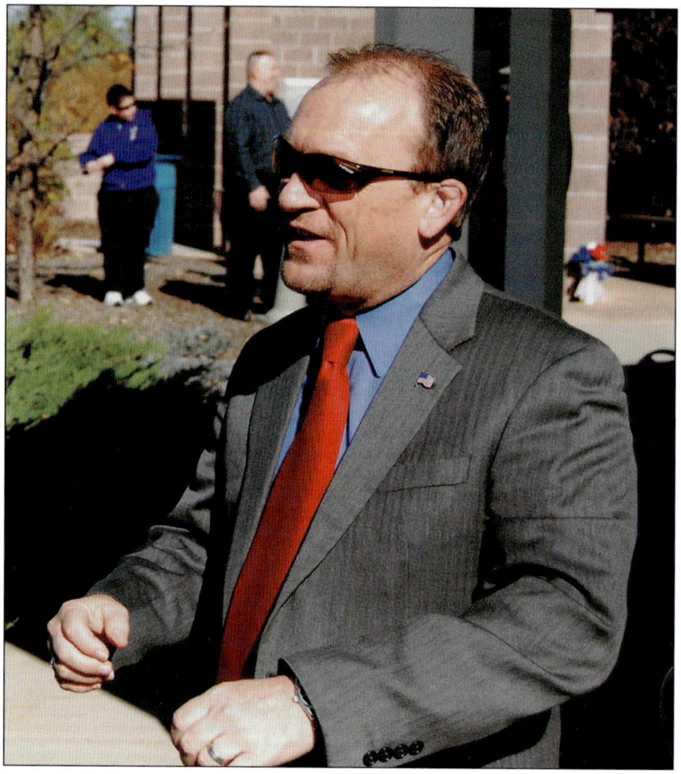

Gregg Hull made his first bid for public office a successful one in 2014 and was doing an admirable job, participating in as many city events as possible, as of this writing. In his brief time in office, Hull has been personable and quick with a joke.

Three

Education in Rio Rancho

The headline in the July 14, 1993, issue of the *Observer* said it all: "It's a District!" *Observer* staff writer Genie Blair Ryan's lead paragraph gave the headline some context: "At 1:55 p.m. on July 9, 1993, Rio Rancho Public Schools (RRPS) was born. It is a day that will be remembered in the history of the city."

On July 9 that year, the state board of education, convening at Bernalillo High School, voted 11-1 to form the school district in a meeting that lasted more than five hours. To take care of the business matters for the fledgling district, the state board named an interim board of education for RRPS: Karla Walker, Barbara Harris, and Robert Fuentes were chosen, with Mark Lautman named as an alternate. Walker and Harris had previous experience as members of the Jemez Valley Schools Board of Education.

The state's newest district (there are 89 school districts in the state as of 2015) would encompass about 6,500 children in kindergarten through eighth grade. The new district, which would officially begin on July 1, 1994, would inherit five elementary schools, Rio Rancho, Martin Luther King Jr., Ernest Stapleton, Puesta del Sol, and Enchanted Hills, and two middle schools, Lincoln and Mountain View, from Albuquerque Public Schools.

The first school, originally consisting of portable buildings, opened in time for the 1972–1973 school year. Rio Rancho Elementary began with just more than 100 first-, second-, and third-graders. The 10-acre campus site was donated by Rio Rancho Estates to Albuquerque Public Schools.

High school students continued to travel down the hill to Cibola High School until Rio Rancho Public Schools built a high school. Rio Rancho High School, starting with grades 9 through 11, opened its doors in August 1997, graduating the class of 1999 two years later.

By the 2014–2015 school year, RRPS had more than 17,000 students housed in a preschool, 10 elementary schools, four middle schools, two high schools, an alternative high school, and Rio Rancho Cyber Academy.

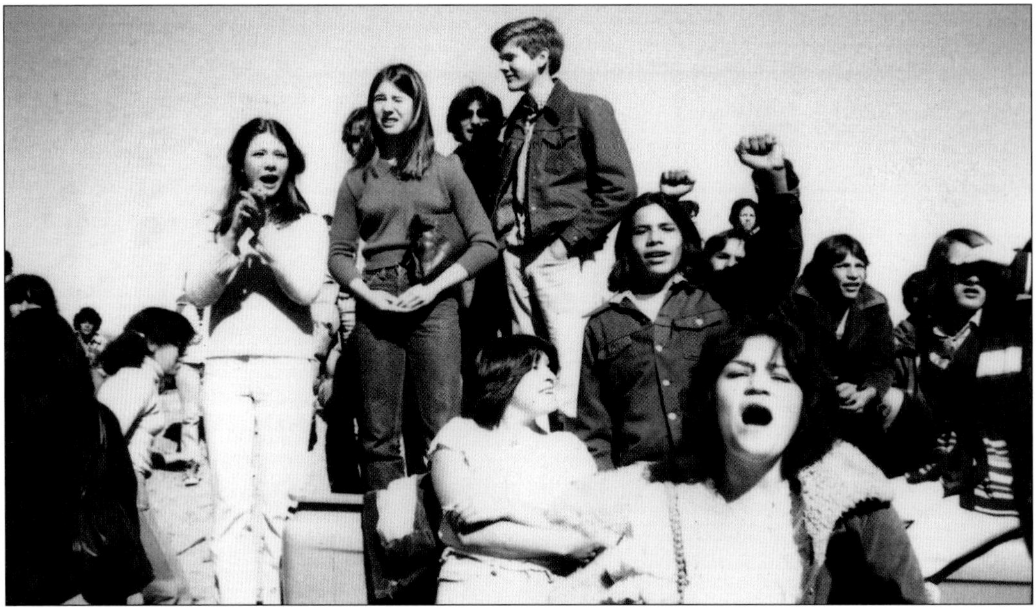

In March 1975, Cibola High School, budgeted at $4.5 million and built for $5.2 million, opened to serve 1,600 students and ended Rio Rancho students' days at West Mesa High School, with a population of 3,585 students in the 1972–1973 school year. Here, Cibola students hold a rally in February 1979.

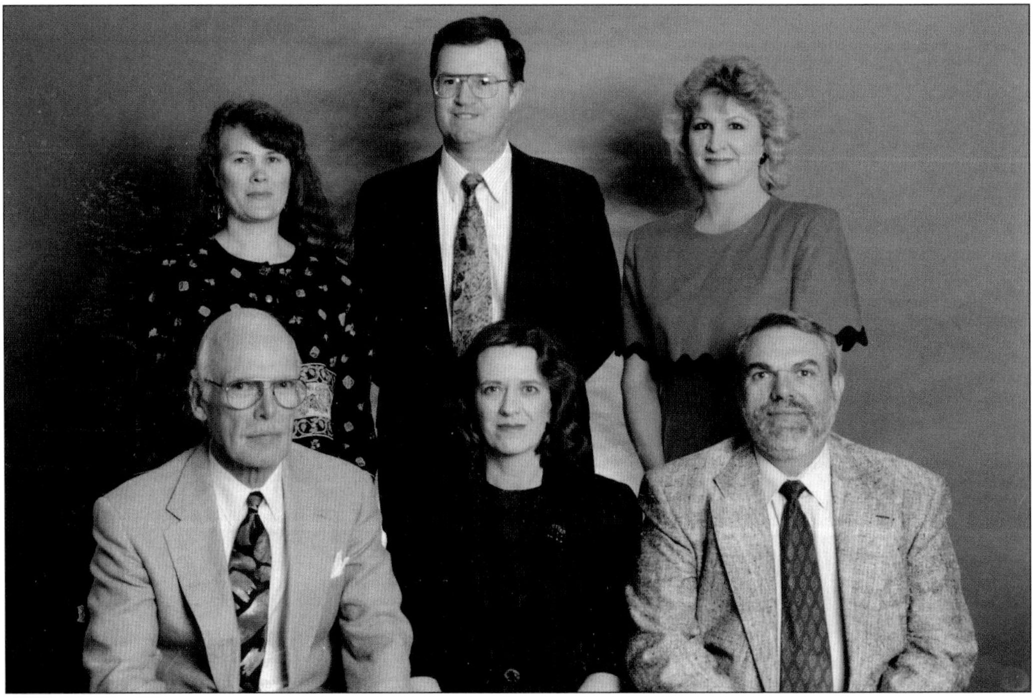

Following forums aimed at educating voters, Karla Walker (District 1), Jewel Hall (2), Carl Harper (3), Robert Herman (4), and Barbara Harris (5) became the first board members. Pictured here from left to right are (first row) Dick Muenzer (board member), Sue Cleveland (superintendent), and Herman; (second row) Harris, Harper, and Walker.

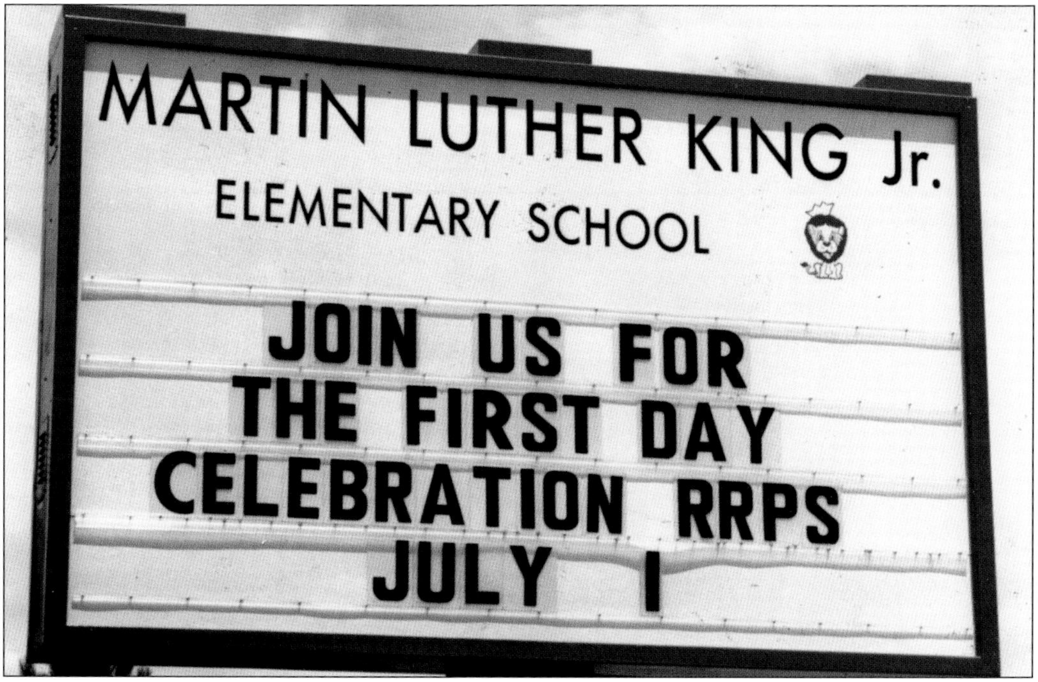

About 300 people attended Rio Rancho Public Schools' First Day ceremonies on July 1, 1994, noted on this sign at Martin Luther King Jr. Elementary, one of 10 schools turned over to the fledgling district by Albuquerque Public Schools. US representative Bill Richardson and New Mexico's First Lady Alice King were among the attendees.

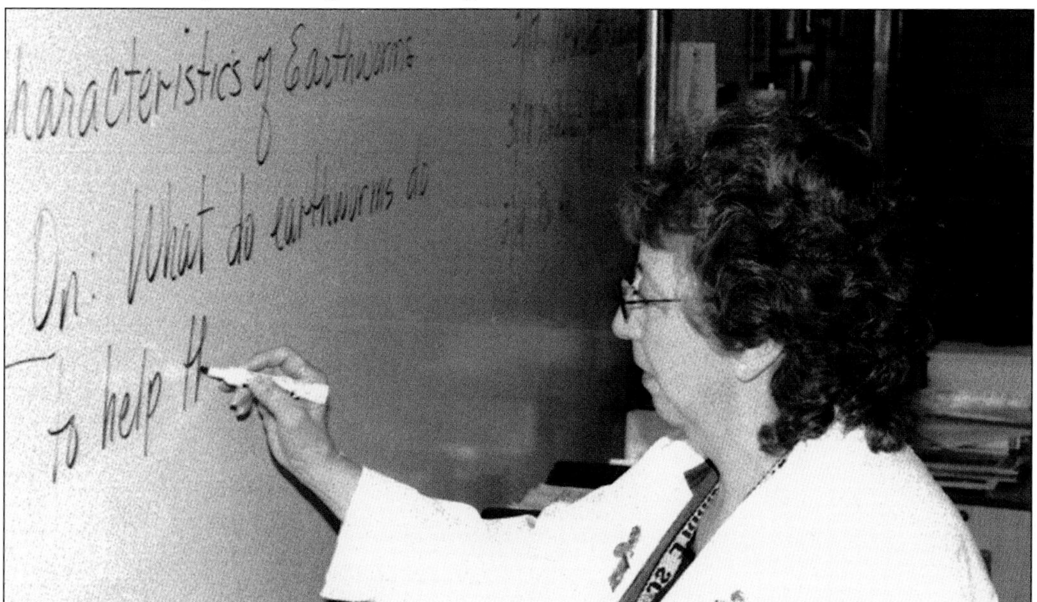

Longtime teacher Dorothy Satriana was a fixture at Lincoln Middle School before it was a part of Rio Rancho Public Schools. The popular science teacher, who did her best to make her middle school students enjoy learning about science, had a wing named after her at the school. She retired in 2013.

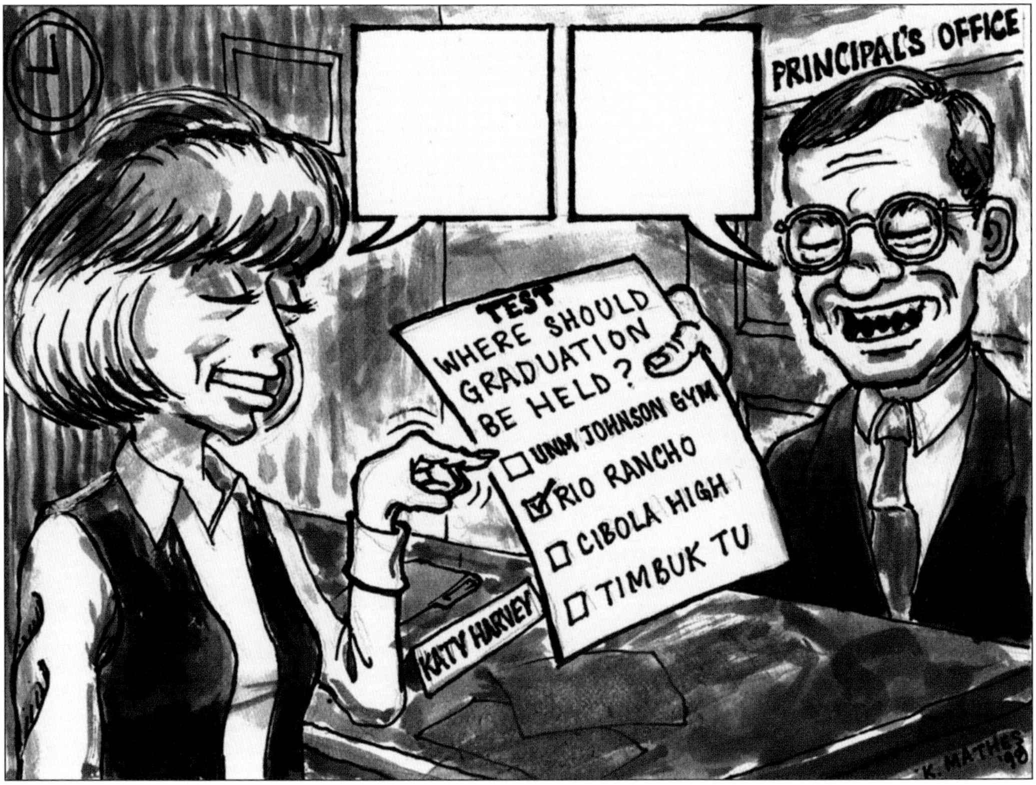

This cartoon depicts the anguish and controversy over where Rio Rancho High School's graduation should be held. Johnson Gym at the University of New Mexico won out, with graduation ceremonies later held at the Pit in Albuquerque and then the Santa Ana Star Center. RRHS and Cleveland's graduation ceremonies are held on back-to-back days in May.

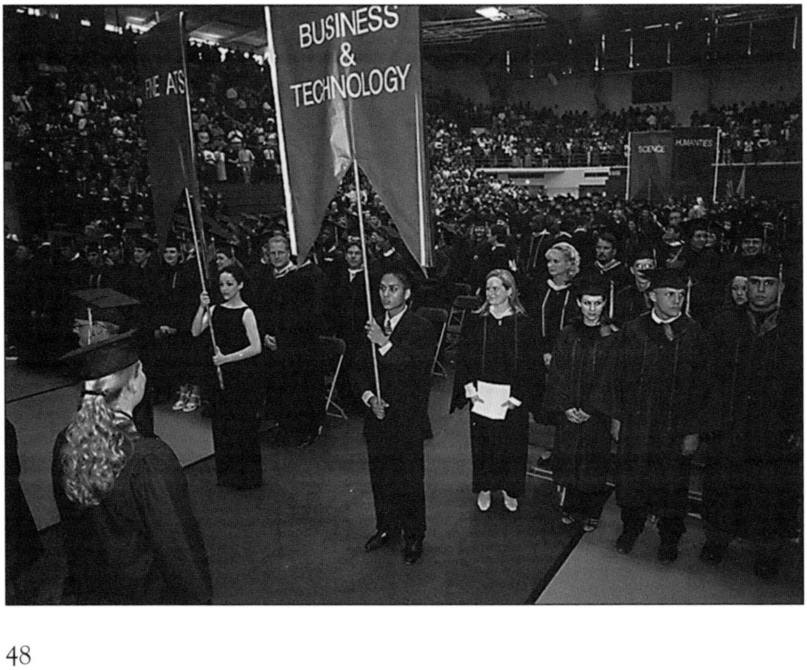

In May 1999, the first Rio Rancho High School graduating class received diplomas in Johnson Gym on the UNM main campus. Later graduating classes picked up their sheepskins at the Pit and then the Santa Ana Star Center. Cleveland High School had its first graduating class in 2011.

Attended also by Secret Service agents, Vice Pres. Dick Cheney (left) visited Rio Rancho High School on October 10, 2000, to get an idea of its cutting-edge technology during a tour of the sprawling campus. Former science department head Russ Fisher-Ives is partially visible over Cheney's left shoulder, listening intently.

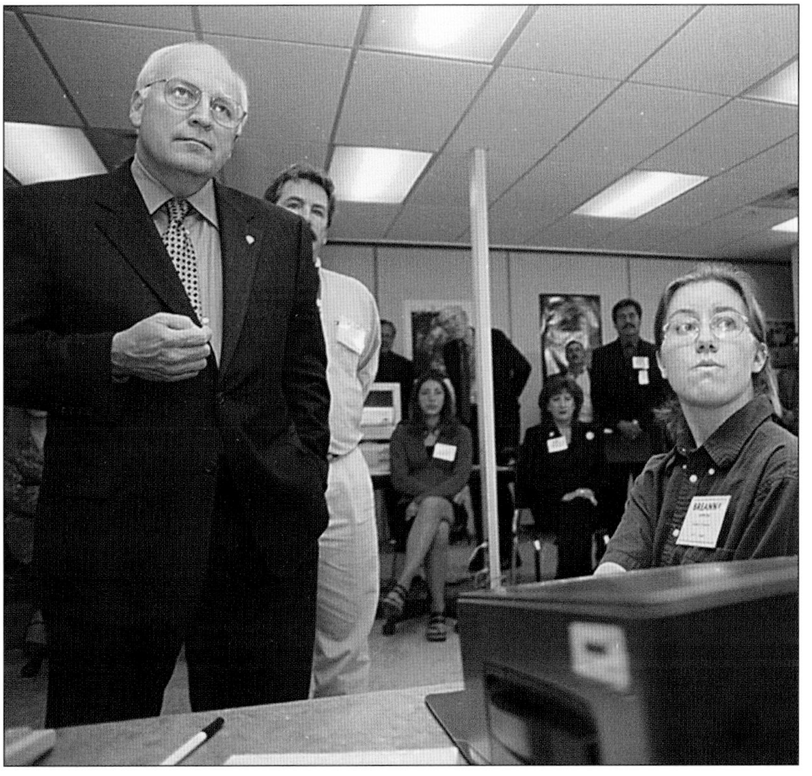

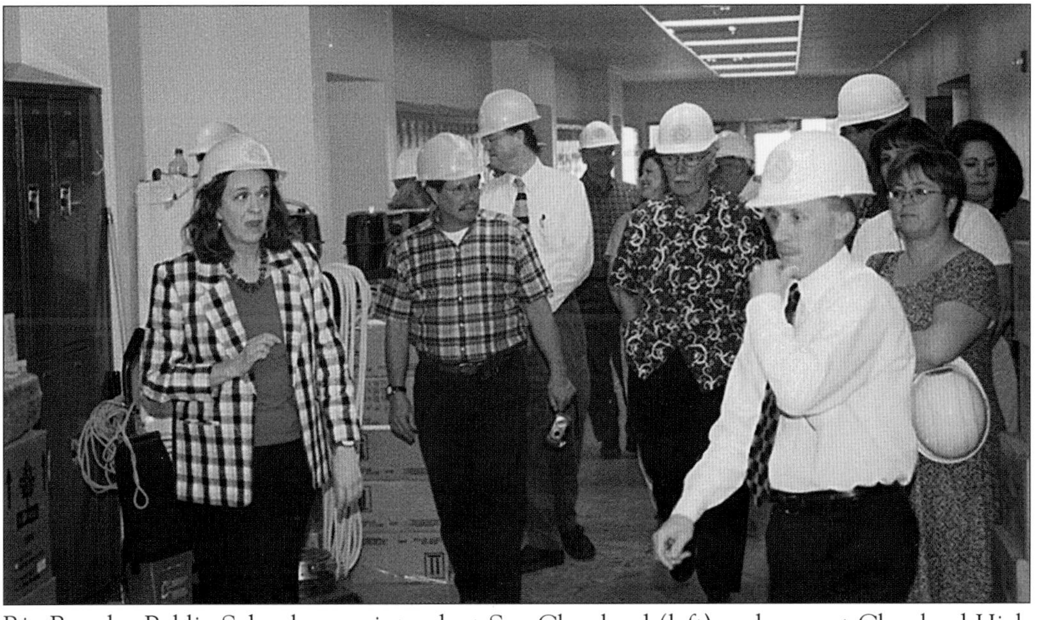

Rio Rancho Public Schools superintendent Sue Cleveland (left) and current Cleveland High School principal Scott Affentranger (far right) led school board members and the media on a tour of what was to be Rio Rancho Mid-High School in May 2002. Affentranger was named principal at Cleveland High School before it opened in August 2009.

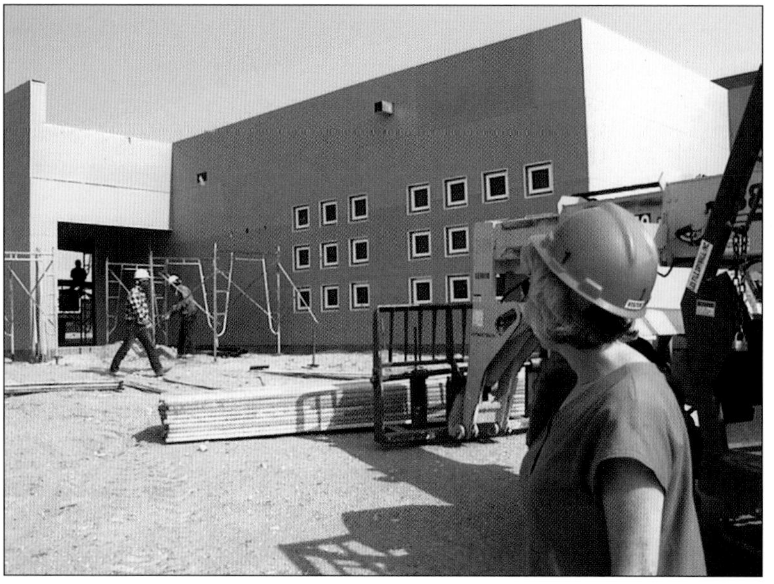

Rio Rancho Mid-High was not the only new school under construction in mid-2002. Here, principal-to-be Linda Banker checks the progress at Vista Grande Elementary in Enchanted Hills. Trent Heffner, a former UNM basketball player and the district's tallest administrator, is the school's current principal, beloved by his staff and students.

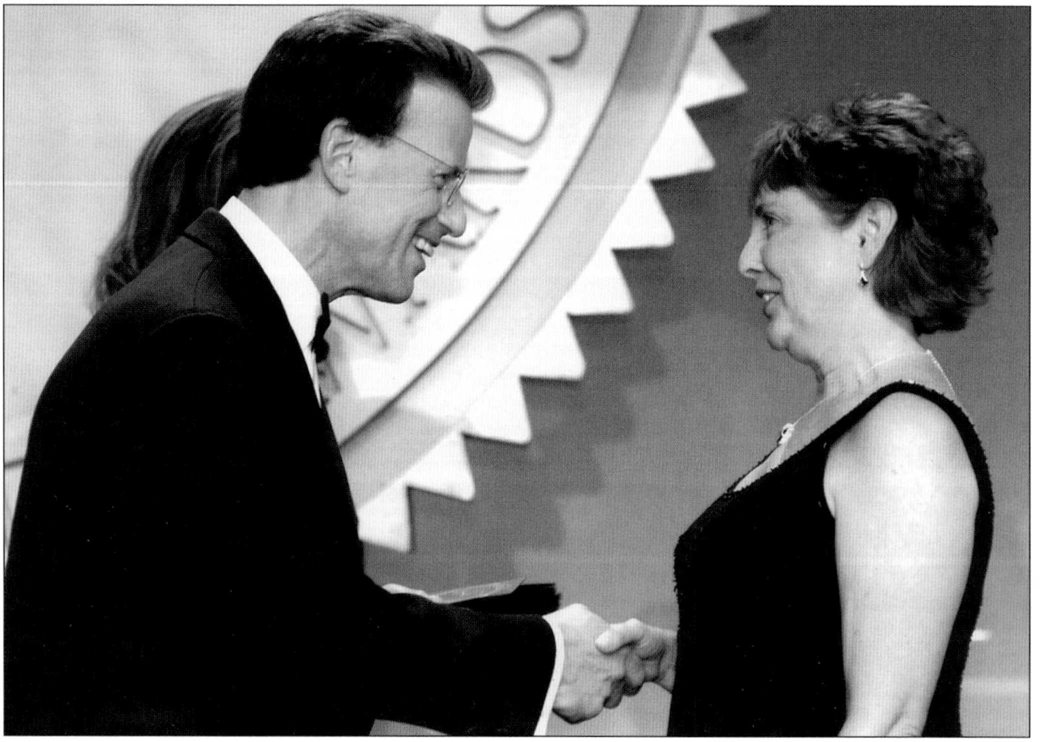

Suzanne Harper, once the principal at Colinas del Norte Elementary, played a big role in establishing a curriculum for Shining Stars Preschool, opened at the former site of Stapleton Elementary in 2005. Here, Harper receives a Milken Family Foundation award in 2002 while at Colinas del Norte; the prestigious award earned her $25,000.

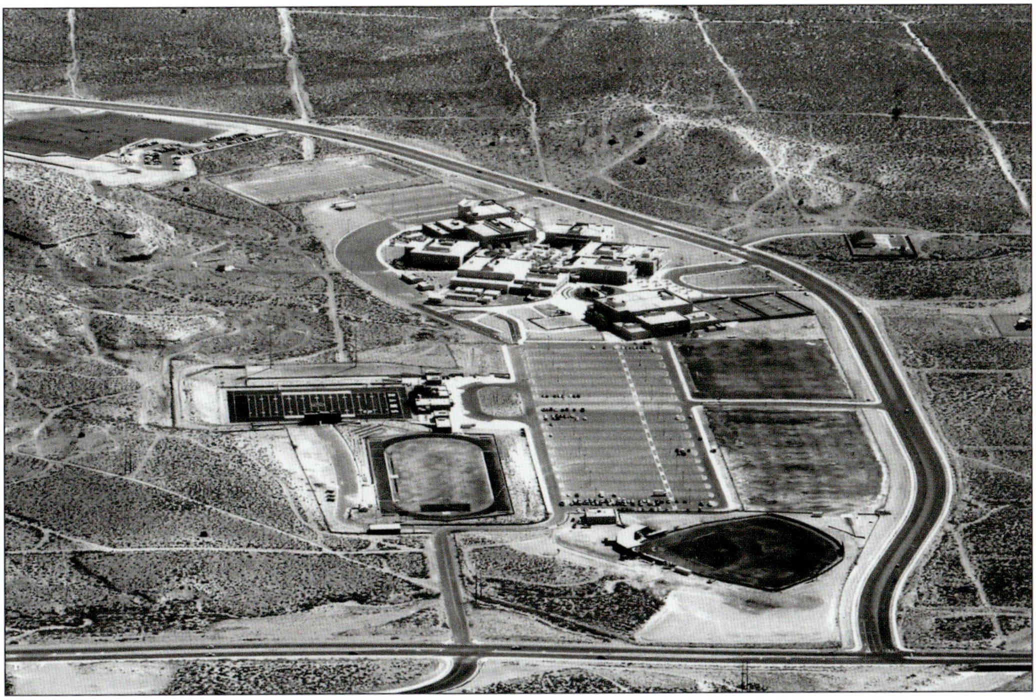

This aerial photograph from 2006 features Rio Rancho High School. Not much has changed on the campus since then, but a plethora of construction has taken place at right and above, including Loma Colorado neighborhoods, a Jesus Christ of Latter-day Saints church, and the Rio Rancho Aquatic Center.

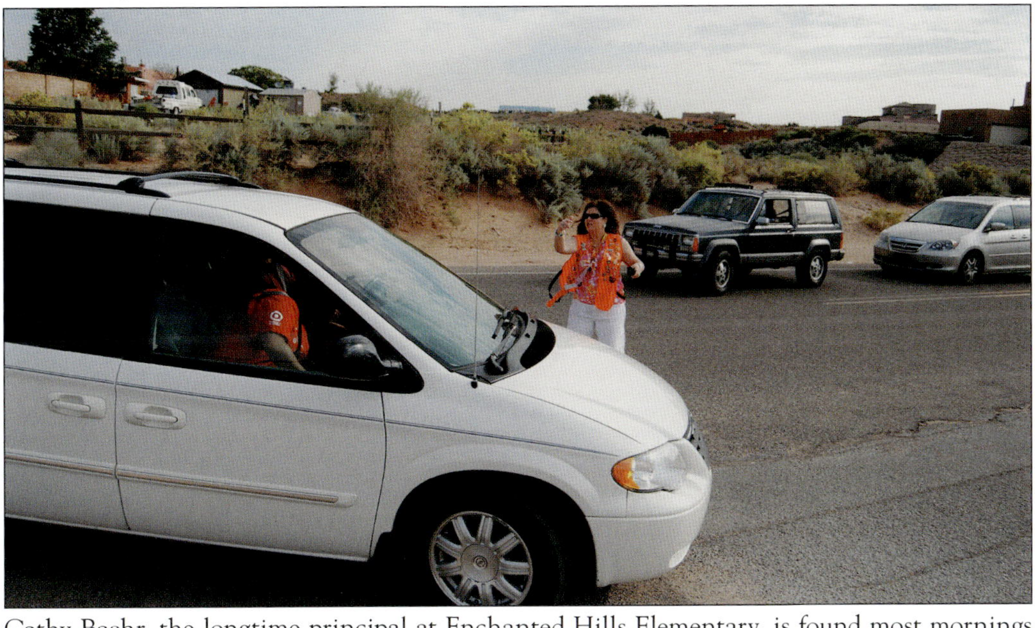

Cathy Baehr, the longtime principal at Enchanted Hills Elementary, is found most mornings directing traffic outside her school. The school has undergone numerous improvement projects, aiding in drainage, a new gym, and roof in recent years. Enchanted Hills is a feeder for Rio Rancho Middle School and Mountain View Middle School.

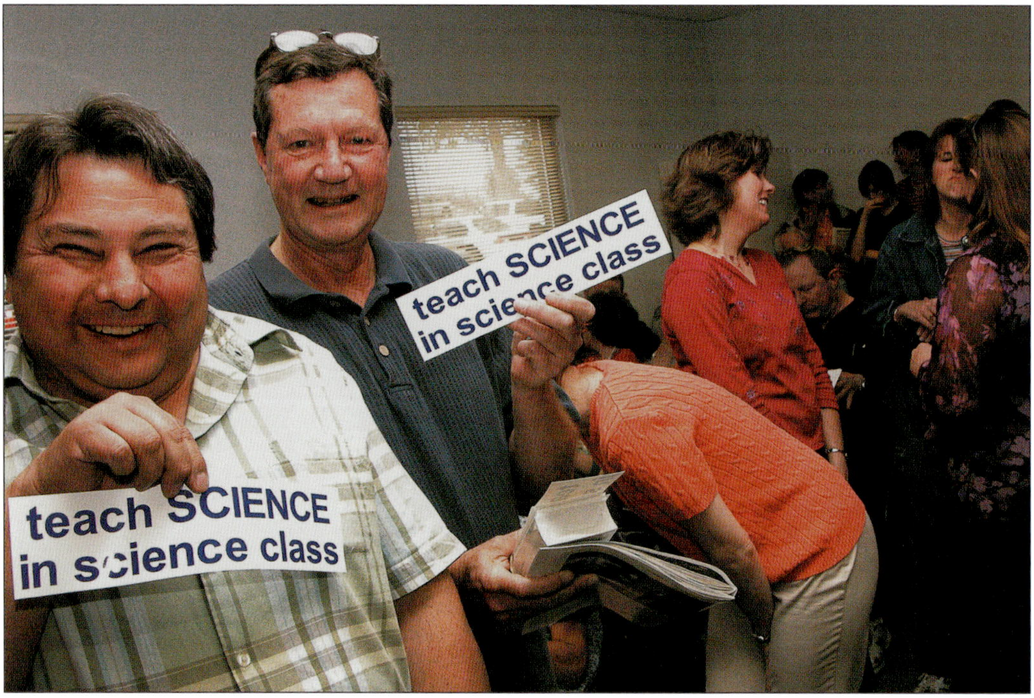

Here is the best way to increase attendance at a school board meeting: discuss topics such as a dress code or, in this case, the controversial Policy 401, when board members debated the teaching of the intelligent design concept versus the traditional concept of evolution in Rio Rancho schools. Evolution won out.

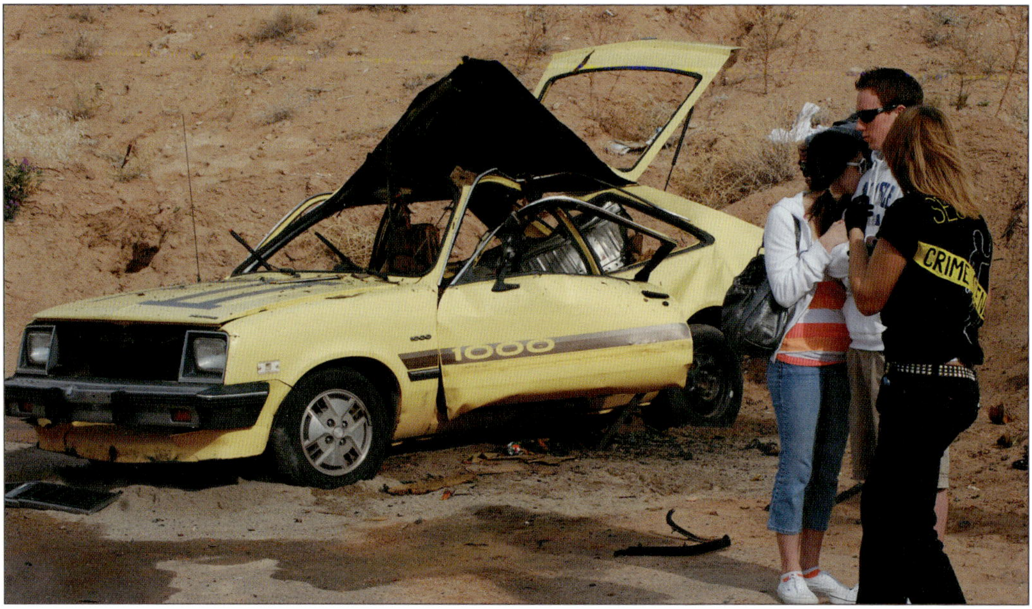

What appears to be the scene of a tragic automobile accident near Rio Rancho High School is actually the site of a staged mishap for Rio Rancho High School forensics teacher Mary Robinson in 2008. Students, intrigued by the television show *CSI*, enjoyed the opportunity to investigate a crime.

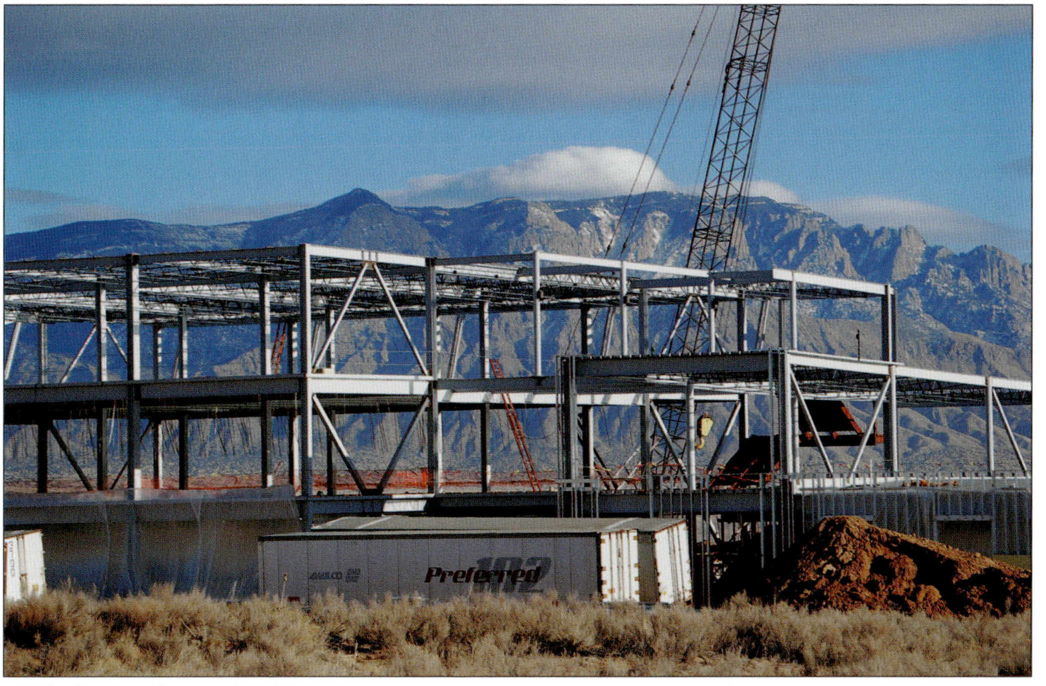

With the rapid growth of Rio Rancho in the early years of the 21st century, Rio Rancho Public Schools administrators realized one high school was not enough. Rio Rancho Mid-High, which siphoned freshmen off the RRHS campus, became another middle school once Cleveland High, pictured here in January 2008, opened in August 2009.

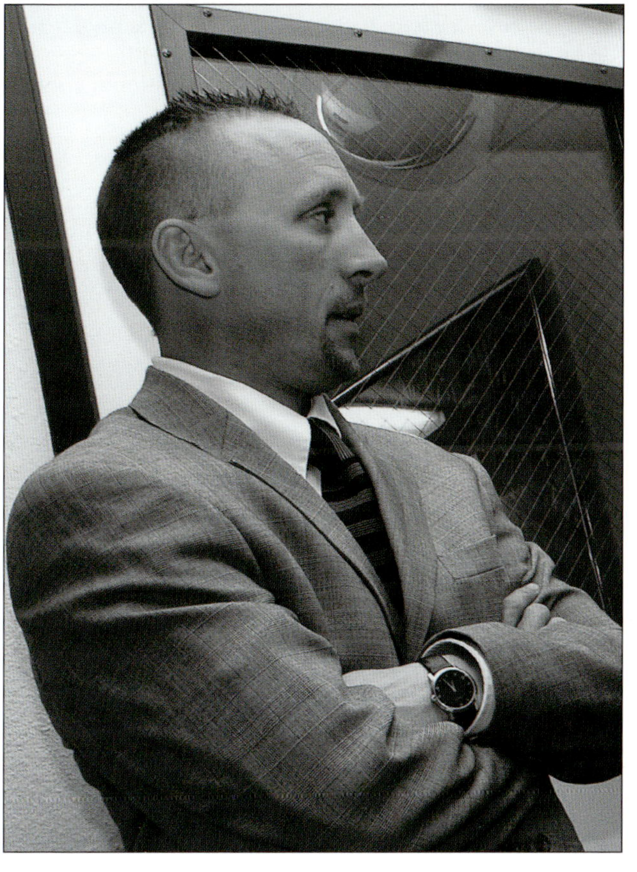

Scott Affentranger, previously an RRHS administrator before becoming the principal of Rio Rancho Mid-High, was selected to be the first principal for Cleveland High School. Credited for the enthusiasm of Storm students at school athletic events and the school spirit in the hallways, Affentranger is a regular in the stands and on the sidelines for school events.

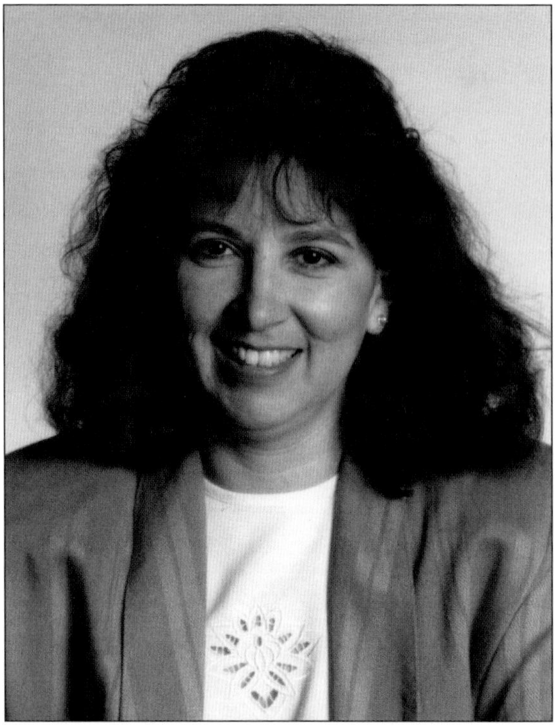

Maggie Cordova was the special-education administrator for Rio Rancho Public Schools and a beloved school official. She contracted breast cancer, battled it valiantly for years, and seemed to be in remission until it claimed her life. Rio Rancho Public Schools named new Maggie Cordova Elementary in her memory in 2005.

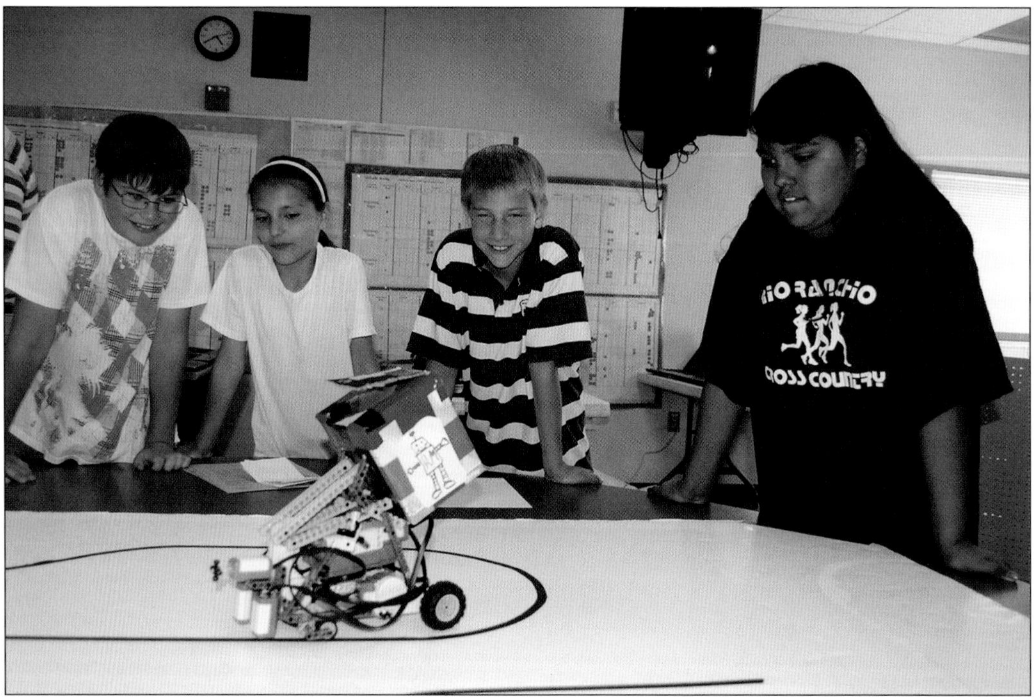

Student interest in robotics has been on the rise for at least a decade—but not always in elementary schools. Puesta del Sol Elementary is an exception; it has a robotics club, which principal Bryan Garcia is understandably proud of. Studying robotics often helps students succeed in math and science.

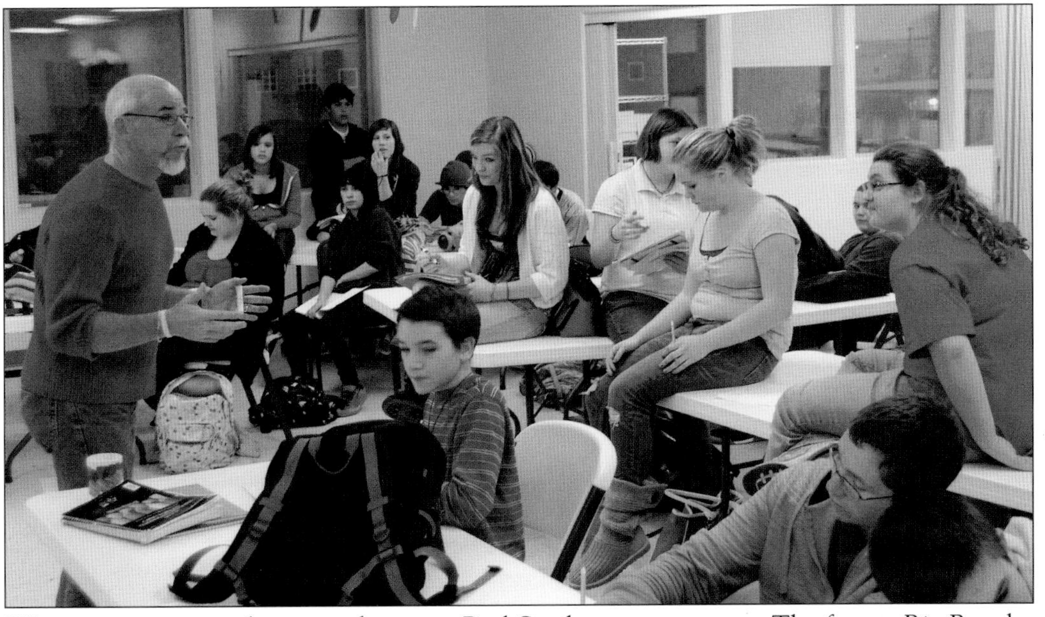

When it comes to enthusiasm, the name Paul Stephenson comes up. The former Rio Rancho High School science teacher became a cofounder of the ASK Academy, a charter school, and is seen here leading a classroom. In addition to his abilities as an educator and school administrator, Stephenson performs the best rendition of the national anthem in town.

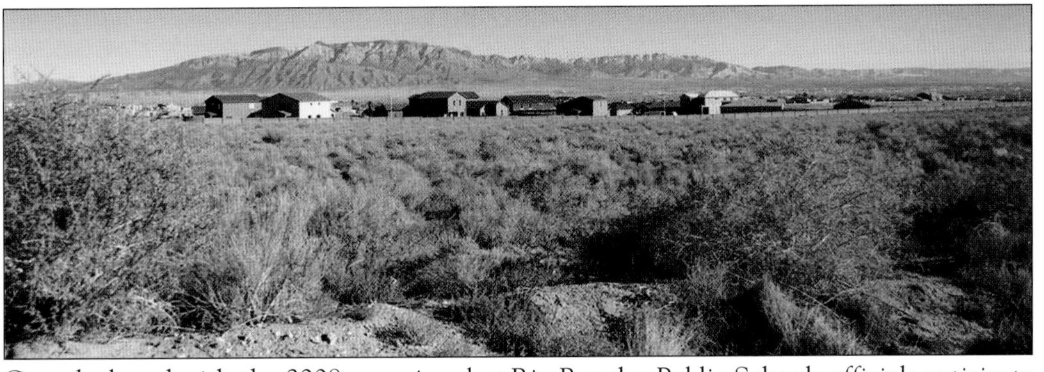

Growth slowed with the 2008 recession, but Rio Rancho Public Schools officials anticipate building an elementary school, to be named after the late Joe Harris, when enough money to staff such a school is realized. The school will be built south of Northern Boulevard, a few blocks west of Unser Boulevard.

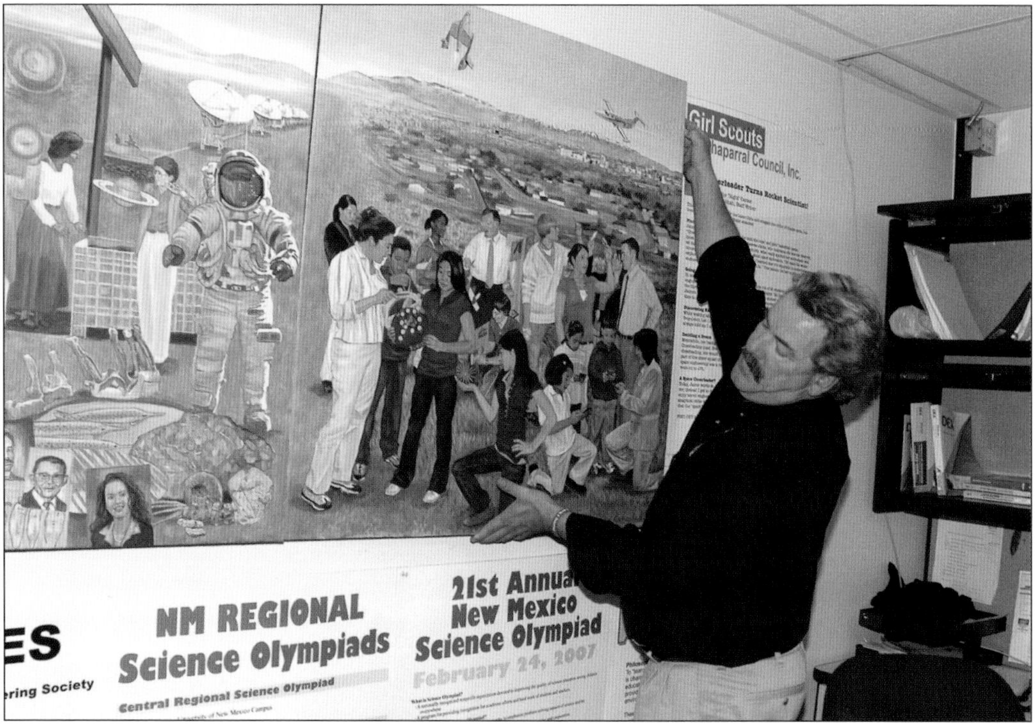

Russ Fisher-Ives resigned as a dedicated science teacher at Rio Rancho High School to help organize the Intel International Science and Engineering Fair (ISEF) held in Albuquerque in 2007. Research expositions for students keep interest in creative thinking alive and well, and Rio Rancho students regularly qualify for the ISEF.

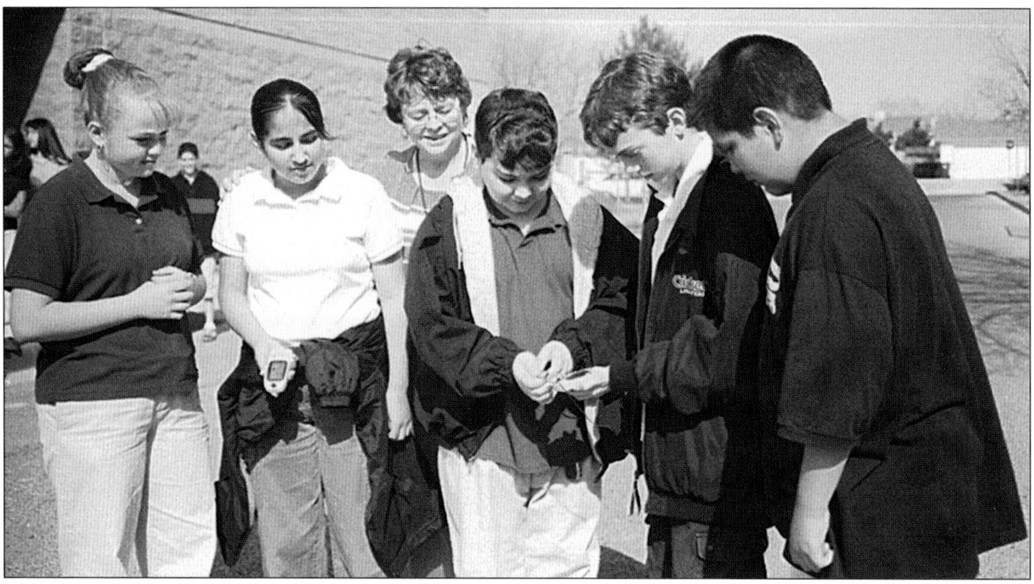
Science teacher Kandy Glazer, behind some of her Lincoln Middle School students, takes a project outside the classroom. Glazer is one of the most enthusiastic science teachers one will ever meet, especially when asked about space travel. In the past, she orchestrated science fairs at the school.

The Rio Rancho High School courtyard is invaded by JROTC Marines for a Veterans Day ceremony. The JROTC program has been successful to say the least, not only at RRHS but also at Cleveland High School. And, Enchanted Hills Elementary even has its own Young Marines program.

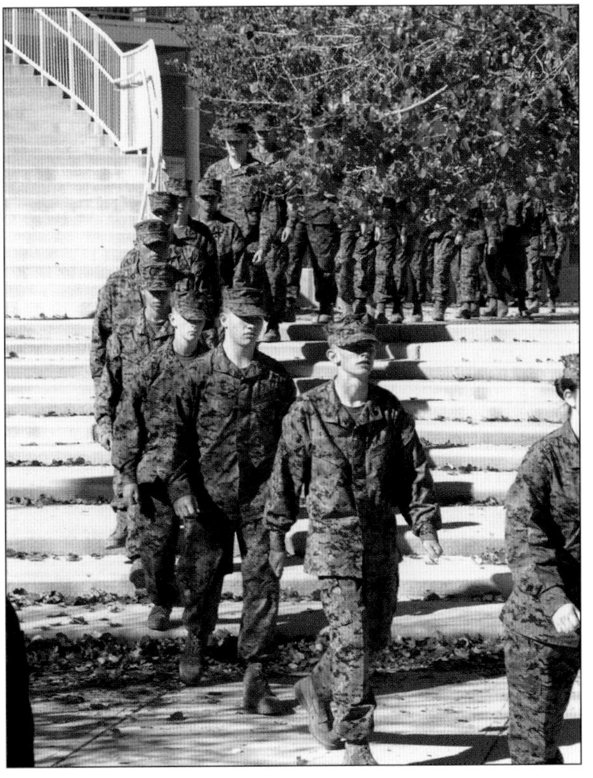

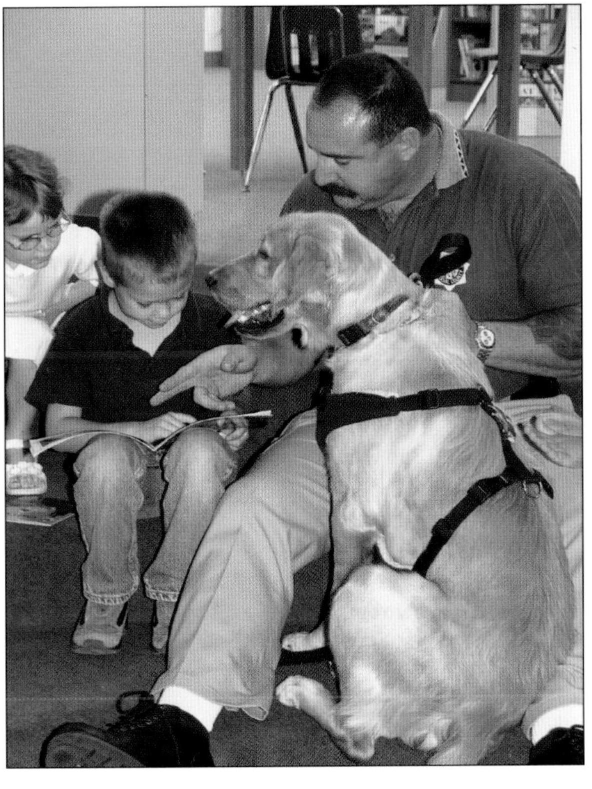

Joe Harris, a popular Rio Rancho police officer and later a Sandoval County sheriff's sergeant, is seen with a KASEY Says golden retriever in the Enchanted Hills Elementary library. Students' interest in reading piqued when they read to dogs. Sadly, Harris was killed in the line of duty in August 2009.

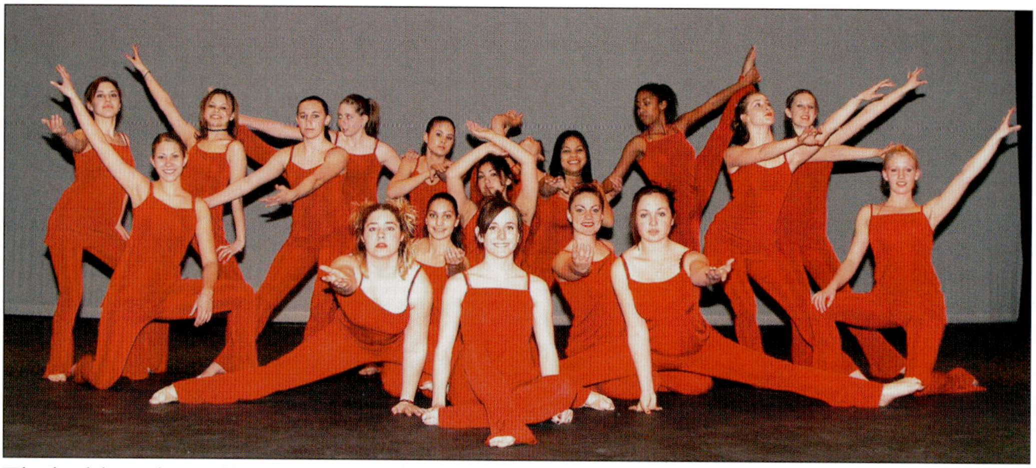

The highly acclaimed Master Dance Class of Rio Rancho High School annually presents energetic, colorful, and creative performances in the school's Performing Arts Center. Lois Moreno not only teaches the class, but also choreographs the shows, often entailing RRHS Master Dance alums. These girls have long since graduated.

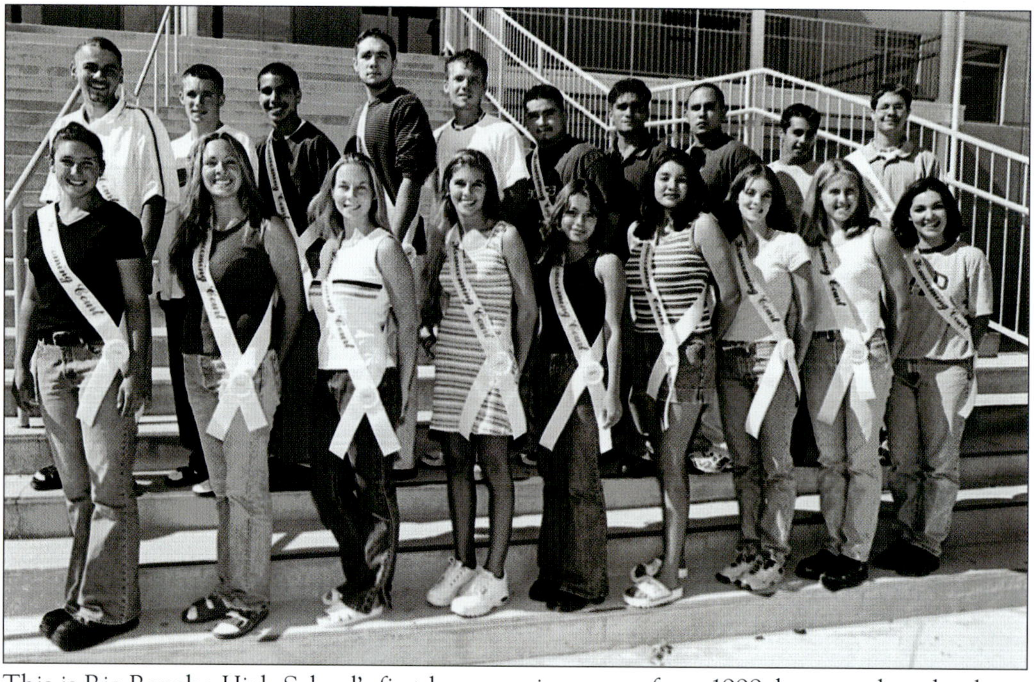

This is Rio Rancho High School's first homecoming court, from 1999, because the school was without seniors in its first year, 1997–1998, and played home games at Bernalillo High until the 1999 football season. The Rams celebrated the 1999 homecoming with a 34-0 rout of Capital High.

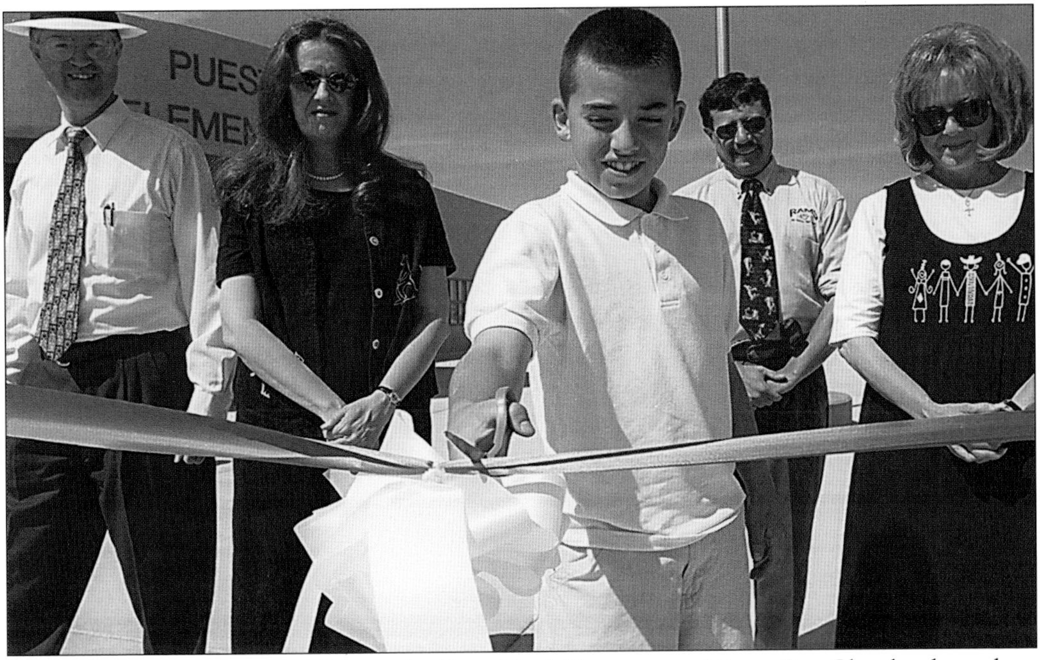

School board members Carl Harper (left) and Joel Sherman and Supt. Sue Cleveland watch as fifth-grader T.J. Baker snips the ribbon for the opening of the second Puesta del Sol Elementary on May 6, 2000. At right is former Sandoval County commissioner and Rio Rancho councilor Patty Thomas.

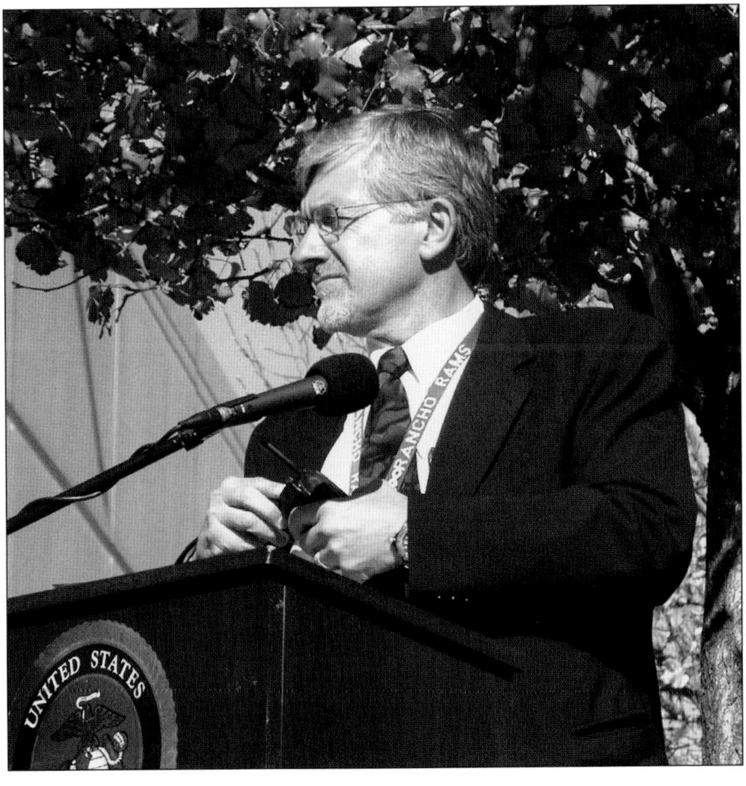

Richard Von Ancken, like so many Rio Ranchoans, came from New York. Von Ancken was the principal at Lincoln Middle School before being selected to succeed Gary Tripp, the school's second principal in school history, following Katy Harvey. Tripp resigned to be executive director of the New Mexico Activities Association.

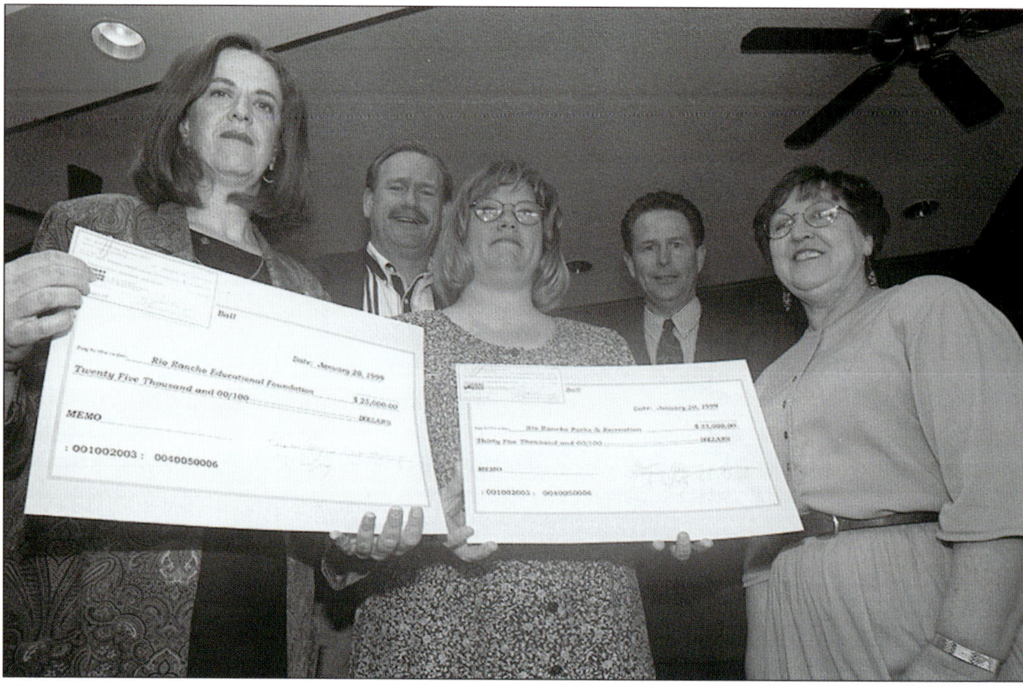

The Rio Rancho Education Foundation annually stages the fundraising Seats & Eats, using proceeds from it to help teachers and administrators fund small projects, buy equipment, make improvements, and more after those lucky teachers and staff members have their requests submitted and approved. RREF members visit the winning teachers' classrooms to surprise them.

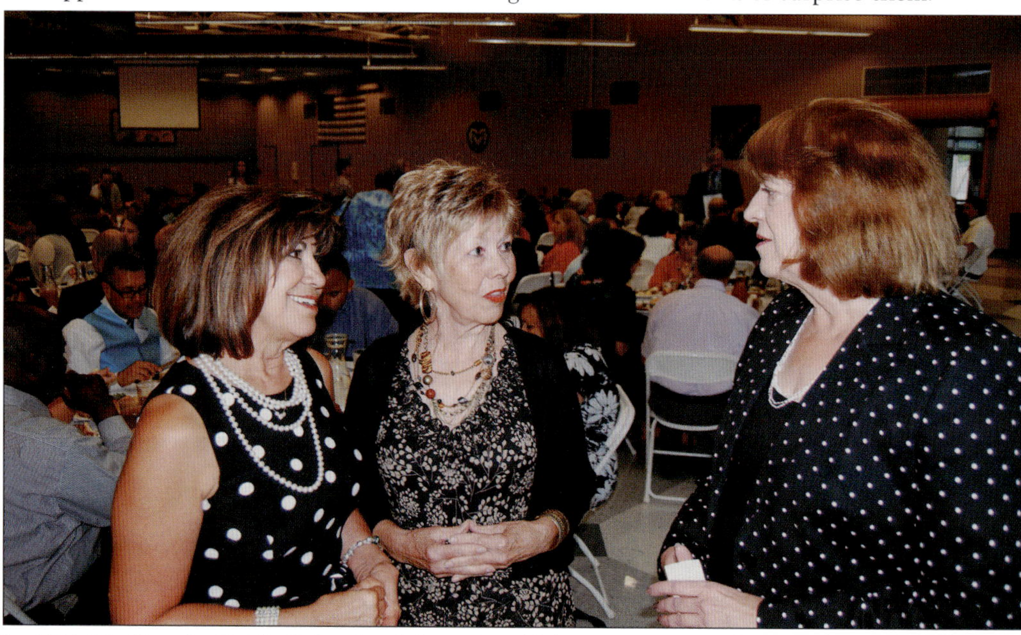

In 2014, Rio Rancho Public Schools celebrated its 20th anniversary with several events, including a banquet in the RRHS cafeteria. Here, former RRPS transportation director and current legislative lobbyist Theresa Saiz (left), the district's first employee, Ema Dreher (center), and Supt. Sue Cleveland talk about the early days.

Four

High School Athletics in Rio Rancho

For the first three decades of Rio Rancho Estates' existence, its high school students were transported to West Mesa High School and later Del Norte and Cibola High Schools. There, student athletes had teammates ostensibly residing on the West Side, in the case of West Mesa and Cibola High Schools, and the Northeast Heights for those driven to Del Norte. In the mid-1970s, Rio Rancho student athletes first played for West Mesa High School, where they were bused until Cibola High School opened in 1974.

Rio Ranchoan Brian Philipbar, whose athletic sons played either at Rio Rancho or Cibola High School, fondly remembers those years, playing for "the beloved Coach Campy [Jim Campanella] from Artesia, who also coached at West Mesa in the early '70s and played for UNM. We were the last group from the West Mesa breakaway, with about half of a great team. He was also the head baseball coach; we played baseball for Bill Gracey at West Mesa as freshmen."

"There were quite a few kids from Rio Rancho on the football team," Philipbar remembered. "The people from 1975 to 1981 were all awesome, not to take anything away from anyone. It was an evolution. Most folks all played football, basketball, and baseball, and we had a few fast cars. Kids would come to school with slicks and open-capped headers and have outright drag races on Golf Course Road." Finally, Rio Rancho High School was built, opening its doors in time for the 1997–1998 school year.

As with a large percentage of new schools, it takes a while to get programs started. New coaches, equipment, and facilities get thrown into a mix of competition that includes schools with established programs. In 2009, the new kid in town, Cleveland High School, opened its doors, and barely two years later, the Storm had a state football championship. Since the 2009–2010 school year, Rio Rancho and Cleveland High Schools have enjoyed a competitive, yet friendly, sports rivalry in District 1-6A.

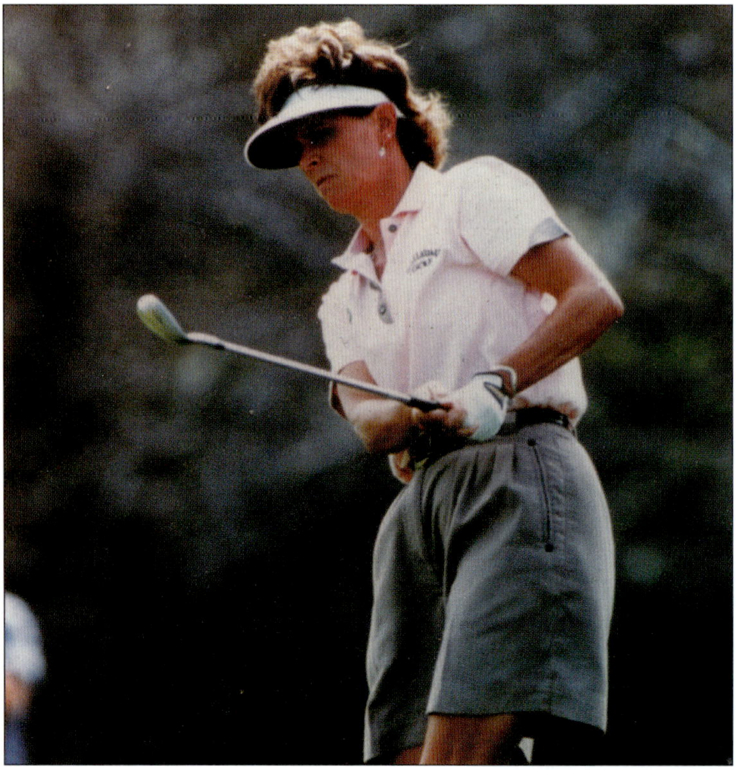

Rosie Jones grew up in Rio Rancho and spent a lot of time honing her game on the Panorama Golf and Country Club course. After graduating from Cibola High School in 1977, she attended Ohio State University before turning to professional golf. She is enshrined in the Cougars' sports hall of fame.

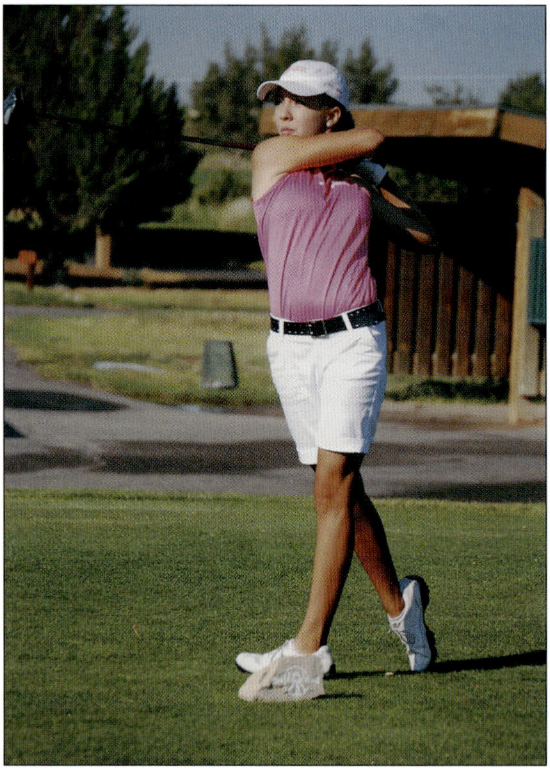

Anyone who follows golf knows this young woman may be the city's next Rosie Jones. Dominique Galloway won three straight state high school championships (2013–2015) and even an Albuquerque City Women's championship before her senior year at Cleveland High School. The talented golfer gave a verbal commitment to the University of Texas.

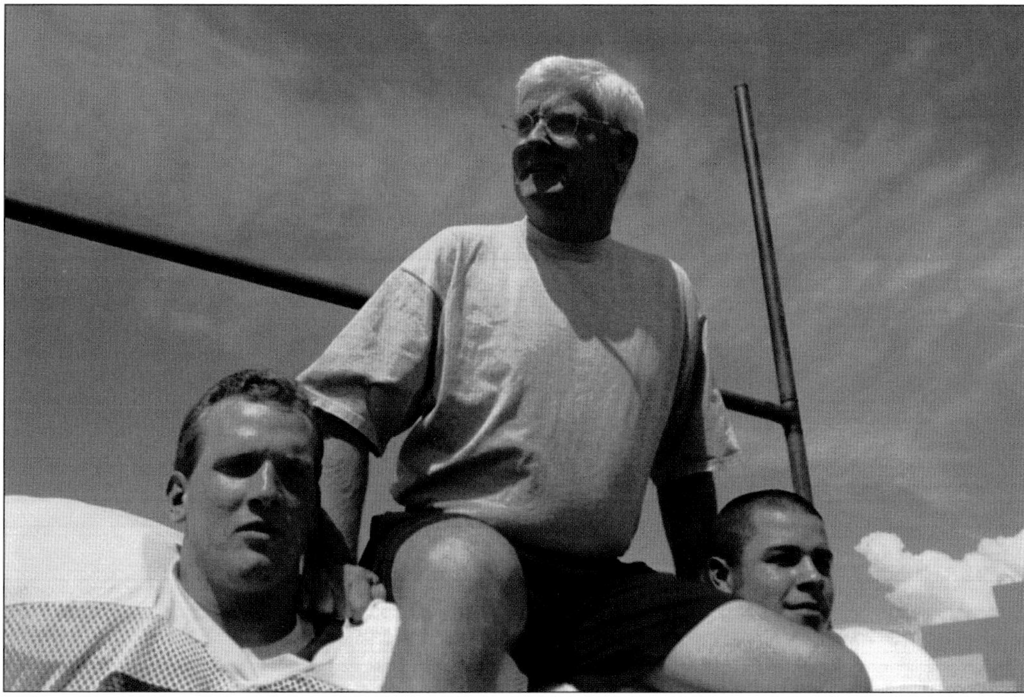

Bill Moon, carried atop the shoulders of two of his Rams, was Rio Rancho High School's first varsity football coach. The Rams struggled in Moon's three seasons and were winless in 1997, the school's debut season. Wilson Holland succeeded Moon in 2001 and led the Rams to their first playoff berth.

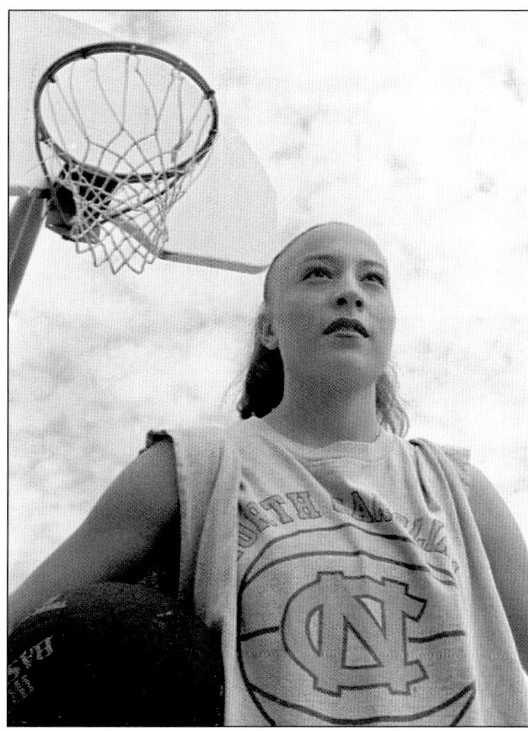

Monique Hernandez endured a lot of criticism from Rio Rancho High School's new fans when she opted to remain at Cibola High School and play for coach Doug Dorame. The slick ball-handling point guard played at the University of Notre Dame (1999–2004), where she was a part of a national championship team.

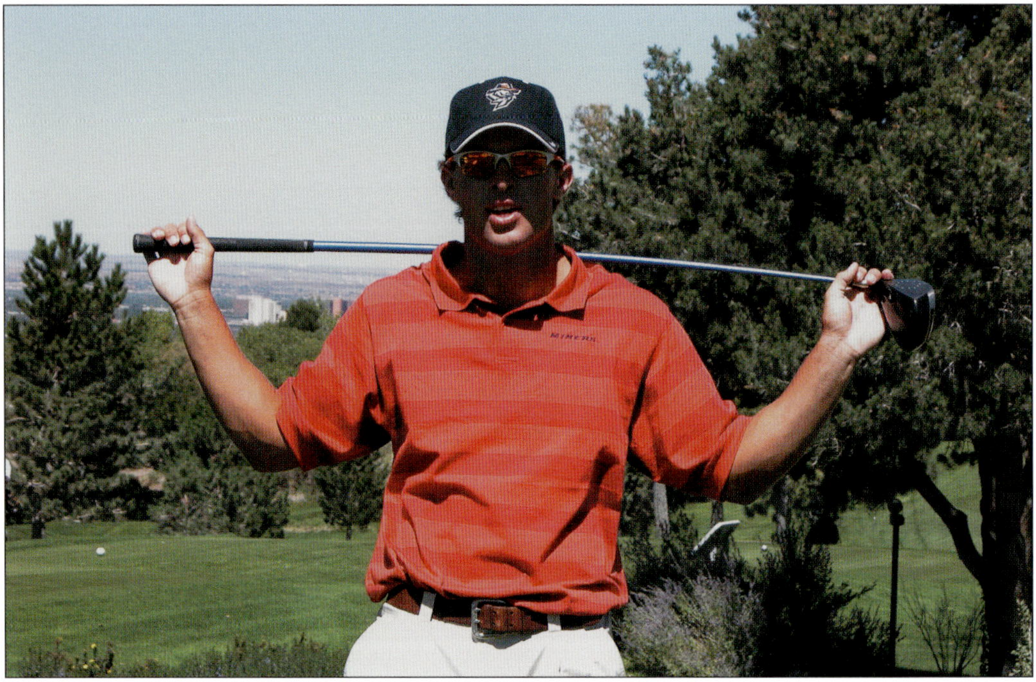

Danyel Longmire won the first individual championship for the Rams in cross country in 1997, and Trent Rommann (pictured) won state golf medalist honors in 2001. Brian Pitts won a state wrestling title in 2000 and repeated his feat in 2001. Rommann played golf for the University of Texas-El Paso.

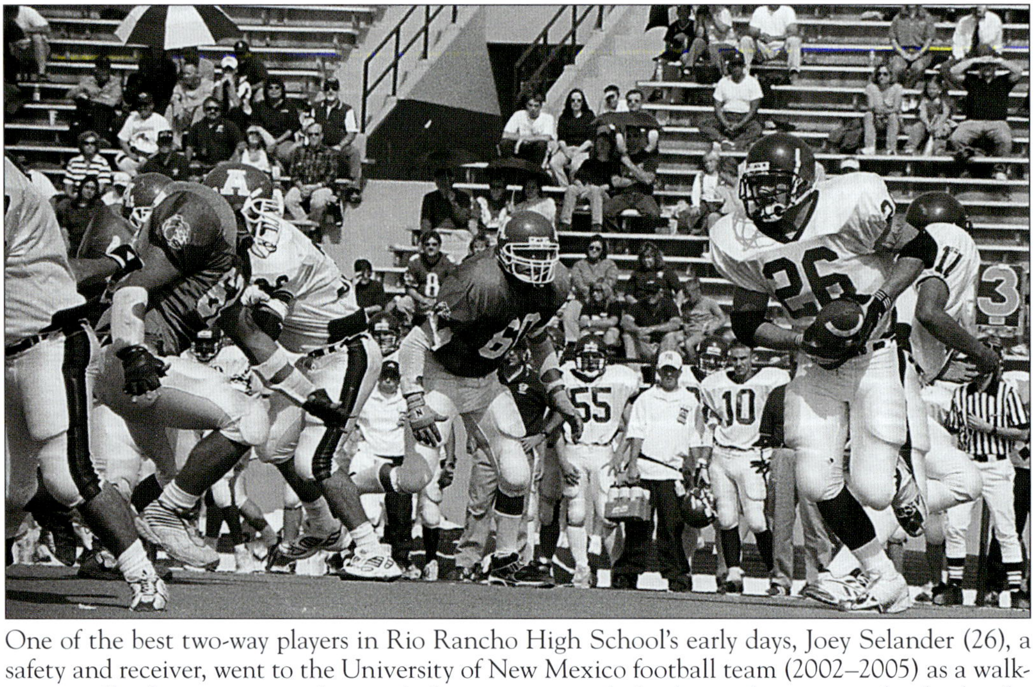

One of the best two-way players in Rio Rancho High School's early days, Joey Selander (26), a safety and receiver, went to the University of New Mexico football team (2002–2005) as a walk-on, initially playing on special teams before earning a scholarship and starting at linebacker for head coach Rocky Long.

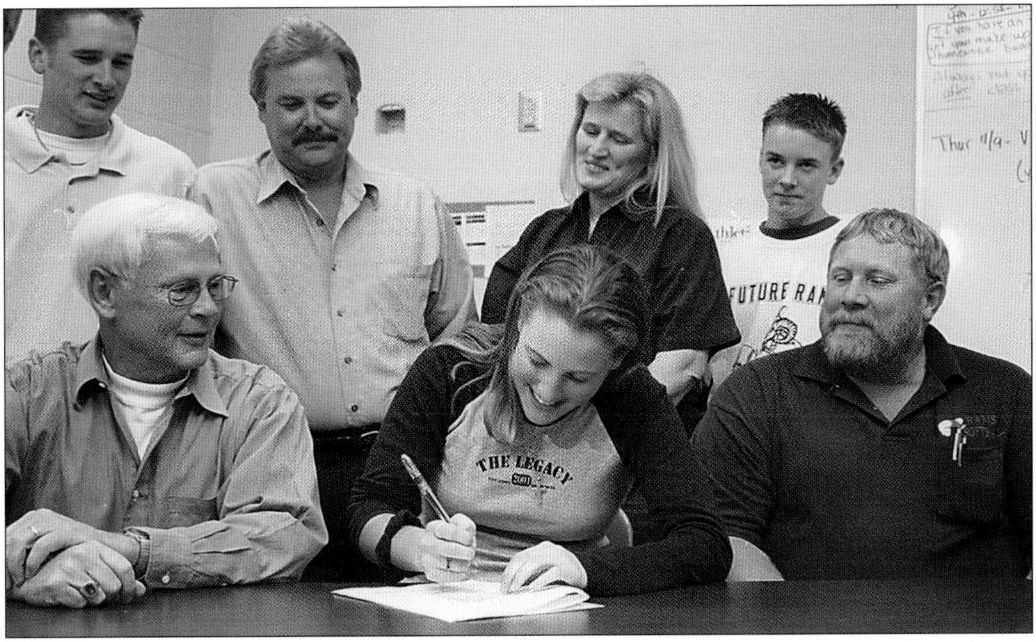

Rio Rancho High School athletic director Gary Hveem (far left) and Rams softball coach Paul Kohman (far right) watch in November 2000 as softball standout Brittany Burtner, who also played a few seasons of basketball, signs her letter of intent to play at Colorado State University. Behind her are her parents and brothers.

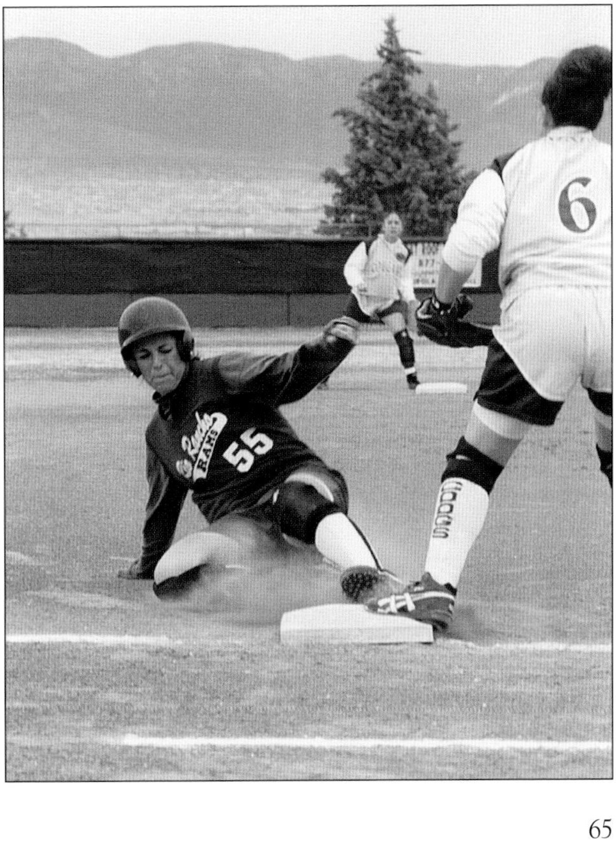

Genevieve Kelly, seen here sliding into third base in a 2001 Rams softball game, followed her teammate Brittany Burtner by also heading up I-25 to Fort Collins, Colorado, pitching for Colorado State University. Those two stars brought prominence to the Rams' softball program, which won its first state championship in 2003.

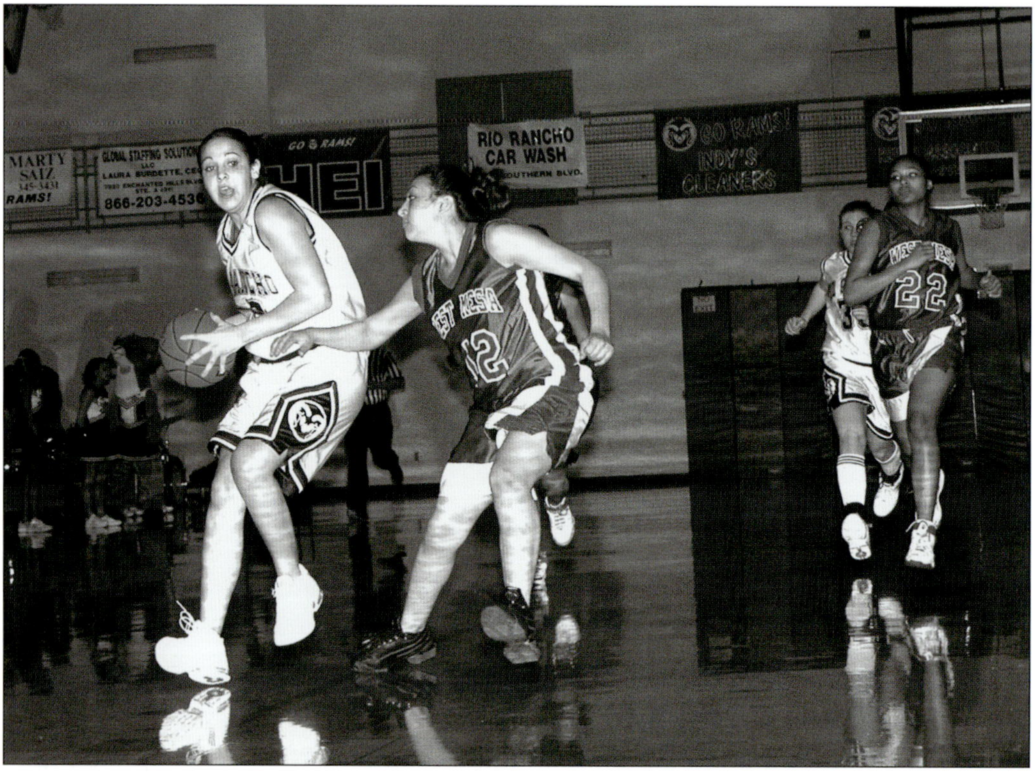

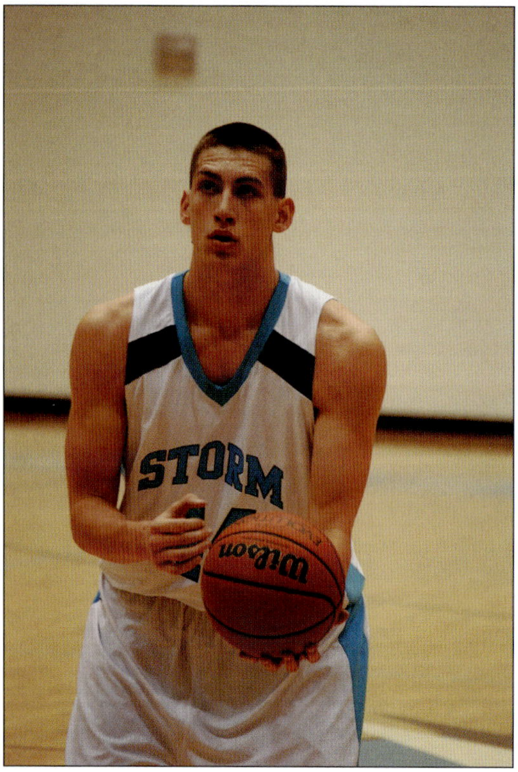

Brio Rode (left) began playing varsity basketball as an eighth-grader and holds the girls' single-game scoring record (35 points). A 2004 graduate, she was a two-time Gatorade Player of the Year. She signed to play at Cal-Berkeley and later played at Seward Community College in Kansas and then San Francisco State.

Six-foot, 10-inch P.J. Horgan was the first Cleveland High School graduate to sign a Division I letter of intent, playing four seasons at the Citadel. The 2011 Cleveland graduate had also played at Rio Rancho High School for head coach Brian Smith. He averaged 20.6 points a game with the Storm.

Brandon McKinney, a 2004 RRHS graduate, was a hard-running halfback who often eclipsed the 100-yard mark for the Rams in their 2002 and 2003 seasons. McKinney played defensive end at New Mexico State University before opting for a career in law enforcement and joining the Rio Rancho Police Department.

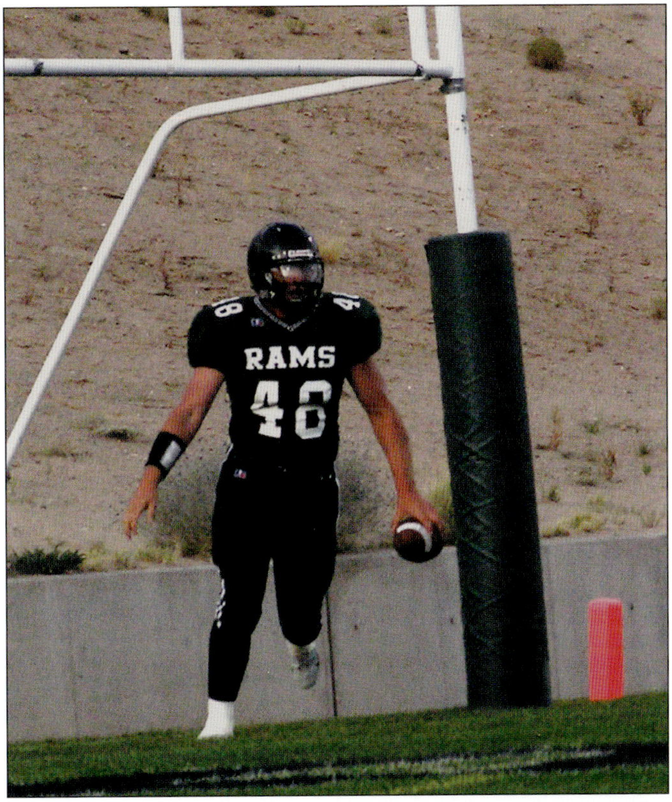

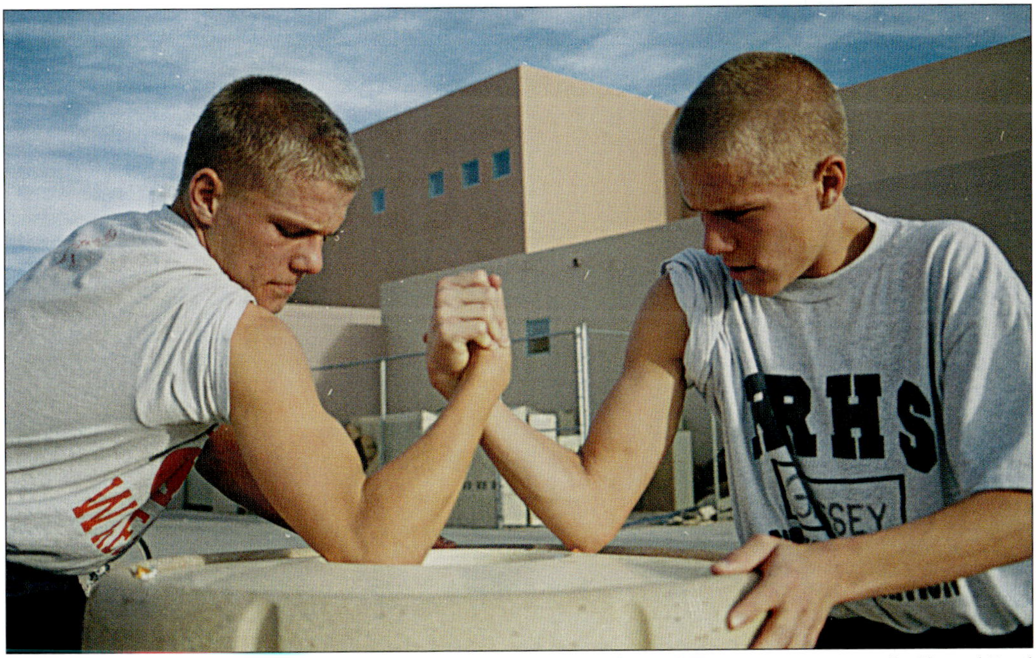

No, this is not an optical illusion. Pictured here are the talented Tice twins, Bryan (left) and Paul (right), who each won individual Class 5A state wrestling titles in 2002. Bryan won another in 2003, the year they graduated; they went on to wrestle for Cal State-Fullerton.

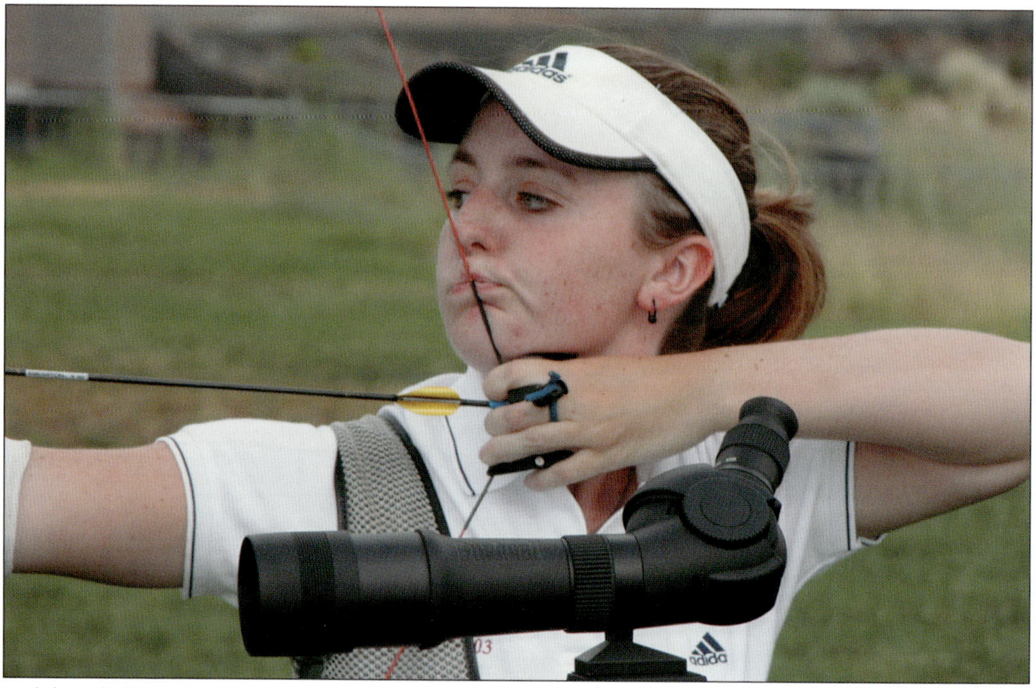

Left-handed Kendra Harvey is Rio Rancho's best archer, and the home-schooled student qualified as an alternate—at the age of 16—for the 2004 Summer Olympics in Greece. As a teenager, she was ranked 14th nationally by USA Archery. Her younger brother Jason later played on the RRHS golf team.

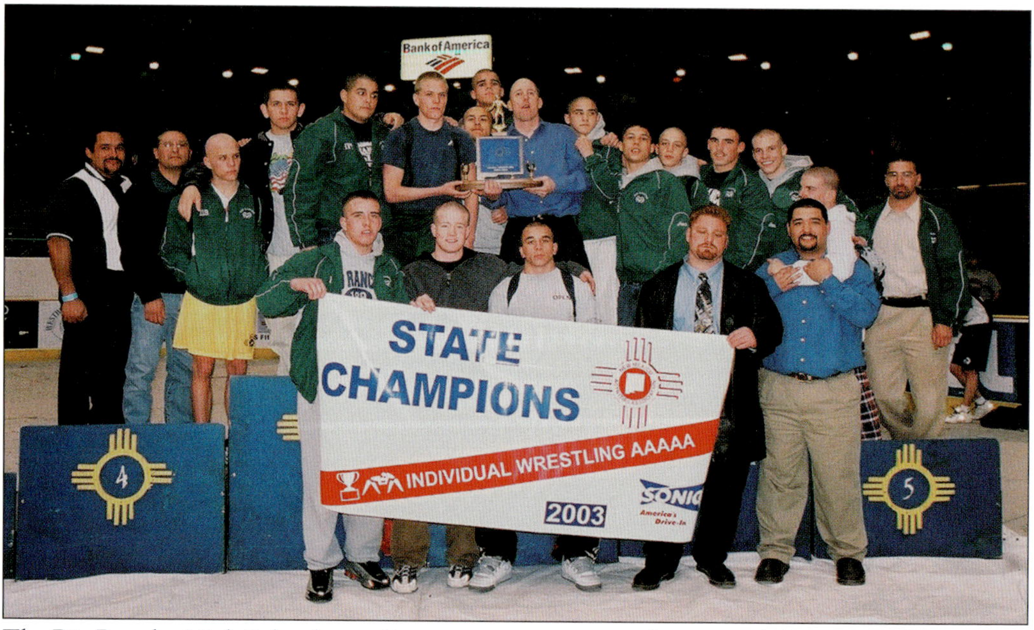

The Rio Rancho High School wrestling team is a state powerhouse, and this 2003 titlist had two individual champions, Bryan Tice at 125 pounds and Lionel Sierra at 140 pounds. Then-coach Dennis Friedland holds the blue championship trophy; former assistant Mike Santos, at the lower right, became head coach in 2011.

Chris Williams was one of RRHS's best athletes, starring in football, basketball, and track and field. Often said to be too small, Williams starred at New Mexico State University and in the Canadian Football League. During a brief stint with the Chicago Bears in 2014, he scored a touchdown returning a kickoff.

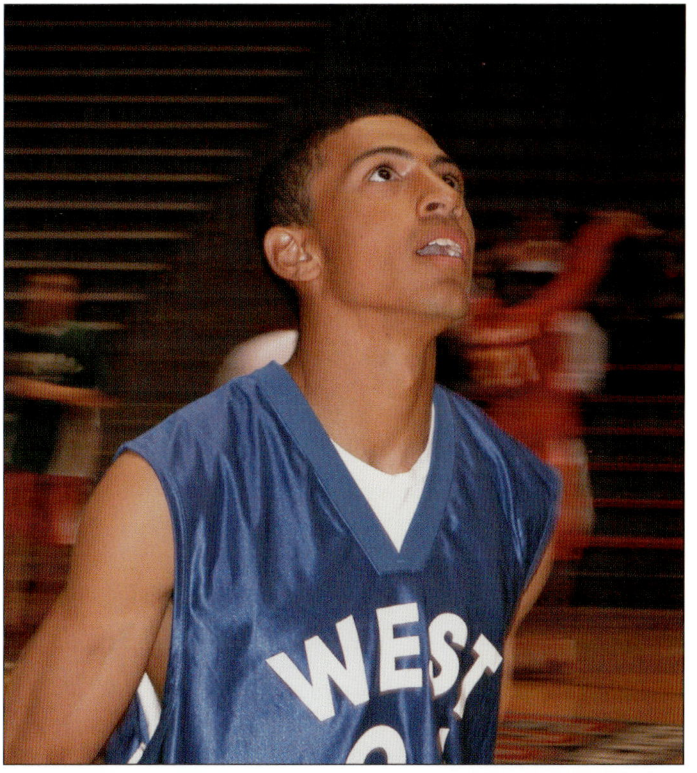

Just as Rio Rancho High School wrestling has risen to the top in New Mexico year after year, so too has the Rams' volleyball program, coached since day one by Toby Manzanares. This is the Rams' 2006 championship team. Through the 2014 season, Manzanares' Rams have won six state championships.

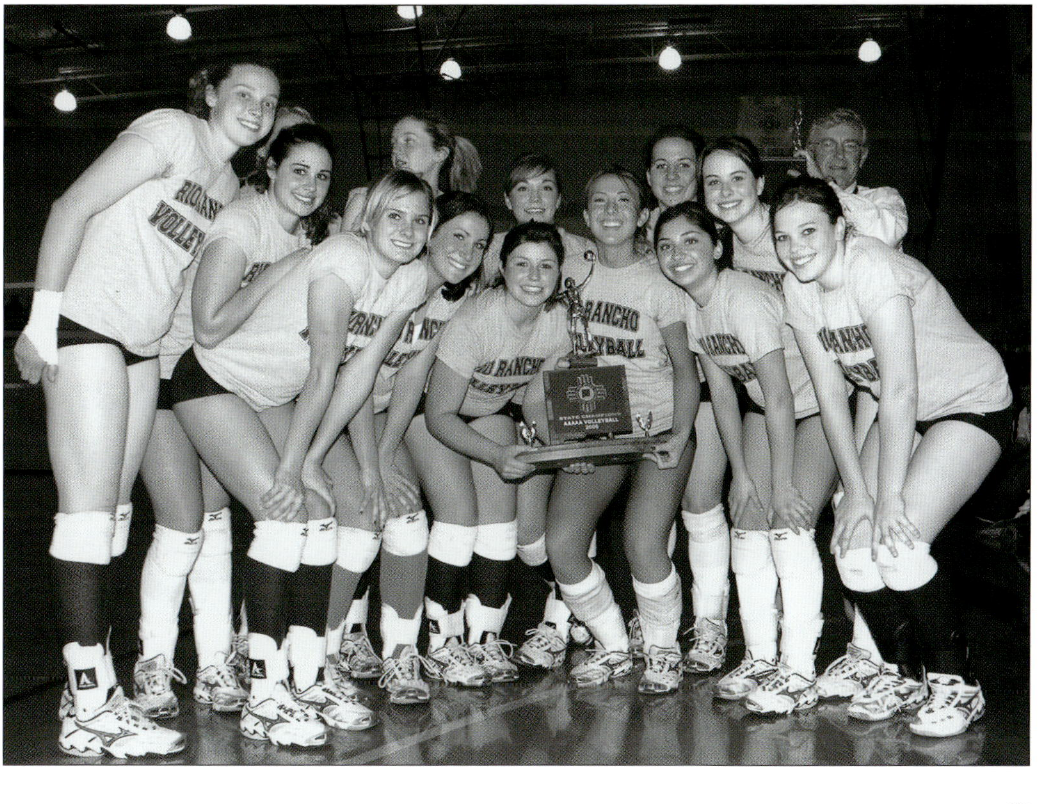

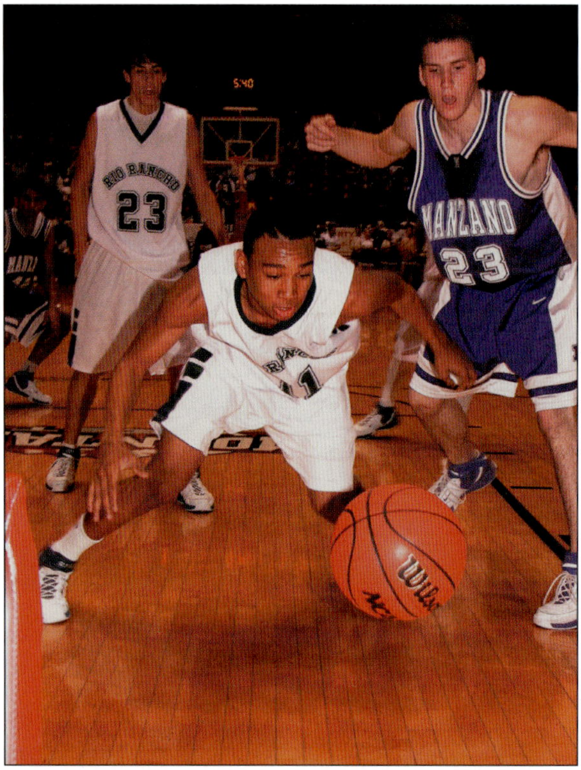

The Rio Rancho High School varsity basketball team had an outstanding 2006–2007 season, winning its final 29 games for an incredible 30-1 campaign and the Class 5A championship. Here, Chris Newsome dives for a loose ball in the Pit in the championship game against Albuquerque's Manzano. Teammate Noah Wolfe (23) watches on.

Yes, hockey is played in the Southwest. Indeed, hockey was played pretty well by Rio Rancho High School, celebrating its high school championship win on the ice in 2007. Tim Camacho was the team's coach; they played most of their games at Blades Multiplex Arenas, a short walk from RRHS.

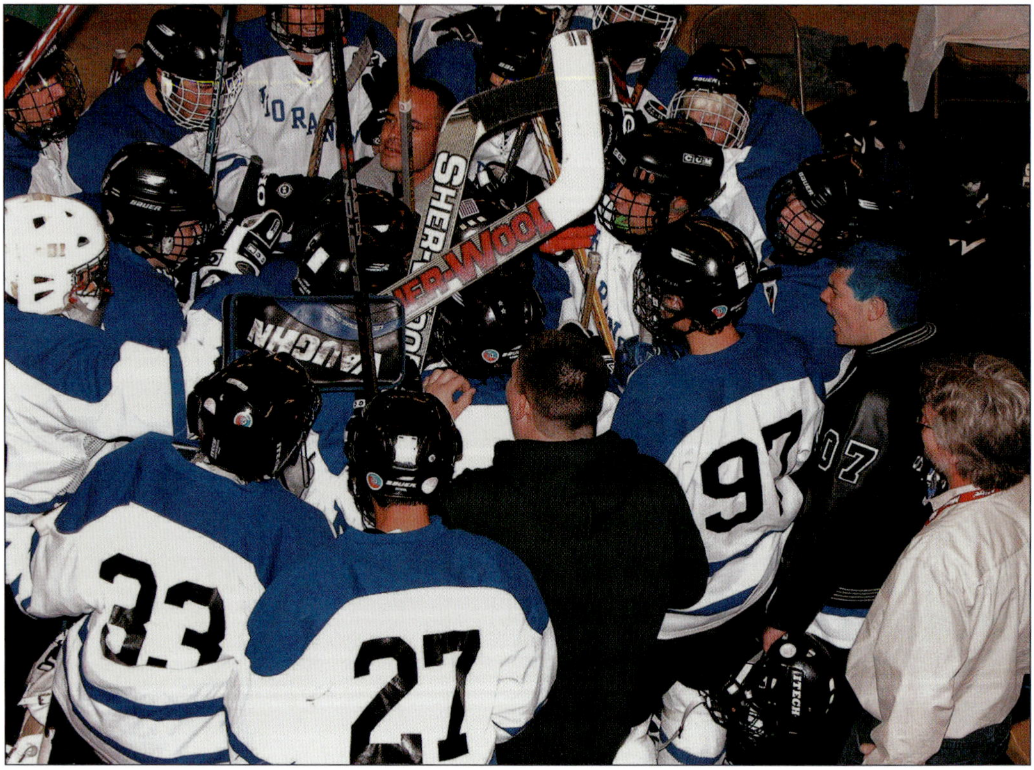

Two-sport star Ashley Rhoades (4) helped the Rams win the 2007 state volleyball title and, after signing a letter of intent to play at the University of New Mexico, returned to the basketball team in the winter. At left is RRHS's Brooklyn Boughter (15). (Courtesy of J.B. Gallegos.)

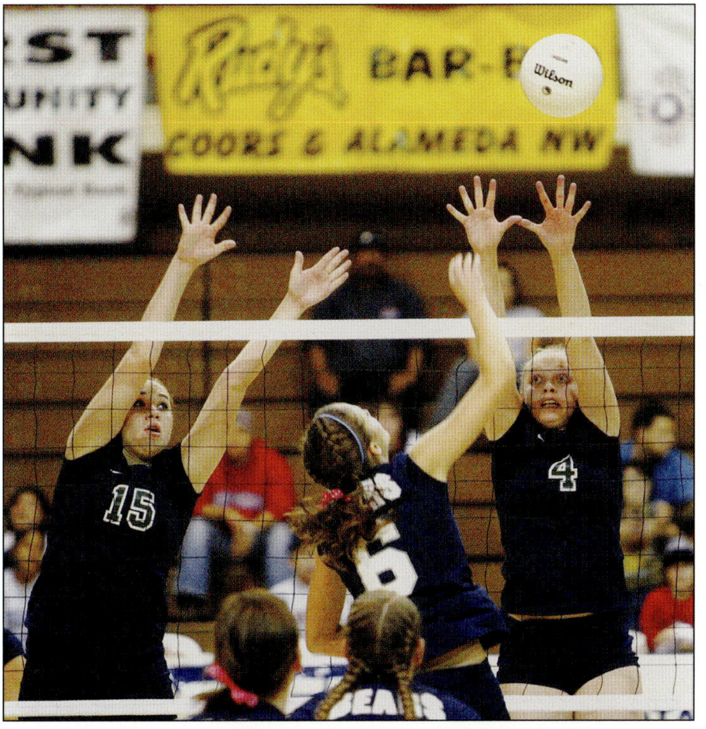

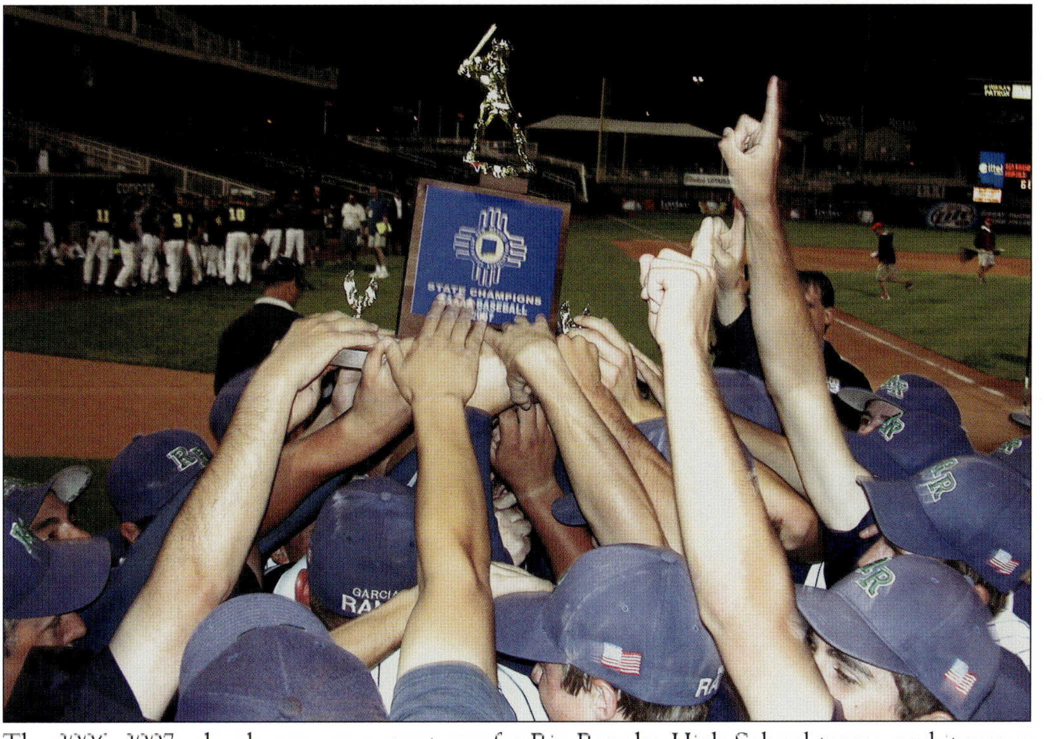

The 2006–2007 school year was a great one for Rio Rancho High School teams, and it won a handful of titles, the last of which was the Class 5A baseball championship at Isotopes Park. Here, the Rams players try to get a hand on the blue trophy symbolic of the title.

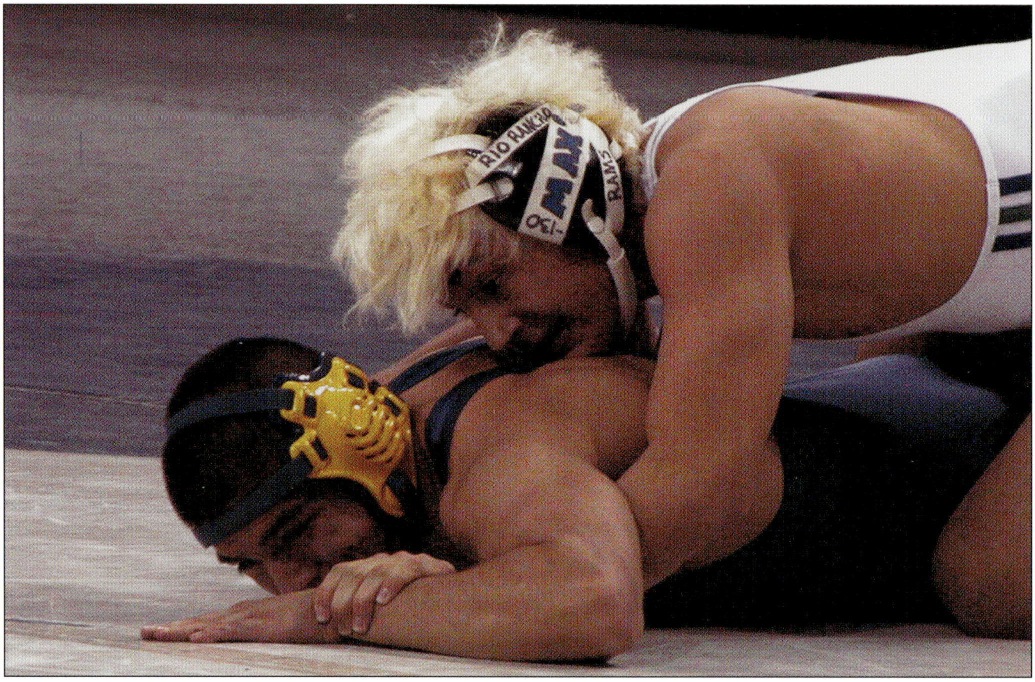

Although his older brother Matt won four individual mat championships from 2004 to 2007, Max Ortega, seen here in white, won five crowns from 2005 to 2009. That is a rare feat in the state of New Mexico, with Rio Rancho and Cleveland High Schools afforded the luxury of using eighth-graders on varsity sports teams.

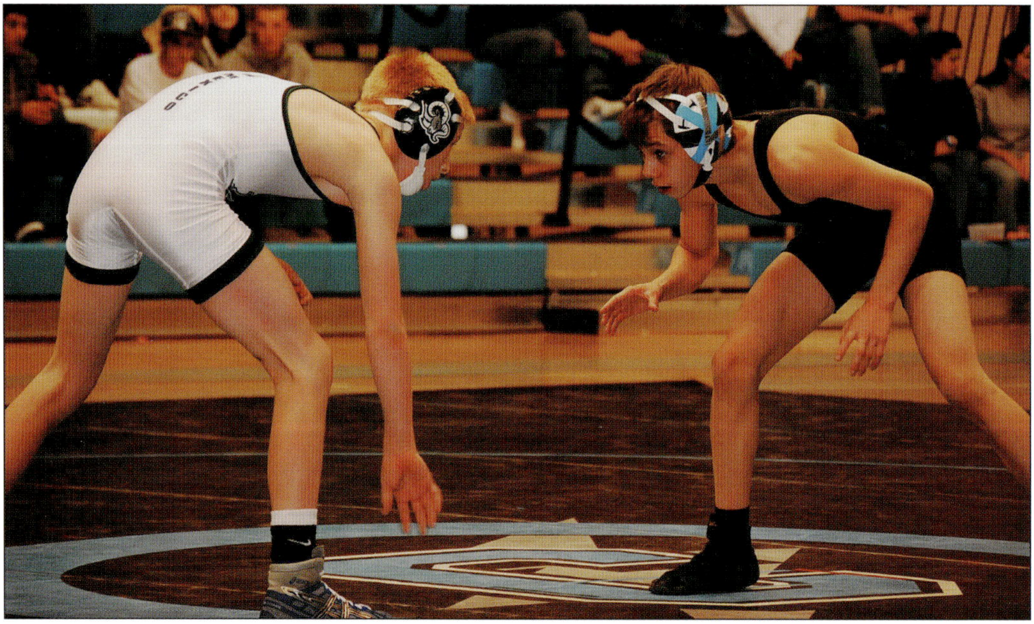

Paul Mascarenas (right), wrestling RRHS's Bo Nickal, not only became Cleveland High School's first individual state champion in 2010 but also matched what RRHS wrestlers Vicente Varela, Matt Ortega, and Louis Trujillo had done: he won four individual state crowns (2010–2013). Mascarenas went on to wrestle at South Dakota State University.

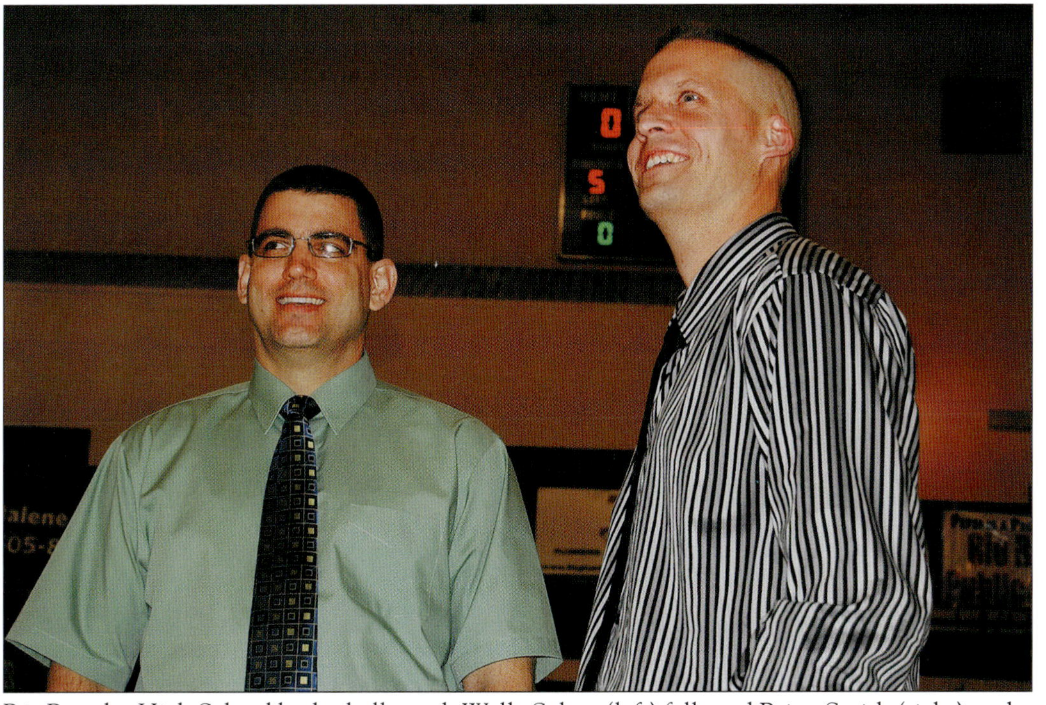

Rio Rancho High School basketball coach Wally Salata (left) followed Brian Smith (right) as the Rams' head coach after Smith became Cleveland High School's first boys' coach in 2009. Salata grew up in Rio Rancho and played basketball at St. Pius High School; his best season with the Rams came in 2014–2015.

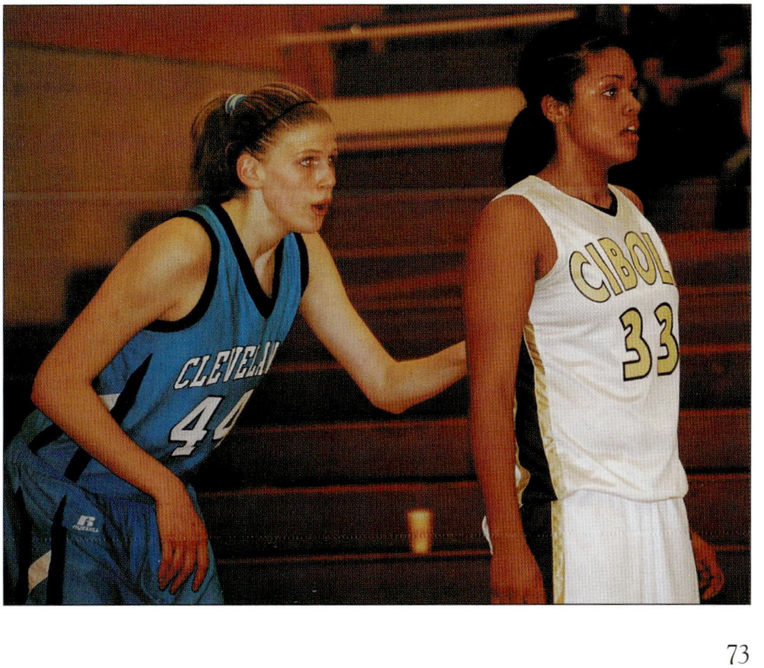

Sara Hattis (left) and her family moved to Rio Rancho from Santa Fe, and she made the most of that move, starring in volleyball and basketball (2009–2011) before going on to play both sports at the University of Texas, where she was a part of a Longhorns' national championship volleyball team.

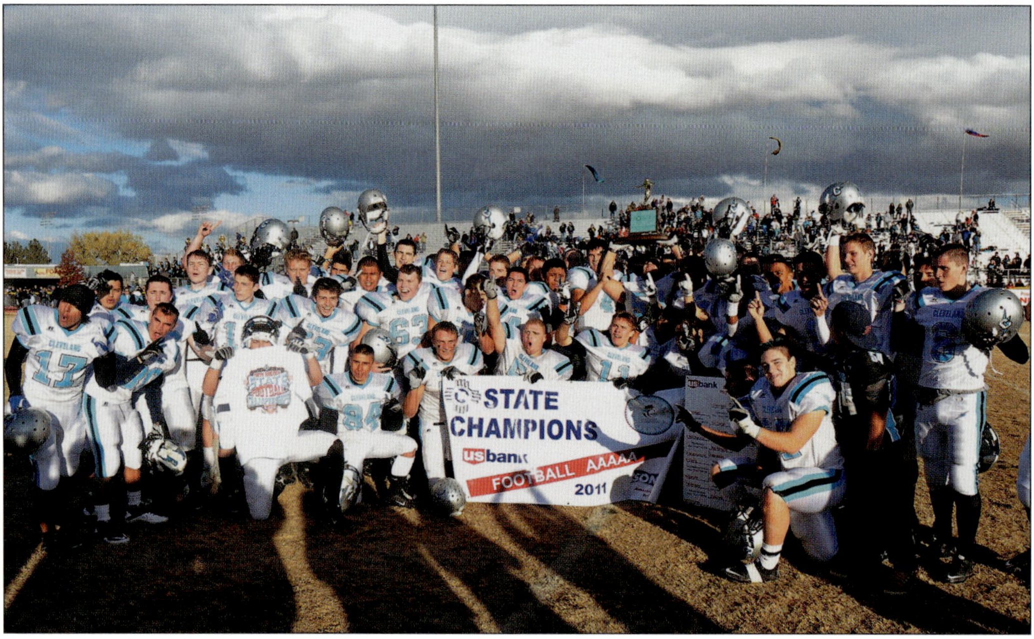

The 2011 Cleveland High football team ran the table, winning all 10 of its regular-season games, capturing the District 1-5A championship, and polishing off three postseason foes to claim the Class 5A title. It took a memorable second-half rally to beat Las Cruces Mayfield on the Field of Dreams in Las Cruces.

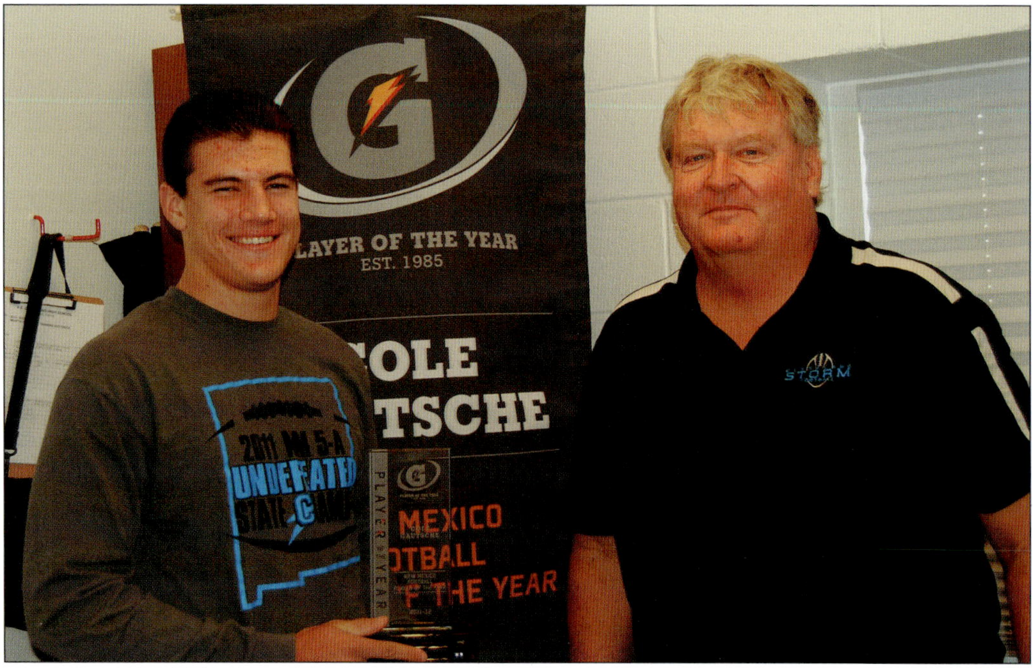

Cole Gautsche (left) was Cleveland High School's quarterback on the 2011 state championship team; Kirk Potter (right) was the coach. Gautsche was named the Gatorade Football Player of the Year in New Mexico for 2011, and he went on to become the starting quarterback for the University of New Mexico.

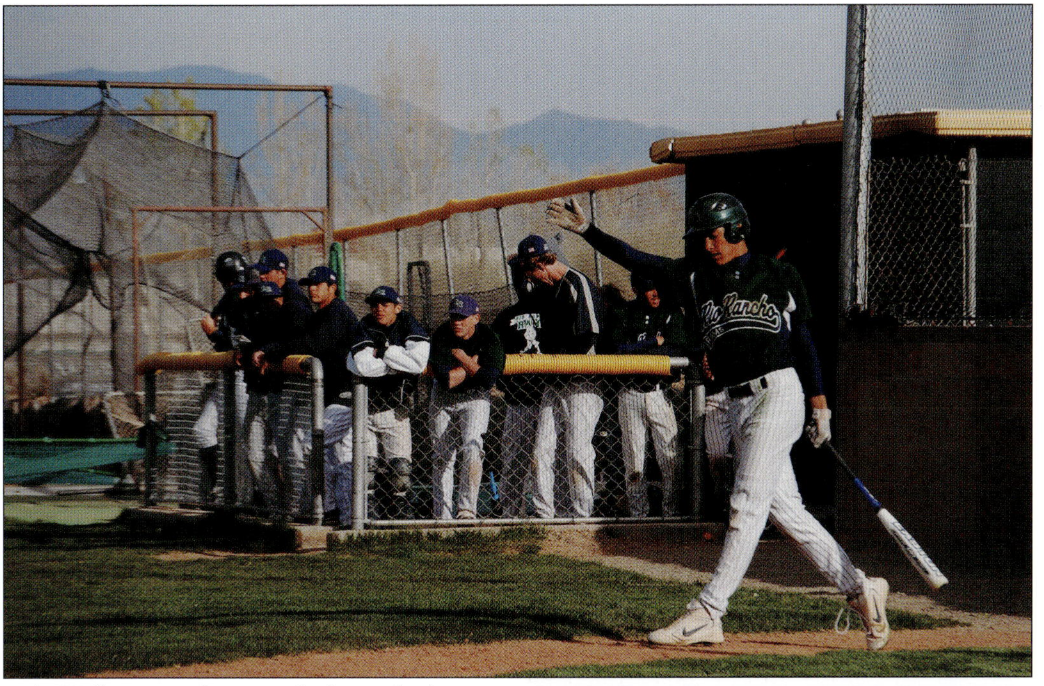

Josh Walker, seen here on-deck, pitched and played the outfield at Rio Rancho High School and played basketball there through his junior year. After one season at Howard Junior College, Walker played three seasons for the University of New Mexico. The Baltimore Orioles selected him in the 22nd round of the 2014 MLB draft.

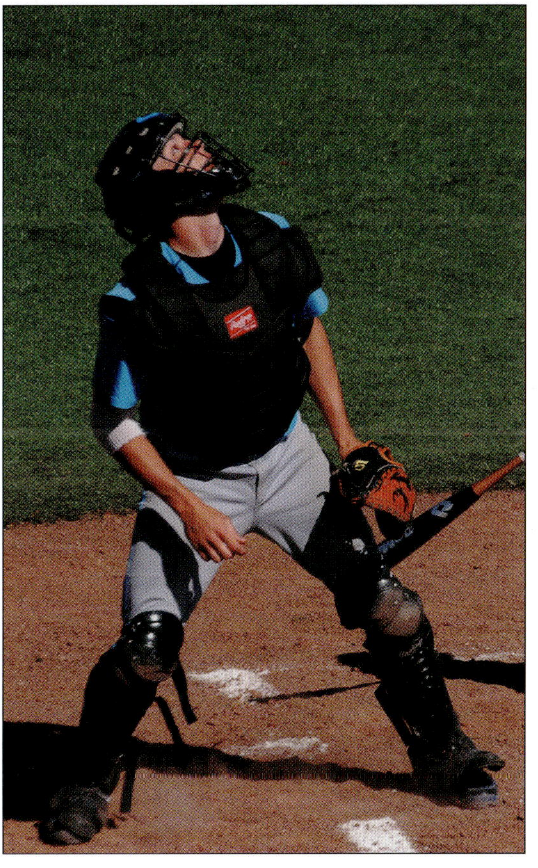

Blake Swihart was a teammate of Josh Walker at Rio Rancho High School, where the two played on the 2009 championship team. Swihart, because of his residence, attended Cleveland High School as a junior and senior. He was the first-round pick of the Boston Red Sox in the 2011 MLB draft.

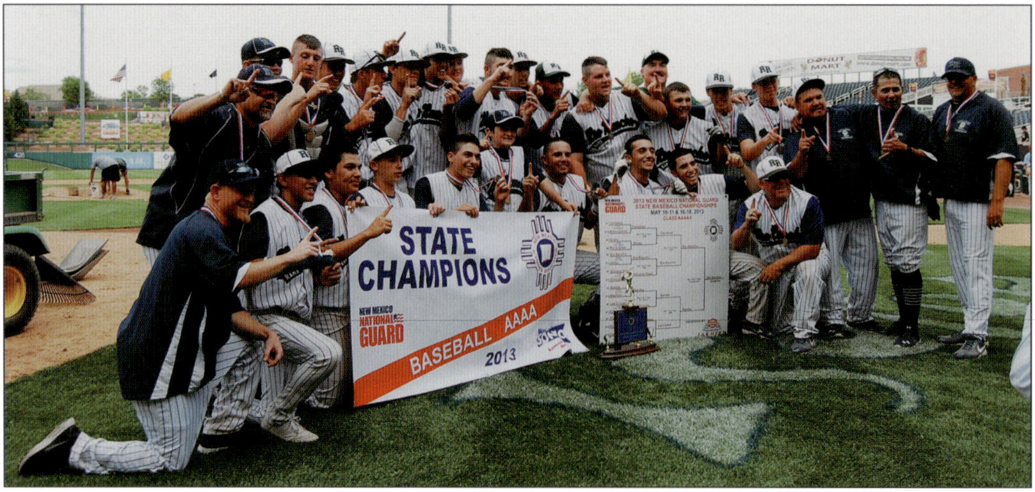

Rio Rancho High School coach Ron Murphy led his baseball team to the 2013 championship at Isotopes Park, although he was ejected from the game against Albuquerque's Sandia High School. It was the third diamond crown for the Rams during Murphy's stint. The Rams also won 5A titles in 2007 and 2009.

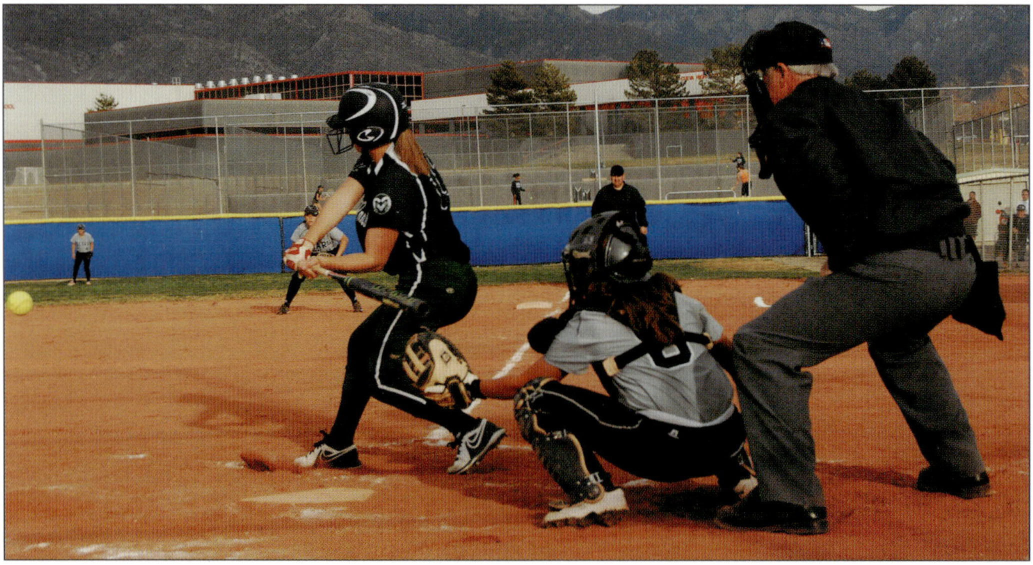

Rio Rancho High School's softball team won the state championship in 2014 thanks in part to the pitching and batting of Nicole Pendley, seen here in a game at Volcano Vista. The Gatorade Player of the Year in the state in 2014, Pendley accepted a scholarship to play at the University of Oklahoma. The Rams won the Class 6A championship in 2015.

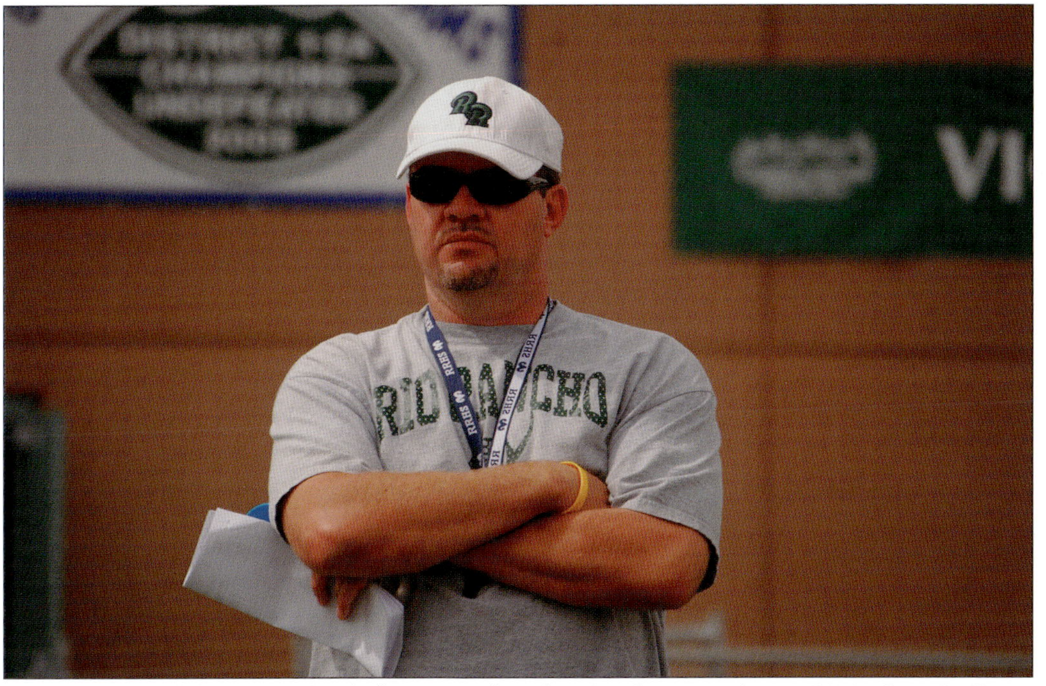

David Howes led the RRHS football team to the Class 6A championship in 2014, when the Rams matched what nearby Cleveland High had done three years earlier: 13-0. Howes was honored as the High School Coach of the Year by the New Mexico Sports Hall of Fame in 2015.

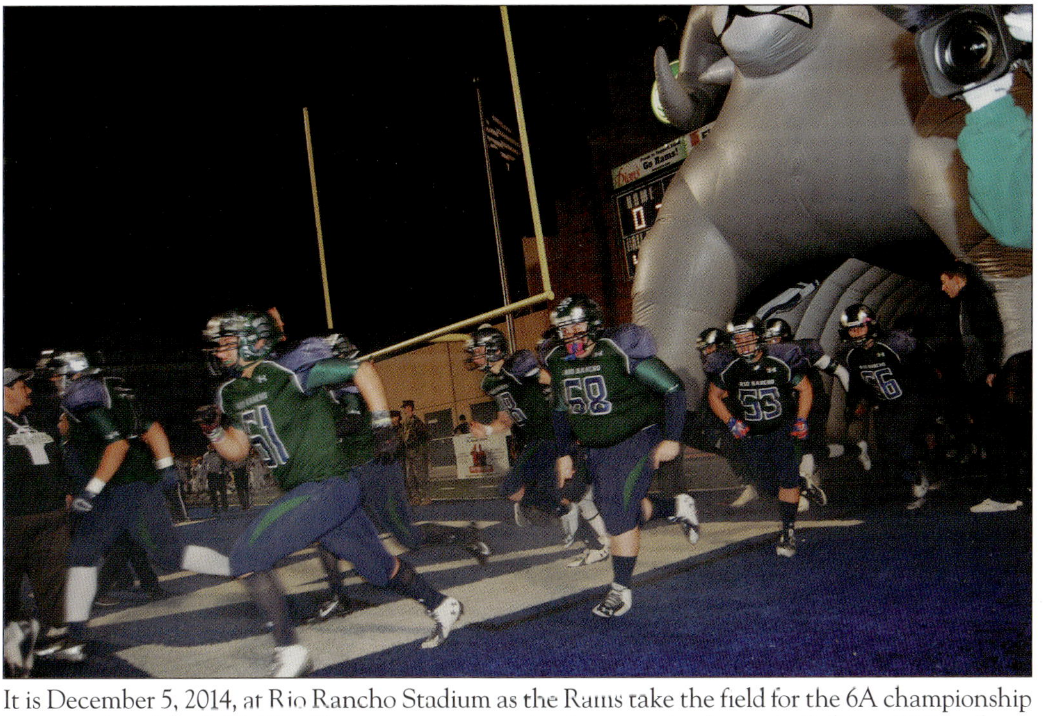

It is December 5, 2014, at Rio Rancho Stadium as the Rams take the field for the 6A championship game against Mayfield. The Rams went on to win the game in dramatic fashion, 33-31, after a snap over the Trojan punter's head sailed out of the end zone for a safety.

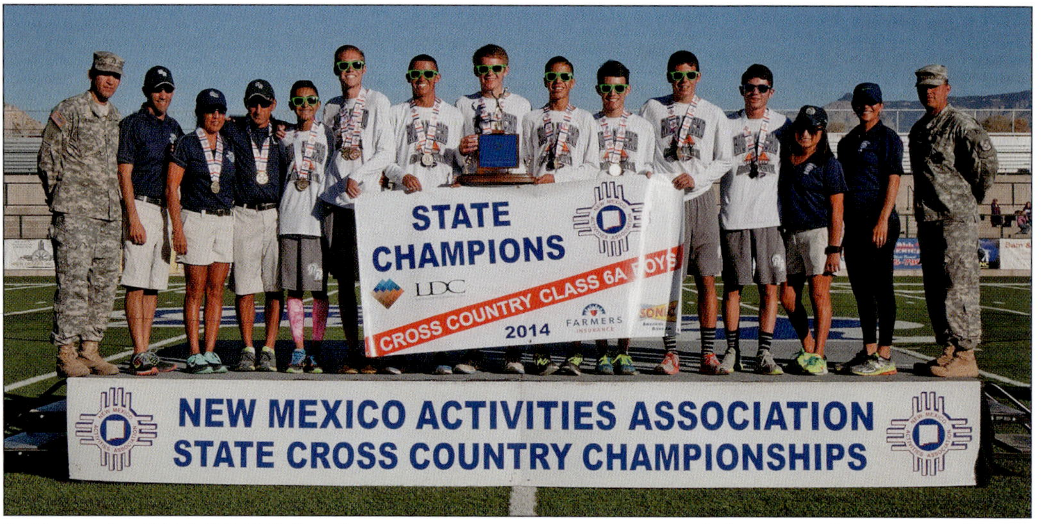

In November 2014, RRHS's boys' cross country team won its second championship in a row. Devin Paredes (fifth from left), finishing second, and teammate Josh Pyeatt (sixth from left), who was sixth, were named all-state for their top-10 finishes. Coach Sal Gonzales was named the state's Cross Country Coach of the Year. (Courtesy of TonyClaire Photography.)

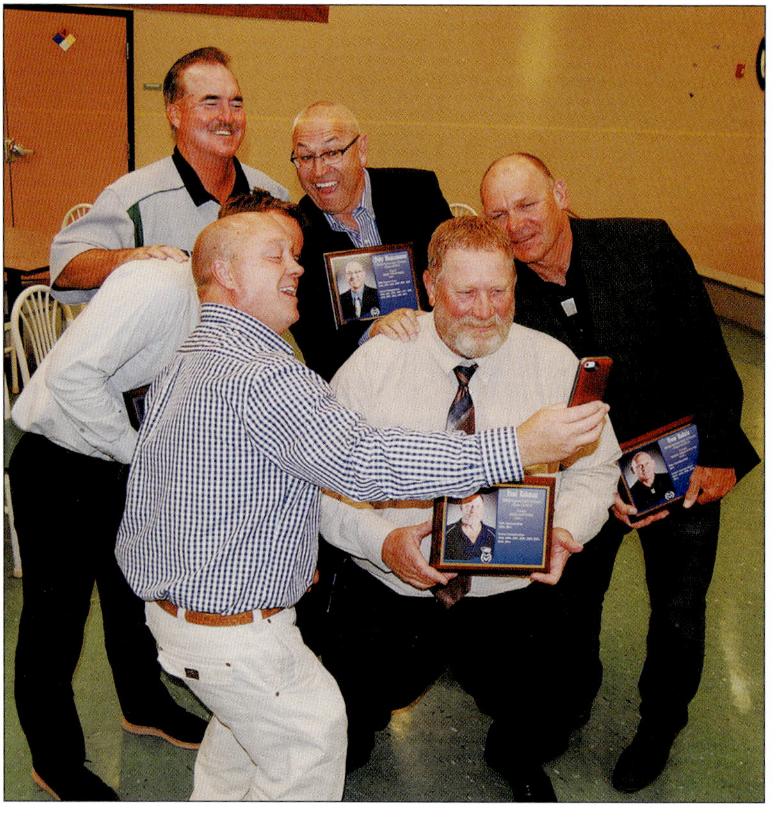

Rio Rancho High School opened its sports hall of fame in 2014. Here, contributor and honoree Tony Otero holds the camera for a selfie as, clockwise from the back left, athlete honoree Trent Rommann and coaches Ron Murphy, Toby Manzanares, Uwe Balzis, and Paul Kohman mug for the camera. Inducted athlete Danyel Longmire was absent.

Five

Santa Ana Star Center

In April 2004, the first part of Rio Rancho's new face was unveiled, as city officials presented plans for a new downtown arena to give the City of Vision a new look.

The project matched the city, Global Entertainment Corp., and its subsidiary, International Coliseums Corp., in a 10-year agreement "for the purposes of managing, administering and coordinating the design and construction, and operating the multi-purpose event center on behalf of the city," according to the project overview section of a 106-page document presented to the governing body by city administrator Jim Palenick.

The arena was seen as the "catalyst to a new city centre/downtown." Palenick, Mayor Jim Owen, and developer/construction manager Rick Kozuback, president and chief operating officer of both Global Entertainment and International Coliseums, said the 165,000-square-foot multipurpose event arena to be constructed near Paseo del Volcan and Unser Boulevard on then-undeveloped land would be the key to a new downtown.

Over the next few years, city hall, Hewlett-Packard, a Central New Mexico Community College branch, a University of New Mexico West campus, and UNM Sandoval Regional Medical Center were built within walking distance of the Star Center. Two miles east, Cleveland High School was completed in time for the 2009–2010 school year. Together, Palenick predicted back then, there would be "an awful lot of good times for everybody in the metropolitan community."

Preliminary arena plans called for 6,500 fixed seats, with the capability to expand to 8,000 for concerts and other staged events, plus 2,000 parking spaces as part of the $42.5 million project. The Star Center found plenty of use; countless concerts, RV shows, Jehovah's Witness conventions, home shows, monster-truck shows, motocross, rodeos and bull-riding events, Disney on Ice events, Cirque du Soleil, "Walking with Dinosaurs," entertainers Jeff Dunham and Larry the Cable Guy, and even Al Gore came to talk about global warming and some of his other concerns for the planet. A few years after the arena was built, Global Spectrum assumed management duties.

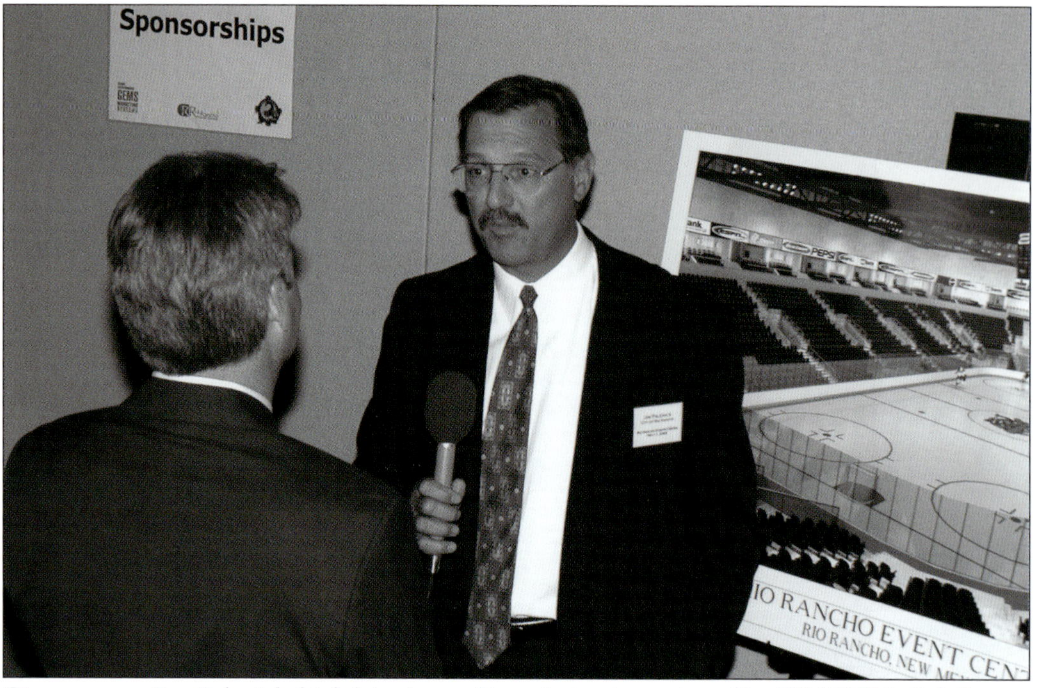

City manager Jim Palenick (right) is pictured here being interviewed by KOAT-TV's Bob Brown during a news conference in 2004, when plans for Rio Rancho's new multimillion-dollar arena and an adjacent entertainment complex, which never came to fruition, were unveiled. Behind Palenick is an artist's rendering of how the interior would look.

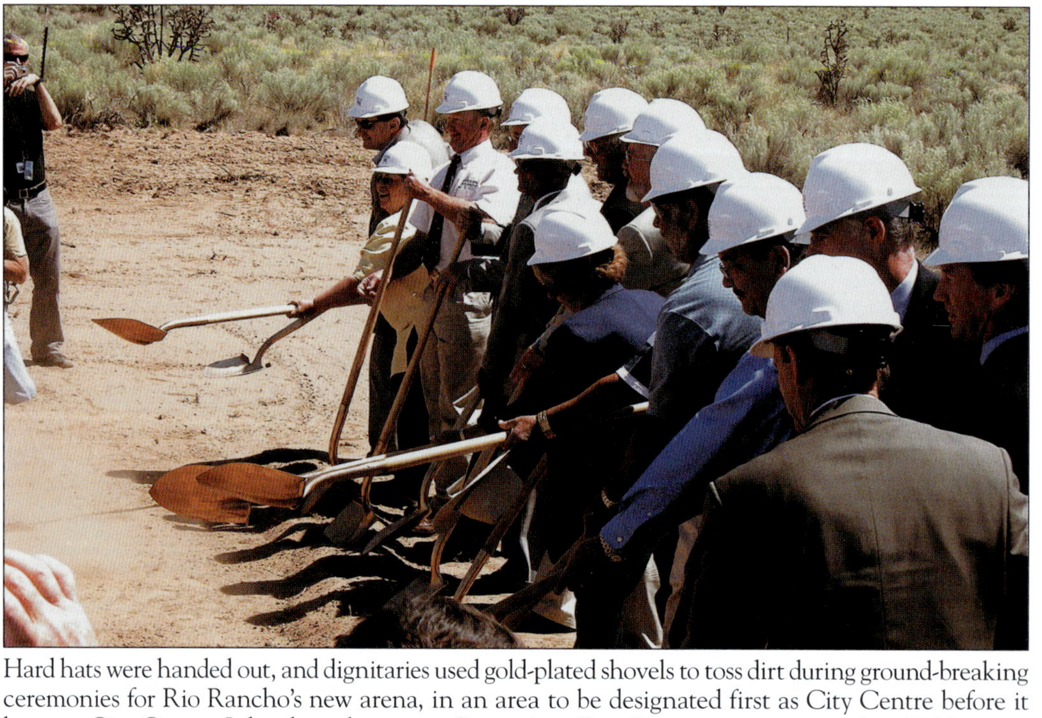

Hard hats were handed out, and dignitaries used gold-plated shovels to toss dirt during ground-breaking ceremonies for Rio Rancho's new arena, in an area to be designated first as City Centre before it became City Center. It has been known as Santa Ana Star Center since it opened in 2006.

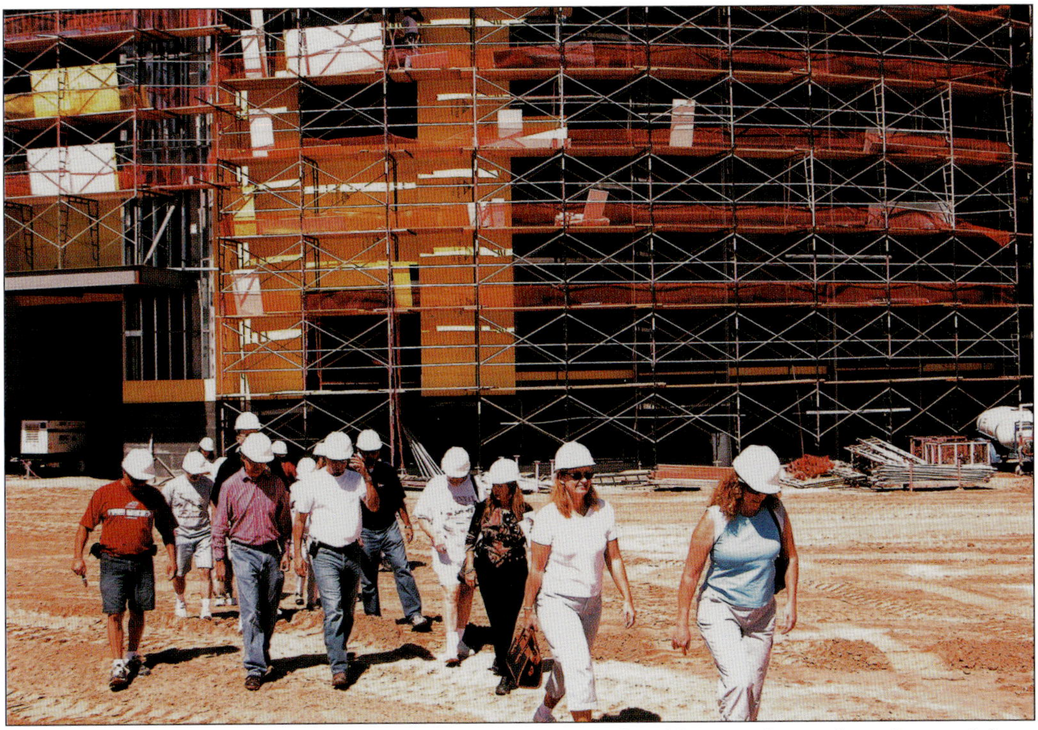

Visitors to ongoing construction at the new arena wore hard hats and were bused to and from the site. Reviews were favorable for the arena, and there was excitement in the air as professional entertainment—the Central Hockey League's New Mexico Scorpions—would be the anchor tenant in the arena.

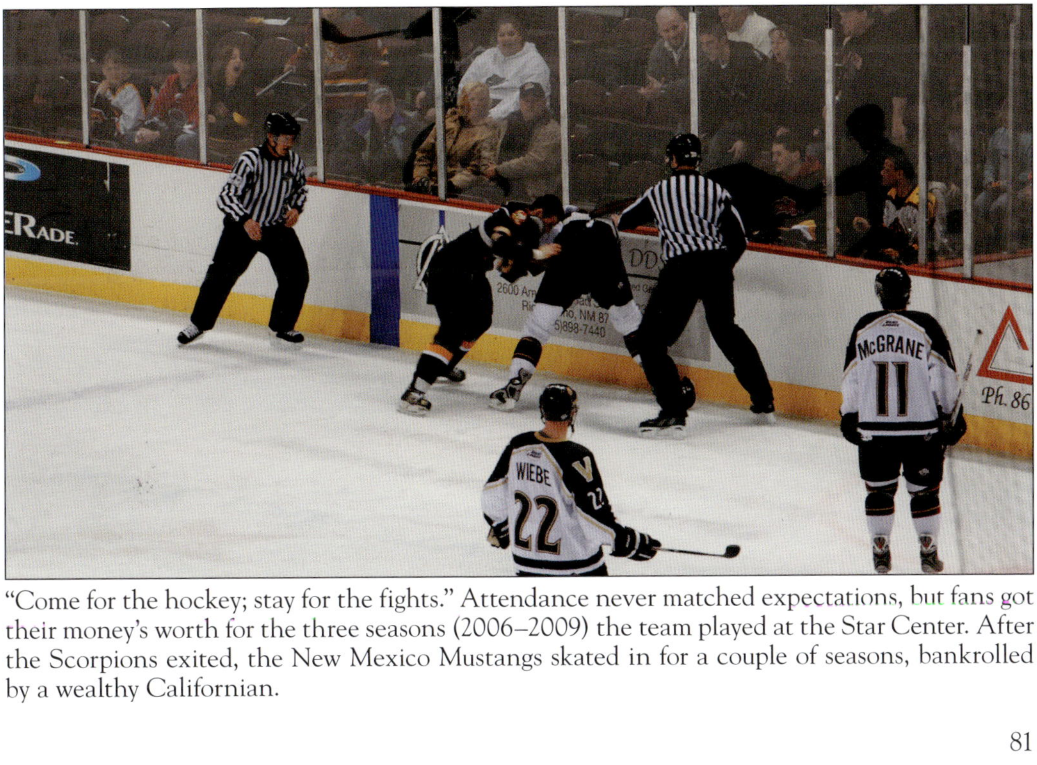

"Come for the hockey; stay for the fights." Attendance never matched expectations, but fans got their money's worth for the three seasons (2006–2009) the team played at the Star Center. After the Scorpions exited, the New Mexico Mustangs skated in for a couple of seasons, bankrolled by a wealthy Californian.

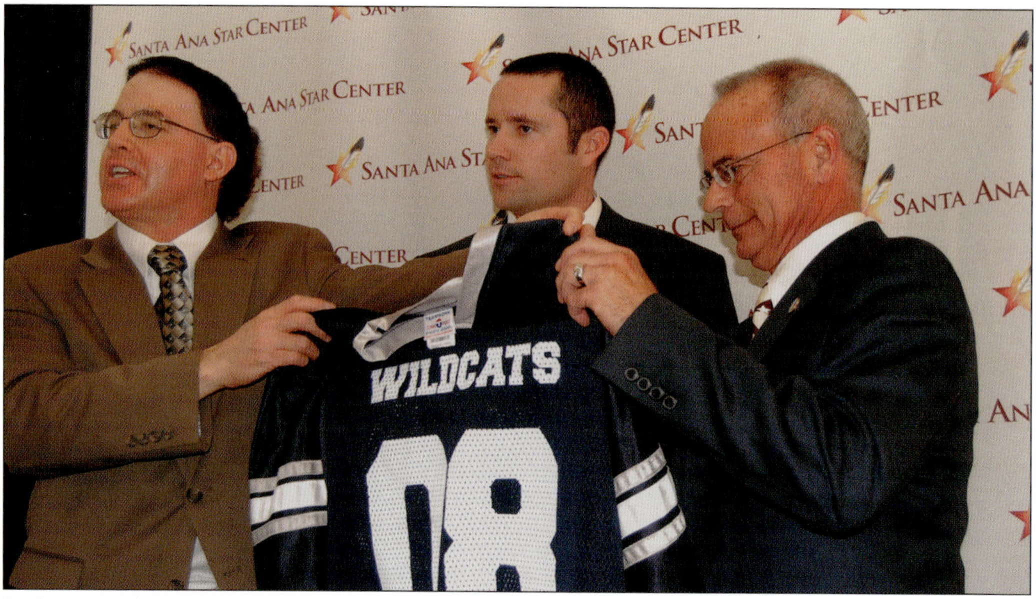

In January 2008, a new tenant announced it would be playing its home games in Santa Ana Star Center. Sadly, the New Mexico Wildcats were poorly run and in Rio Rancho for only one season. Still, it was long enough for acting-mayor Mike Williams (right) to don a Wildcats jersey.

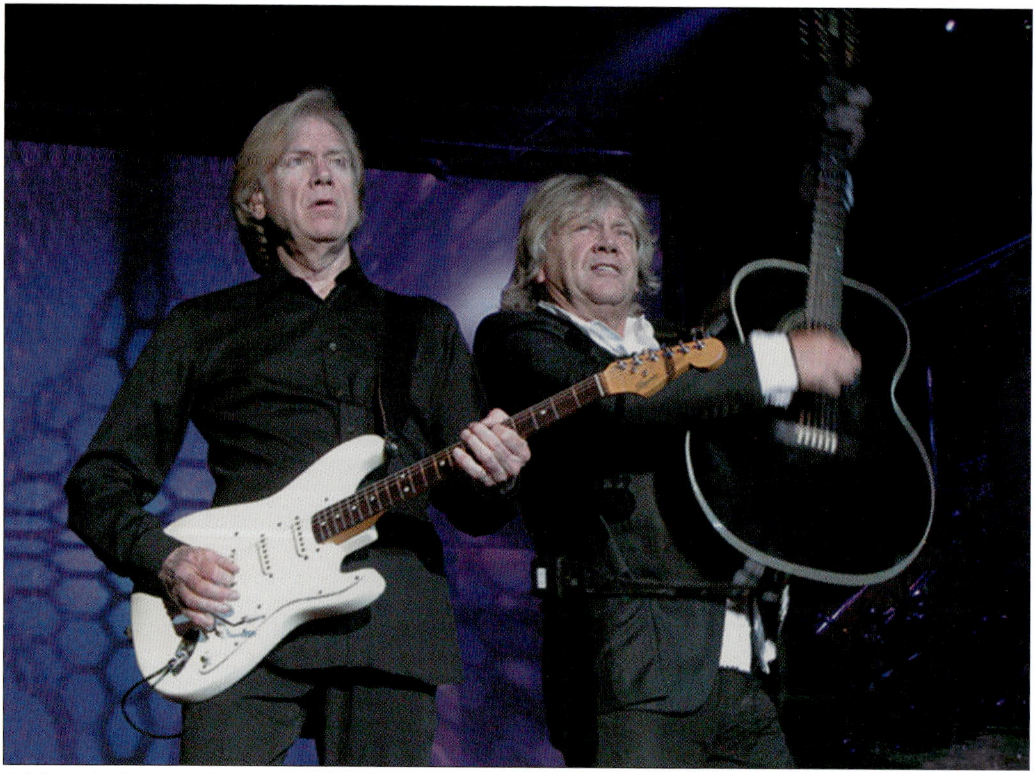

Although the Star Center has held countless concerts since it opened in the fall of 2006, one of the most memorable was a 2007 show by The Moody Blues, who showed that men in their 60s could still rock and roll. The British group played its hits from the late 1960s and early 1970s.

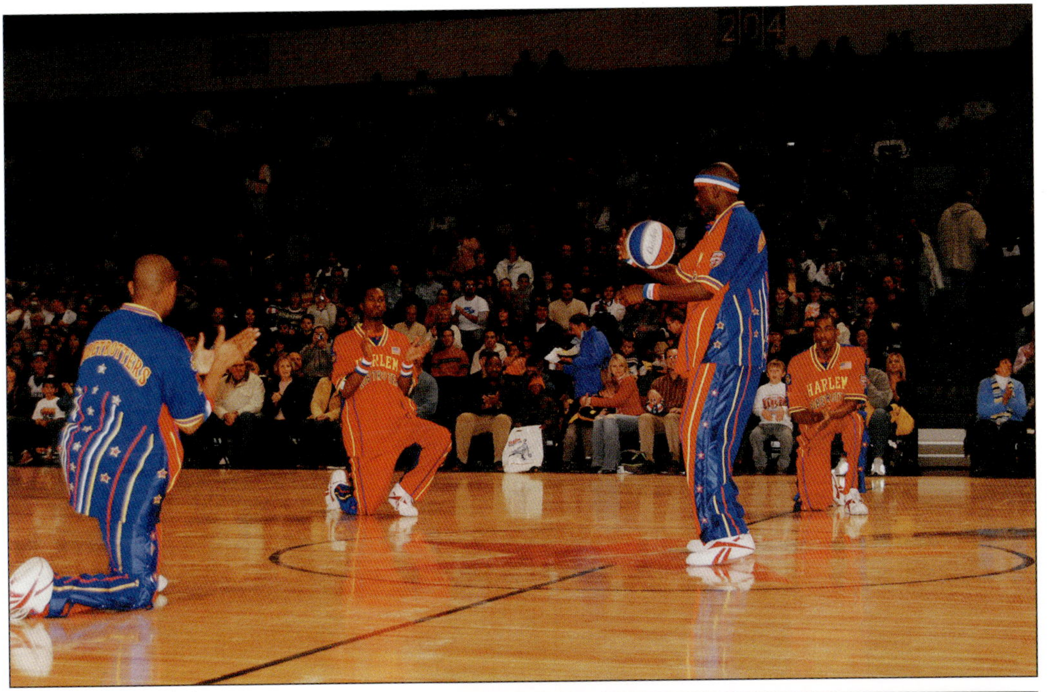

The Harlem Globetrotters, famed basketball magicians, first dazzled Star Center crowds in January 2008, demonstrating their hardwood mastery and mingling with the crowd, especially the youngsters. Of course there was the obligatory bucket being lugged around by a Trotter. Did it have confetti or water?

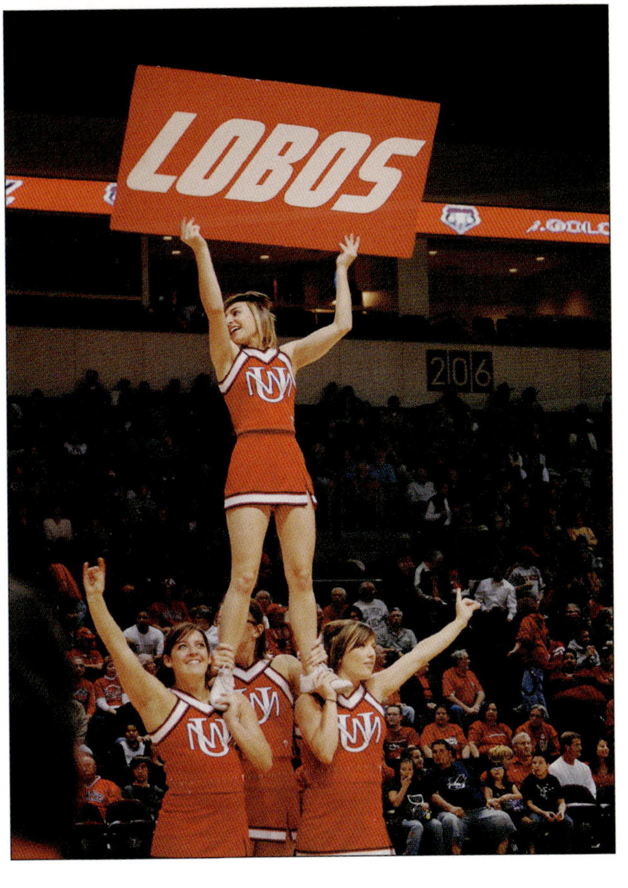

With University Arena in the midst of a $60-million renovation in March 2009, the University of New Mexico women's basketball team played a WNIT contest at the Star Center, delighting Rio Ranchoans but frustrating Lobo fans who had to drive all the way to Rio Rancho to see it.

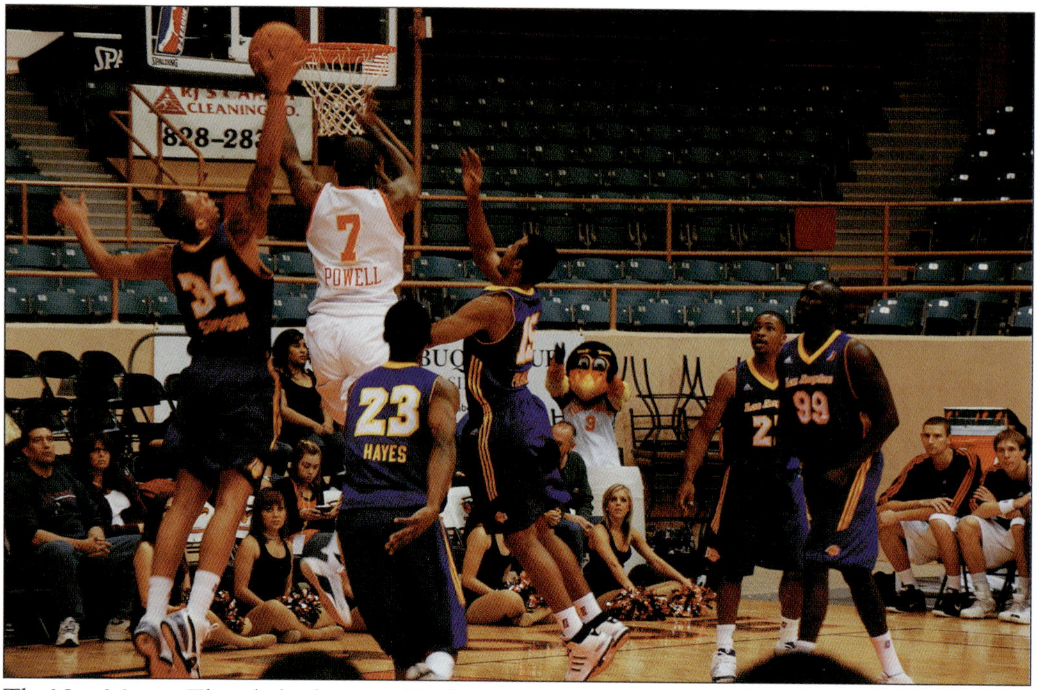

The New Mexico Thunderbirds, owned by Sam and Jackie Bregman, moved from Tingley Coliseum to the Star Center for the 2009–2010 D-League basketball season, although some nights it seemed like nobody knew a top-quality, professional basketball game was being played in Rio Rancho. The team lasted one season in Rio Rancho.

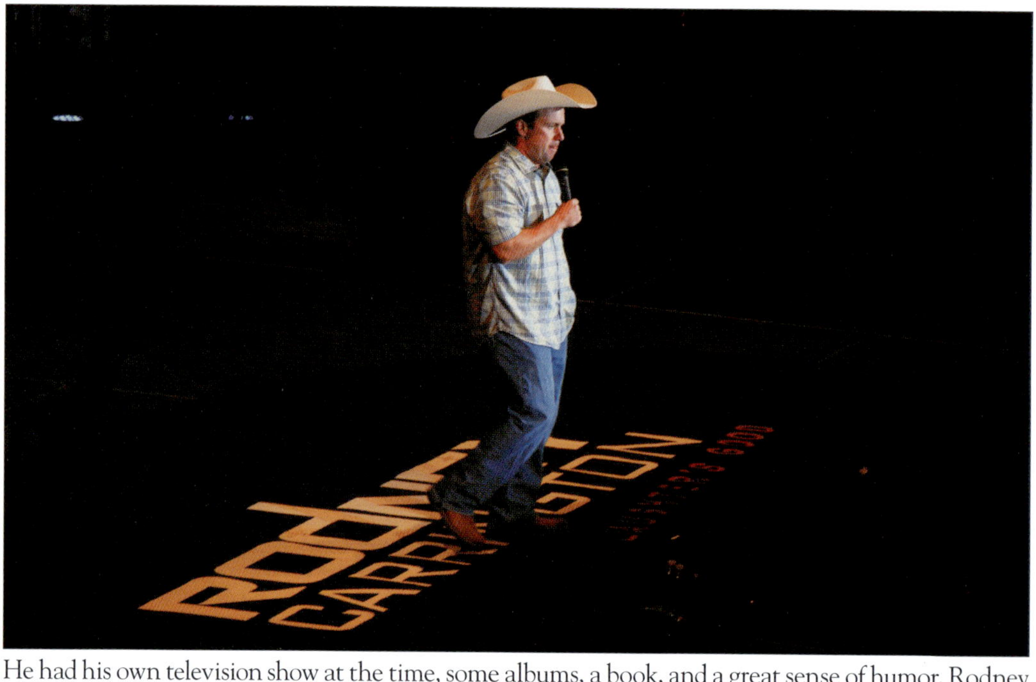

He had his own television show at the time, some albums, a book, and a great sense of humor. Rodney Carrington cracked up Star Center attendees at his July 2011 concert. Larry the Cable Guy, Jeff Dunham, George Lopez, and other comedians have kept the Star Center buzzing with laughter.

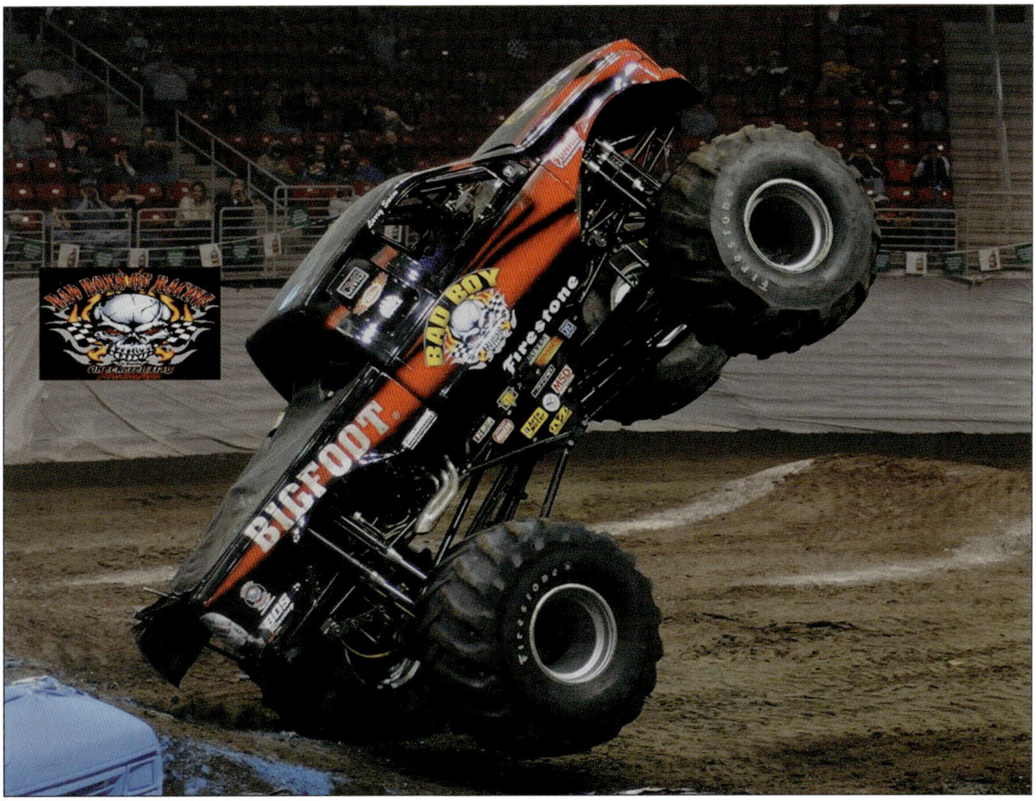

The monster trucks are regulars at the Star Center, always attracting a lot of fans. Many of them want to see Bigfoot, seen here doing a wheelie. The Star Center often follows a weekend of monster trucks with a rodeo or bull-riding event, making good use of the dirt on the floor.

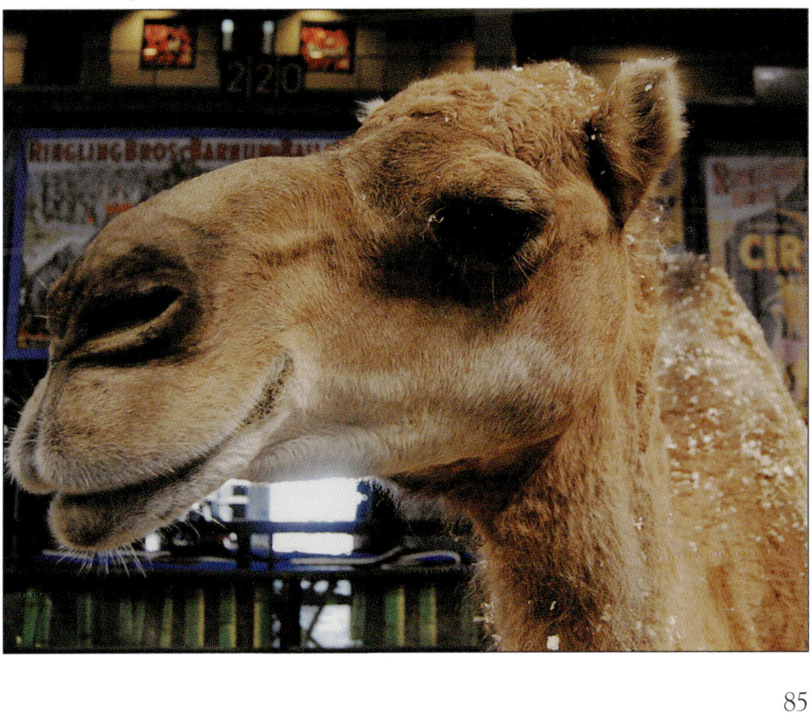

In the summer of 2013, Ringling Brothers Barnum & Bailey circus made a stop at the Star Center, and Jewel the camel was among its many stars. Ringling Brothers was one of several circuses to visit Rio Rancho in recent years; Cirque du Soleil also schedules stops annually for its myriad shows.

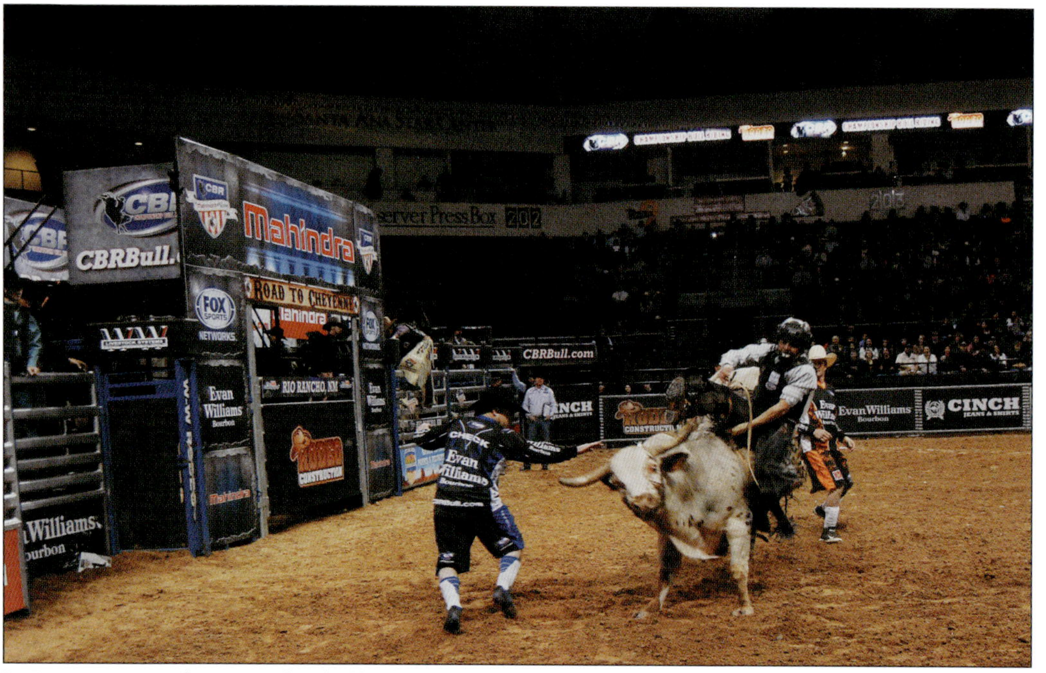

In January 2014, championship bull riding began appearing annually at the Star Center. Operated by legendary bull rider Tuff Hedeman, the CBR brings in 24 of the best riders, and approximately 2,300 fans were at the Star Center in January 2015 to see the second Bucking on the Rio Grande.

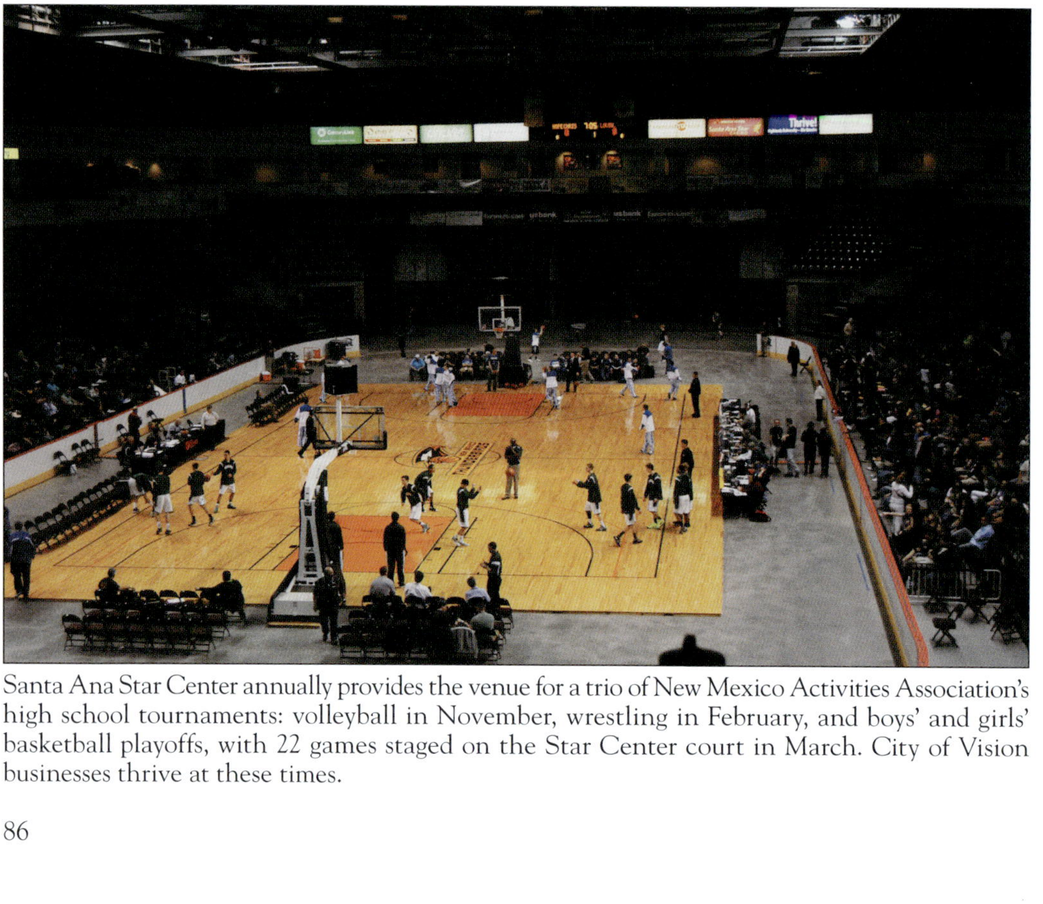
Santa Ana Star Center annually provides the venue for a trio of New Mexico Activities Association's high school tournaments: volleyball in November, wrestling in February, and boys' and girls' basketball playoffs, with 22 games staged on the Star Center court in March. City of Vision businesses thrive at these times.

Six

Treasures in the City

It seems ironic that the famed Spanish explorer Francisco Vázquez de Coronado once passed through the Rio Rancho area seeking treasure, which he did not find—and there are treasures of another sort that lure and keep people here. They may never be thought of as treasures, per se, but there are countless amenities and wonders within the City of Rio Rancho's borders that should be considered as such.

Earlier chapters touted the estimated 360 sunny days a year, the great schools, top-notch athletes who have grown up here, and more. City streets are relatively safe, fire-and-rescue crews are quick to respond when and where they are needed, and veterans have found the respect they deserve. Shopping is also readily available, with grocery stores, hardware stores, auto-body shops, and even some big-box stores, unlike the city's early days when everything residents needed was down the hill in Albuquerque.

There is never a shortage of entertainment, either, with a plethora of high school sports and the luxurious Santa Ana Star Center arguably regarded as the best entertainment venue in the state. In the event one needs immediate health care, maybe even surgery, there are two hospitals in the city: Presbyterian Rust Medical Center and the University of New Mexico Sandoval Regional Medical Center.

Here are some of the city's many treasures, some of which are depicted in the following pages: Rio Rancho Aquatic Center, Blades Multiplex Arenas, the bosque, Club Rio Rancho, Galloping Grace Youth Ranch, Haven House, J&R Vintage Auto Museum, Esther Bone Memorial Library and Loma Colorado Main Library, Meadowlark Senior Center, 20-plus city parks, Premiere Cinemas, Rio Puerco escarpment, Rainbow Park Observatory, Veterans Monument Park, and Waterwise Garden.

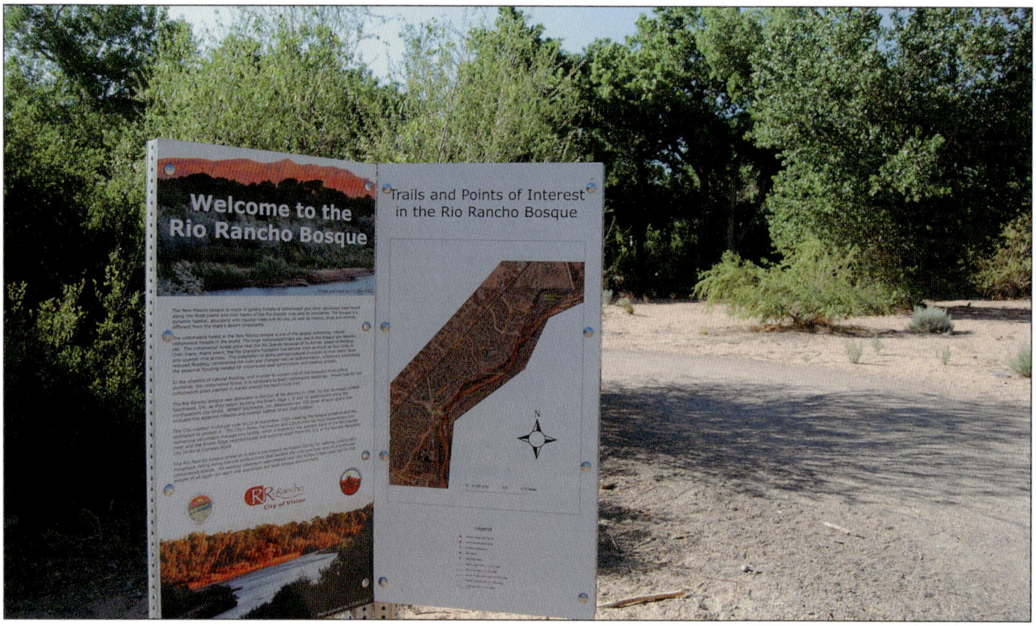

The bosque may be the best-kept secret in the city, with many residents unaware of the peace and tranquility, as well as wildlife, found along the Rio Grande. Tended by volunteers belonging to FORROS (Friends of Rio Rancho Open Space), the group's mission is to provide an enjoyable place for residents and wildlife.

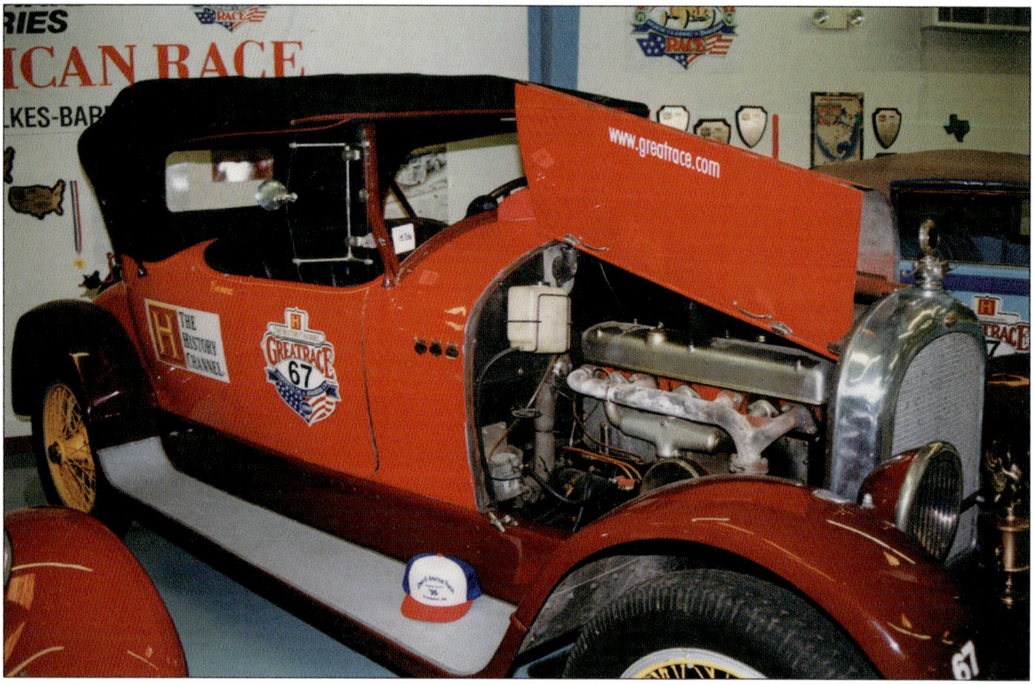

Talk about well-kept secrets, Gab and Evonna Joiner, native New Mexicans, have called Rio Rancho home for several decades. Gab, who passed away in May 2015, bought his first antique car in 1959, a 1926 Model T Ford coupe, which he later traded for a 1928 Chevrolet. J&R Vintage Auto Museum has approximately 70 vehicles on display.

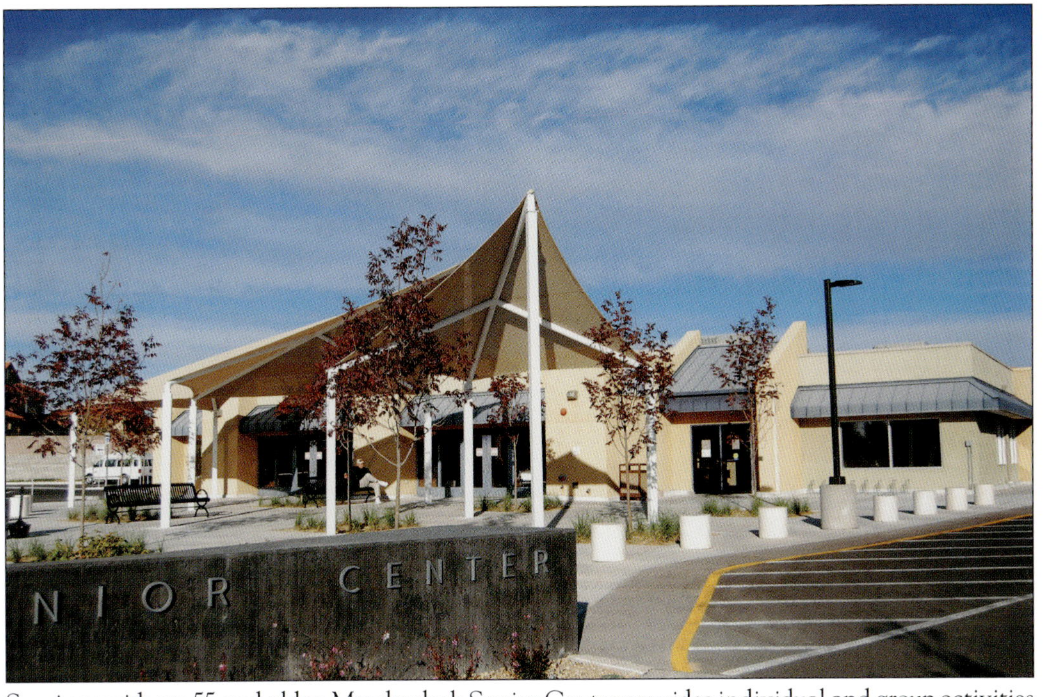

Serving residents 55 and older, Meadowlark Senior Center provides individual and group activities that include health and wellness, arts and humanities programming, intergenerational programming, social activities, day trips, educational opportunities, financial and benefits assistance, information and referral services, volunteer opportunities, transportation services, and a meal program. Annual membership fees are inexpensive.

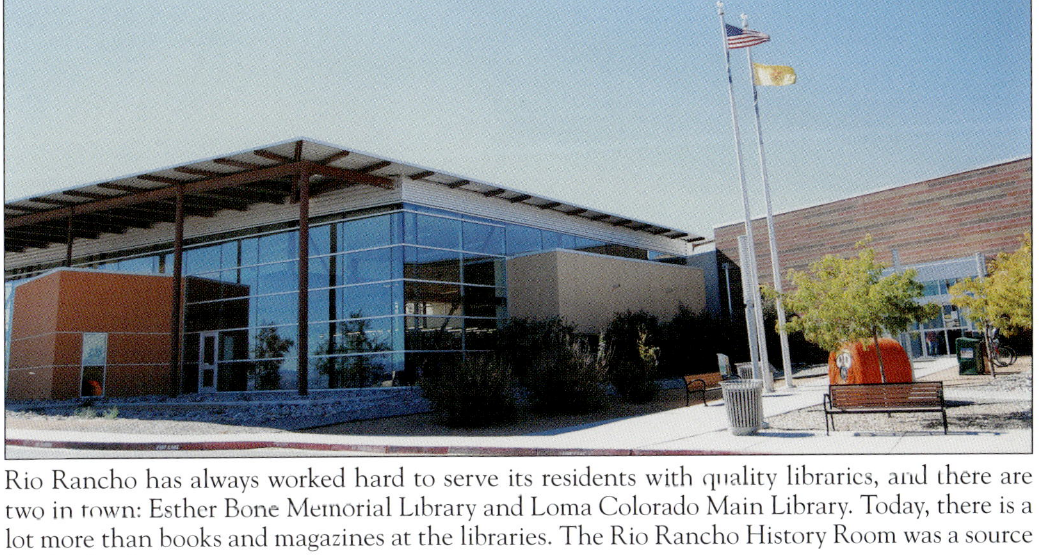

Rio Rancho has always worked hard to serve its residents with quality libraries, and there are two in town: Esther Bone Memorial Library and Loma Colorado Main Library. Today, there is a lot more than books and magazines at the libraries. The Rio Rancho History Room was a source for this book.

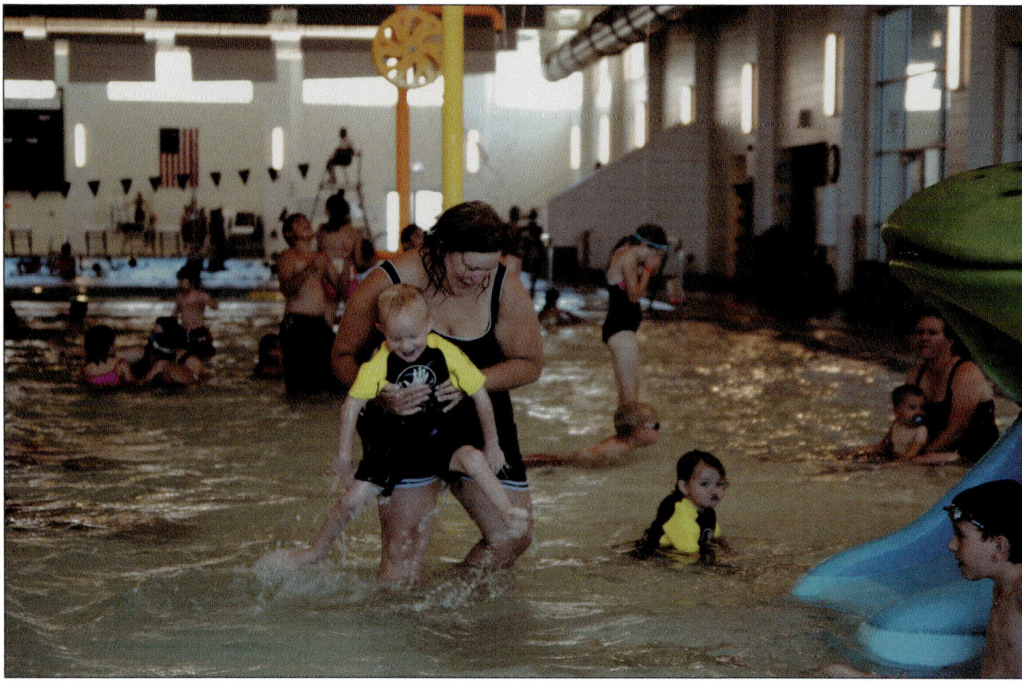

Completed in March 2008, this indoor swimming center came to fruition after the city council approved a $9.2-million contract with Bradbury Stamm. The aquatic center is on Loma Colorado. In March 2006, voters passed a $7-million bond issue to fund construction; Pulte Homes donated an additional $3 million.

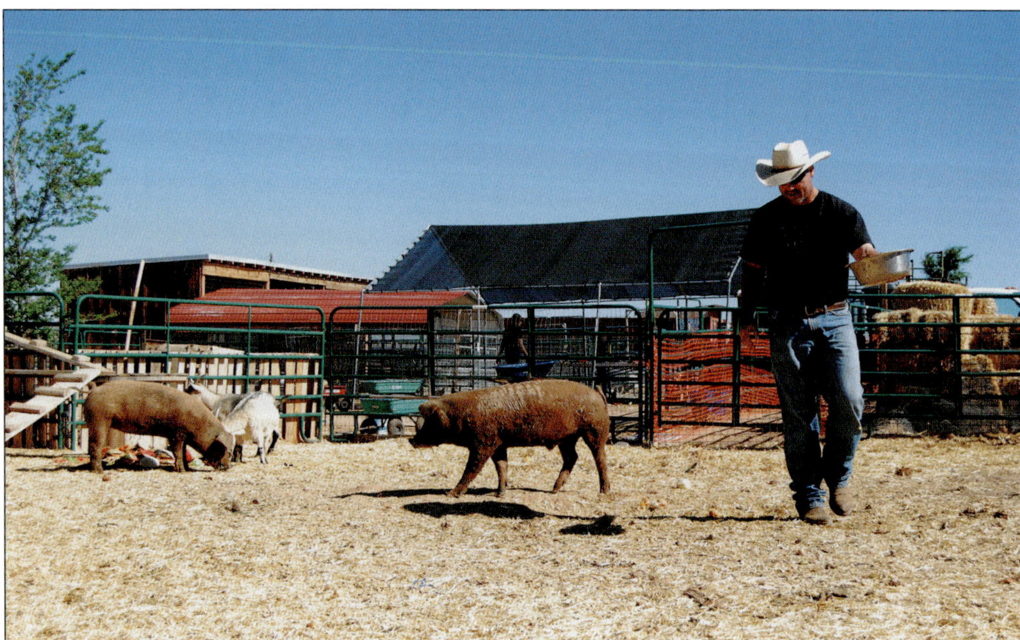

Galloping Grace Youth Ranch was built in 2007, and it is a working horse ranch. Founder Max Wade is seen here in the foreground. At the ranch, work and fun go hand in hand. The mission of Galloping Grace Youth Ranch is to bring pure joy to children, and it has succeeded.

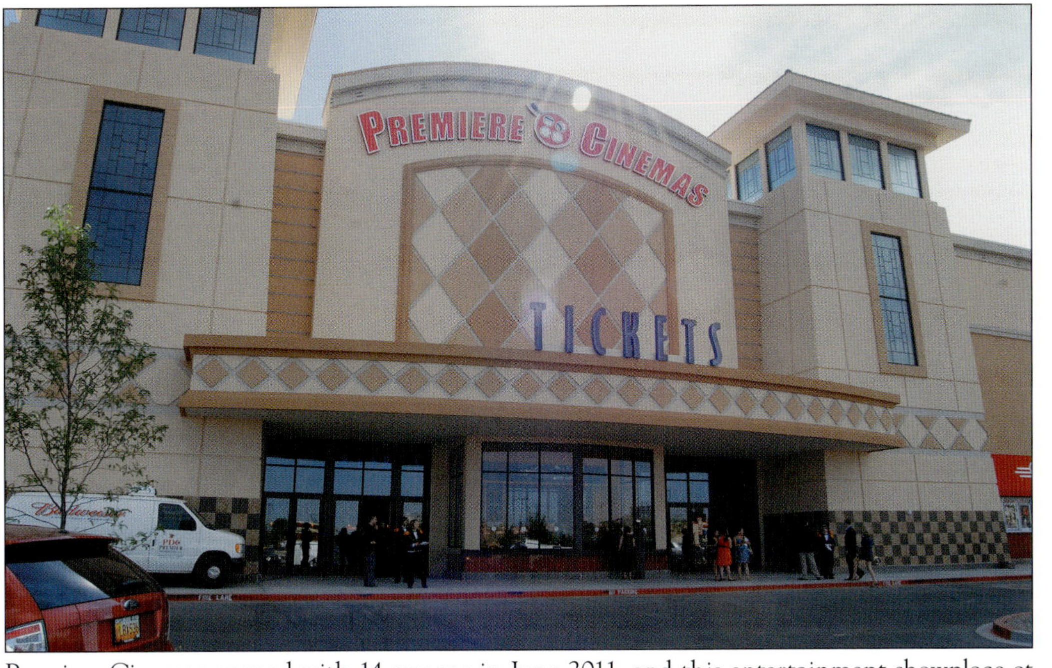

Premiere Cinemas opened with 14 screens in June 2011, and this entertainment showplace at Southern and Unser Boulevards can be seen for miles coming from almost any direction and represents a milestone—the city was without a movie theater since the early 1990s—in Rio Rancho's progress and evolution.

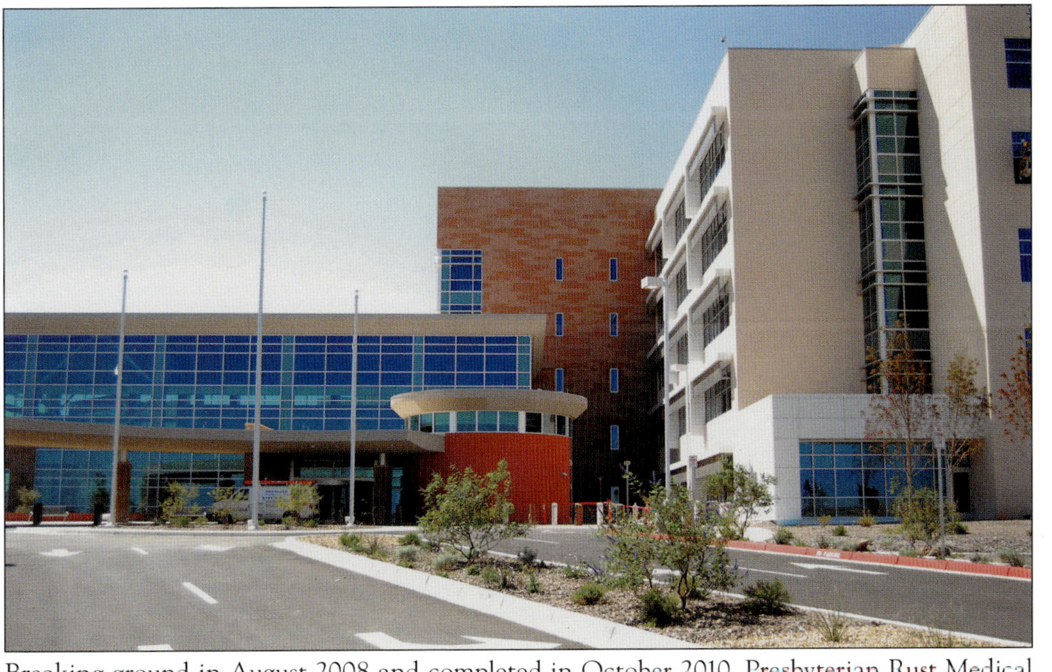

Breaking ground in August 2008 and completed in October 2010, Presbyterian Rust Medical Center addressed hospital needs of Rio Rancho as the city's first full-service community hospital. The hospital initially had 120 private patient rooms with the most modern care in labor and delivery, surgery, emergency care, and key medical specialties.

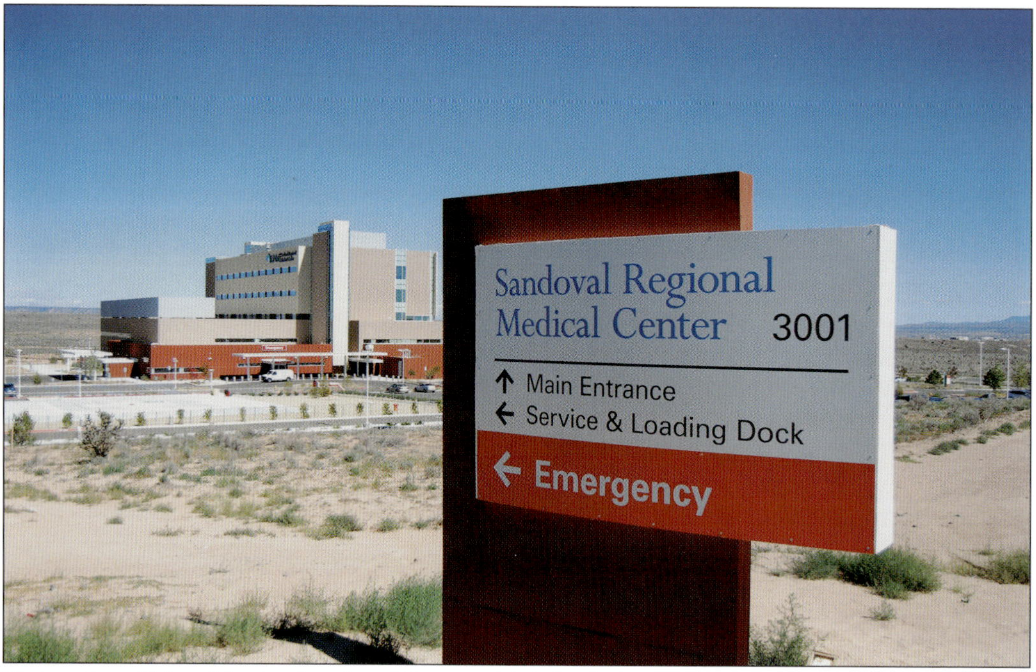

University of New Mexico-Sandoval Regional Medical Center (SRMC) is a community-based academic health-care facility served by hospital-based UNM faculty physicians and community-based independent physicians. SRMC houses 72 acute-care inpatient beds that service two medical/surgical units, an intensive-care unit, and an inpatient senior behavioral health unit. The facility opened in July 2012.

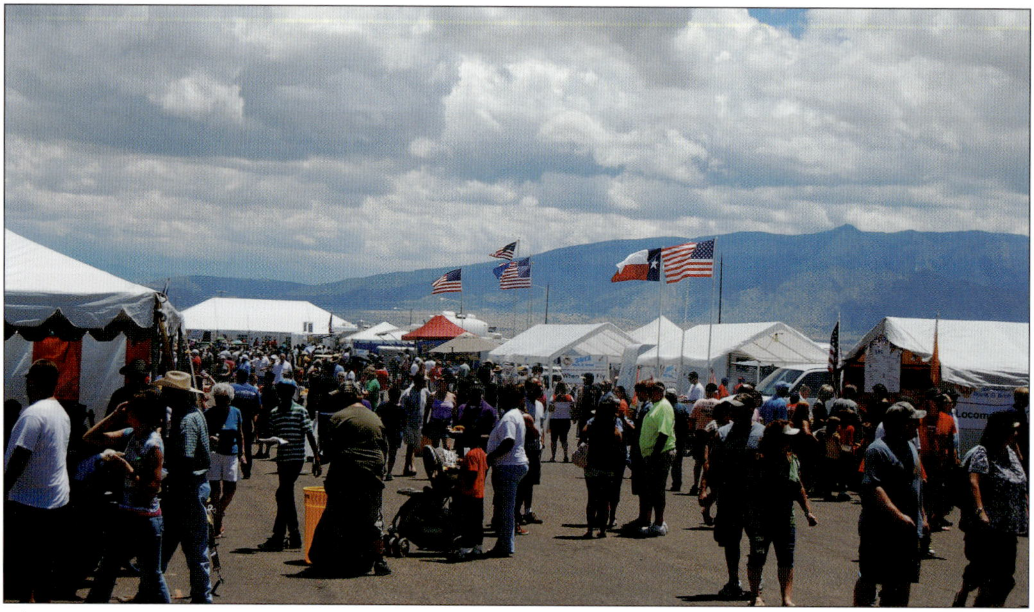

The annual Pork & Brew, attracting thousands and held at several venues until finally opting for the large spaces outside and even within Santa Ana Star Center, offers visitors a plethora of pork, as well as beef, chicken, and other delicacies plus a beer tent, entertainment, and more every July.

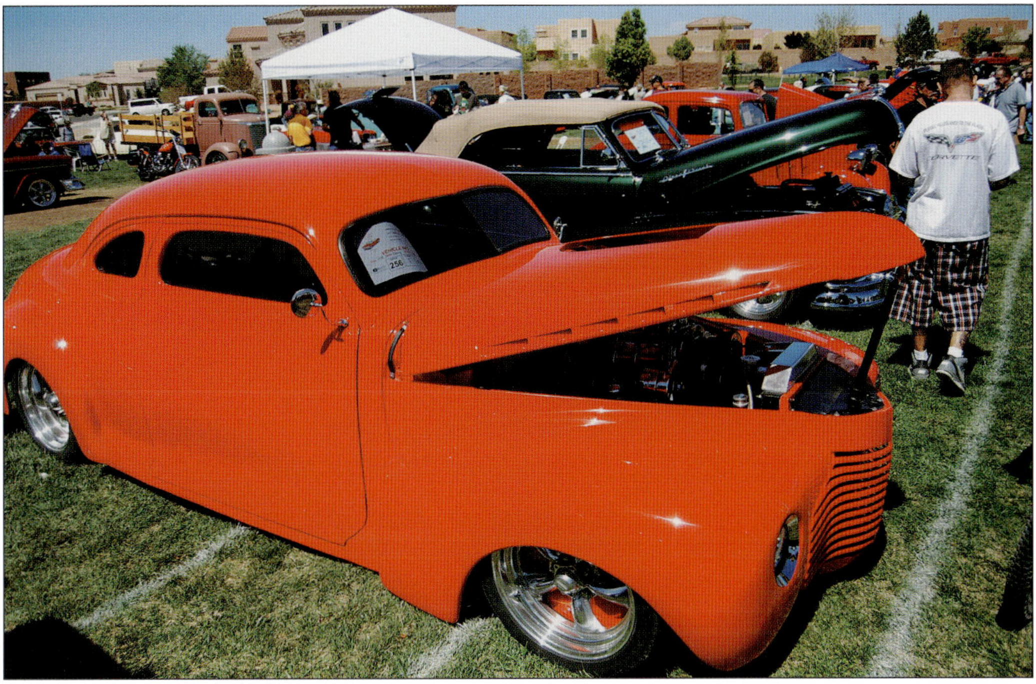

The annual Park 'n the Park is held every April at Cabezon Park. Close to 300 antique and classic vehicles, dazzling with their wild colors and chrome, compete in various categories for trophies. Walking up and down the aisles of cars, one can hear a father telling his son, "I had a car like that once."

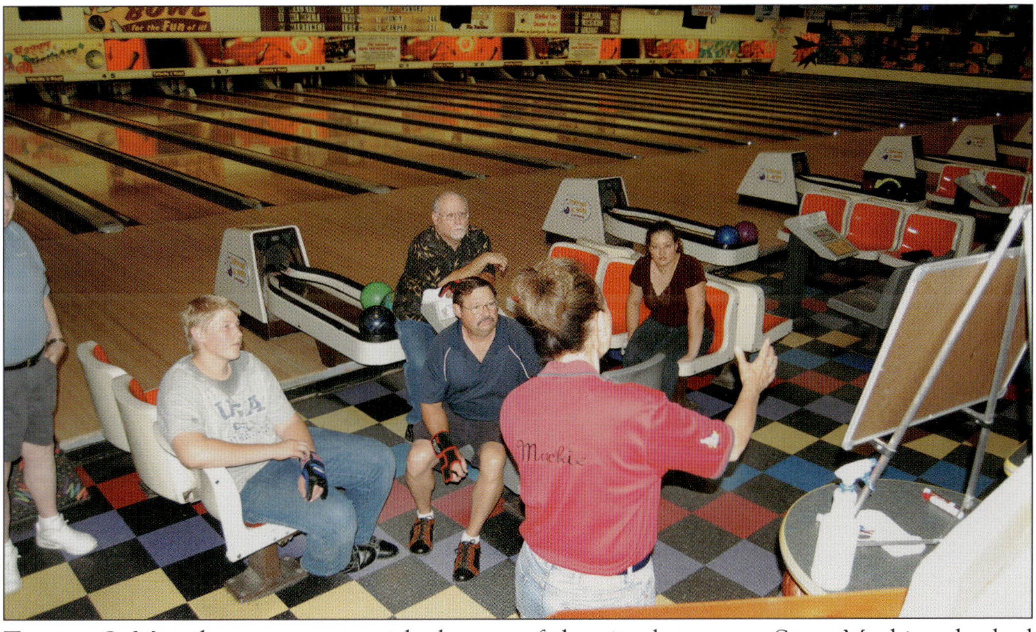

Tenpins & More has not grown with the rest of the city, but owner Steve Mackie, who had 24 synthetic lanes installed at his center in 2014, sees growing interest in the sport every year. The annual New Mexico Open is staged here every August, with $10,000 or more going to the winner.

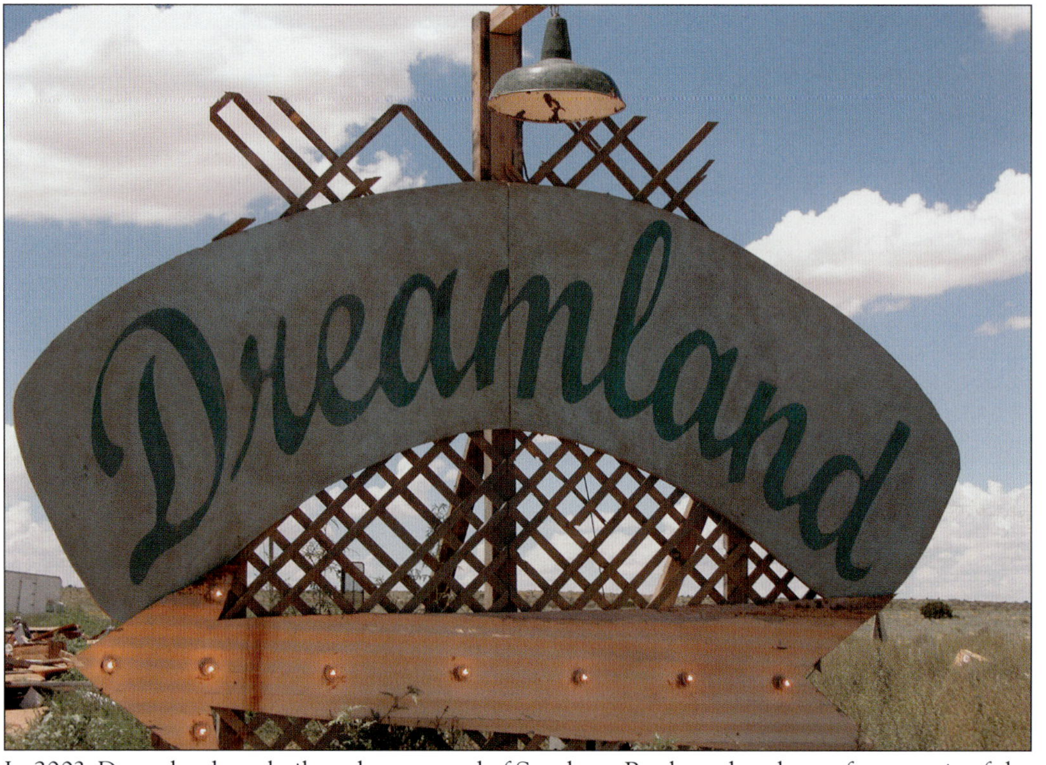

In 2003, Dreamland was built at the west end of Southern Boulevard as the set for a movie of the same name and one of many movies filmed in Rio Rancho. *The Spy Next Door* and *Ghosts of Mars* and television shows such as *Hart to Hart* and *Breaking Bad* also used Rio Rancho sites.

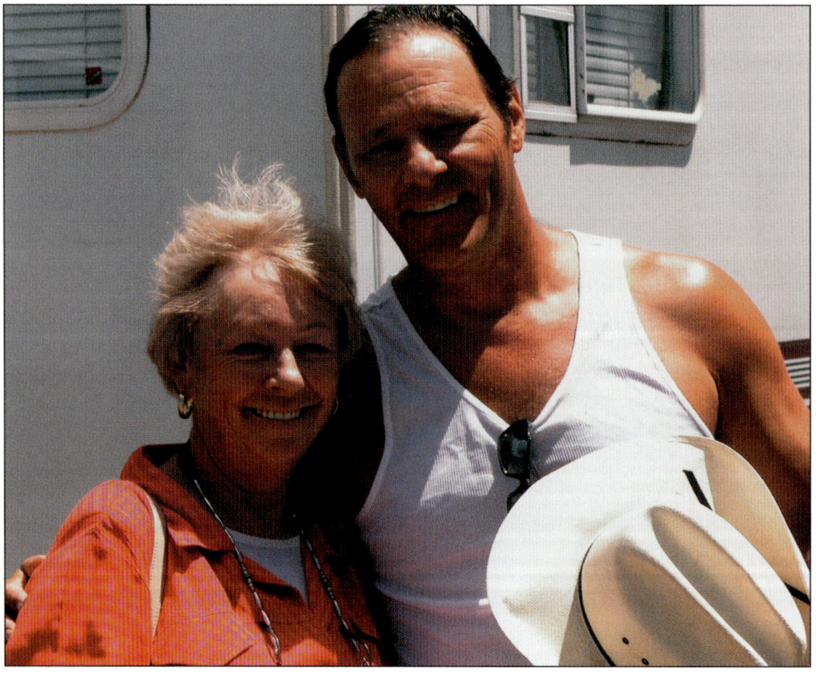

Film and production crews had a good friend in Judi Snow (left) in the early 2000s, when she worked tirelessly with television and movie people to help them find places that suited their needs, even if was just lodging. Here, Snow is seen with actor Chris Mulkey on the *Dreamland* set.

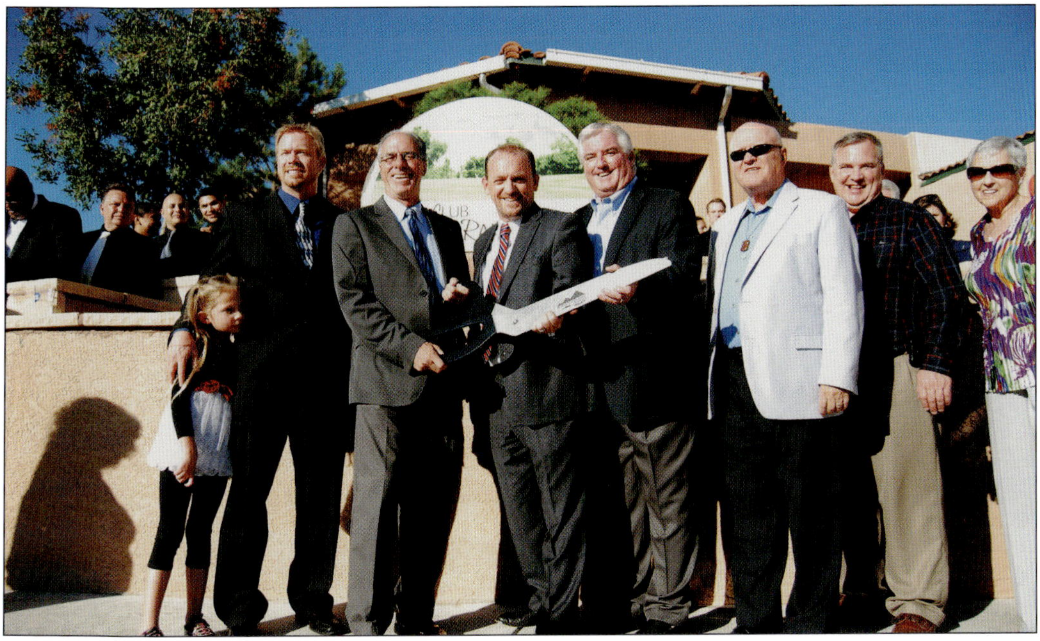

Known in the past as Panorama Golf and Country Club, Rio Rancho Country Club, and Chamisa Hills Country Club, Club Rio Rancho was acquired in 2014 by partners Jhett Browne (left) and Bob Gallagher (right), at opposite ends of the scissors, with Mayor Gregg Hull between them. Improvements have gone on throughout the property.

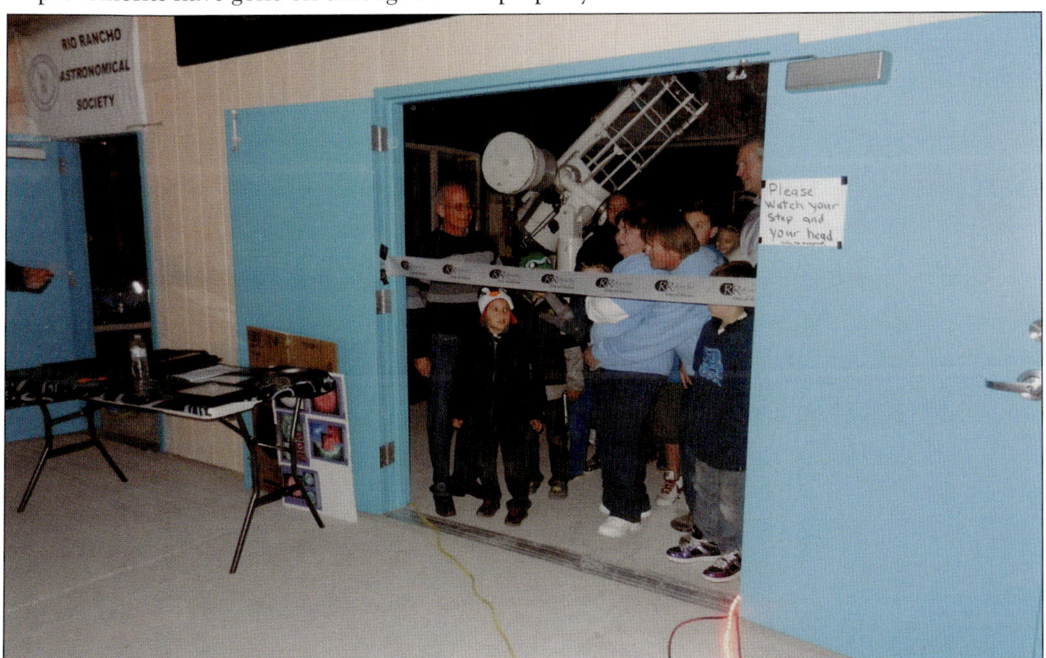

At 301 Southern Boulevard, Rainbow Park Observatory was officially dedicated on November 9, 2013. The observatory is open to the public during the Rio Rancho Astronomical Society's regular monthly meeting, traditionally held on the Friday closest to the first quarter moon. Detailed scheduling and meeting information is available at www.rrastro.org.

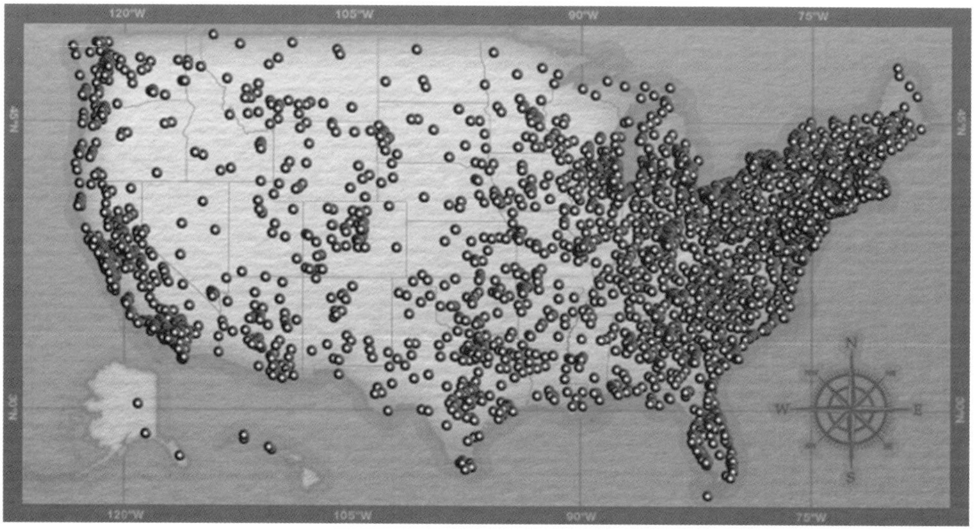

Consistent with our mission to preserve history on a local level, this book was printed in South Carolina on American-made paper and manufactured entirely in the United States. Products carrying the accredited Forest Stewardship Council (FSC) label are printed on 100 percent FSC-certified paper.

MADE IN THE USA